The
EVERYTHING®
Crossword Challenge Book

Dear Reader:

Just as art and literature are recognizable and attributed to their creators, so, too, is the art form known as the crossword puzzle. The humor, patterns, themes, fills, clues, triviata, and titles all reflect the personality that the constructor has imbued the puzzle with. Some even reference the parts of the country where the constructors come from. We proudly identify the constructors of all of the puzzles in this book as acknowledgment of these noble artisans, just as a portrait would not be complete without a signature.

Many different constructors have contributed to this book, using their own unique styles and standards. I have tried to preserve the uniqueness inherent to the constructors. It should keep the book feeling fresh and new throughout. I hope you enjoy the puzzles as much as I did. Perhaps you'll even want to start making your own crossword puzzles . . . but that will have to wait for another book.

So, grab a pencil or pen and let's get started!

Puzzlingly yours,

Douglas Fink

The EVERYTHING® Series

Editorial

Publishing Director	Gary M. Krebs
Managing Editor	Kate McBride
Copy Chief	Laura MacLaughlin
Acquisitions Editor	Kate Burgo
Production Editor	Jamie Wielgus

Production

Production Director	Susan Beale
Production Manager	Michelle Roy Kelly
Series Designers	Daria Perreault
	Colleen Cunningham
Cover Design	Paul Beatrice
	Frank Rivera
Layout and Graphics	Colleen Cunningham
	Rachael Eiben
	Michelle Roy Kelly
	John Paulhus
	Daria Perreault
	Erin Ring
Series Cover Artist	Barry Littmann
Puzzle Designer	Douglas R. Fink

Visit the entire Everything® Series at www.everything.com

THE

EVERYTHING®

CROSSWORD

CHALLENGE

BOOK

Take it to the next level!

Edited by Douglas R. Fink

Adams Media
Avon, Massachusetts

This book is dedicated to my wife Susan, daughter Hannah, and son Ethan, for their love and support. It is also dedicated to my parents and brothers who instilled in me a sense of creativity, puzzle solving, and humor. Yay team!

An Everything® Series Book.
Everything® and everything.com® are registered trademarks of F+W Publications, Inc.

Published by Adams Media, an F+W Publications Company
57 Littlefield Street, Avon, MA 02322 U.S.A.
www.adamsmedia.com

ISBN: 1-59337-120-9
Printed in the United States of America.

J I H G F E D C B A

Library of Congress Cataloging-in-Publication Data
Fink, Douglas.
The everything crossword challenge book / Douglas R. Fink.
p.   cm.
(An everything series book)
ISBN 1-59337-120-9
1. Crossword puzzles. I. Title. II. Series: Everything series.
GV1507.C7F55 2004
796.732 22
2004008221

This publication is designed to provide accurate and authoritative information with regard to the subject matter covered. It is sold with the understanding that the publisher is not engaged in rendering legal, accounting, or other professional advice. If legal advice or other expert assistance is required, the services of a competent professional person should be sought.
—From a *Declaration of Principles* jointly adopted by a Committee of the American Bar Association and a Committee of Publishers and Associations

Many of the designations used by manufacturers and sellers to distinguish their products are claimed as trademarks. Where those designations appear in this book and Adams Media was aware of a trademark claim, the designations have been printed with initial capital letters.

This book is available at quantity discounts for bulk purchases.
For information, call 1-800-872-5627.

Contents

Acknowledgments

I would like to thank the following constructors for their contributions: Adrian Powell, Alan Olschwang, Dave Fisher, Jerry Rosman, Lane Gutz, Leslie Nicoll, Mark Milhet, Matthew Skoczen, Merle Baker, Michael Wiesenberg, Grace Becker, Norm Guggenbiller, Roy Leban, Sylvia Thompson, Verna Suit, and Viv Collins.

Crossword Compiler and Across Lite were used in the creation and/or processing of many of the puzzles.

Introduction

▶ THERE ARE TWO TYPES of people: those who like crosswords, and those who do not yet know that they like crosswords. This book is for those who already know that they like crosswords. My first book (*The Everything® Easy Crosswords Book*) is for those who do not yet know that they like crosswords, or have not yet put in the time to learn "the tricks of the trade." By "tricks of the trade," I mean curveballs that may be in clues, themes, fill styles (including rebus puzzles, where a multi-letter string can fill in a white square, listed on pages 94, 134, 152, 170, 173, 189, and 224), or vocabulary and trivia that come with practice when solving crosswords.

The author must confess that for a lot of his life, he fell into the "do not yet know" category. I did not like the fact that a new vocabulary needed to be learned just to start solving the infernal creations known as crosswords. Not only that, but I'd studied Spanish instead of French in high school, seemingly putting me at a disadvantage. It was not until I started commuting into Boston by train that I decided to give crosswords a chance. After all, I was already a big fan of word puzzles, had been part of the National Puzzlers' League, and was particularly fond of anagrams (this was before I got into palindromes). I started playing around with crossword construction and started putting crosswords and other puzzles into the company newsletter that I was editing. I improved through trial and error, still lacking certain fine-tunings like "symmetry should be maintained in the grid."

The "Challenge" in the title does NOT mean that the book is chock-full of entries that will have you scratching your head, saying,

"Gee, I'm missing a letter here, where some tiny river I've never heard of crosses this obscure foreign leader I've never heard of." There may be some obscure entries, but hopefully not enough to make a puzzle impossible to break open or impossible to finish.

I have enlisted the aid of fellow constructors to increase the textures of the puzzles as you experience them. Like pizza toppings or ice cream flavors, I'm guessing that you'd like more variety than the clues and themes that I'd come up with purely on my own. Well, I'm letting you know the constructors so you can look for them in the future and identify your favorites.

The first two puzzles are warm-ups, a little smaller than the 15x15s that make up the rest of the book.

Have fun, and good luck!

E

Chapter 1

Bursting at
the Themes

The Optimist *Dave Fisher*

ACROSS

1. King Khan?
8. Propane safety additive
9. Cold War phase that wasn't so cold
10. Smelly locker item
11. Gull
12. Watering holes
15. *Jeopardy*'s Trebek
16. Exploding cigar? (that's fishy)
20. Took over
21. Acknowledged
22. Rent
23. Vlad the ___
26. Not on the rocks
27. Fill
31. Chanter
32. Earthy colors
33. Stretched to the limit

DOWN

1. *The ___ Must Be Crazy*
2. First nudist camp?
3. Item under a fridge magnet
4. Dickens novel for optimists?
5. Crave
6. Monica Lewinsky was one
7. Isaac and Otto
12. Mongol
13. *Home ___*
14. Sissy Spacek's USO girl
17. Praise
18. John the plowman
19. Stranger
23. Make demands
24. Bully
25. The last governor of Hong Kong
28. Henry VIII's second
29. Camellia and Earl Grey
30. While beginning

❖ Solution on page 265

2

Ringmaster *Dave Fisher*

ACROSS

1. Capital of Venezuela
8. Colorful shellfish
9. Knocked down
10. Bodybuilder's activity
11. Pay for a hand
12. Bid first
15. ___ arrest
19. Dum or dee
20. Raise
21. Put forth
24. Copycat
25. Wine and dine
29. Coastal
30. Missing in the military?
31. Type of front
34. Heart of Dixie
38. Rhine siren
39. *Gimme* ___ (Stones hit)
40. Heidi Fleiss et al.

DOWN

1. Muscle prone to cramps
2. First homicide victim
3. Pan's opposite
4. The Ringmaster?
5. Bushman Powell
6. Concerning
7. Paper plant
12. Opus opener?
13. Mutt's mitt
14. Before
16. Nice concept
17. Sorrowful word
18. Dip. or doc.
21. Hindu habit
22. ___ *the Roof* (Drifters hit)
23. Cabochons and peridots
26. Word repeated by a placater
27. ___-Magnon
28. Conger
31. Eagle Joe
32. Hilo hello
33. More uncommon
35. Singing voice
36. Gather
37. Broadcasts

❖ **Solution on page 265**

Dollar Exchange — Merle Baker

ACROSS

1. Line crosser?
5. Slack-jawed one
10. Unpaid TV ads
14. Salad fish
15. Chicago airport
16. Typeface
17. "You said it!"
18. Terrier type
19. Stephen King book
20. Superfluous ornamentation
23. CD-___
24. Bewitched witch
25. Dressed to the nines
27. Stubble remover
30. Late-night name
31. Stitch
34. Juliet's cousin
36. Christmas season
39. Texas shrine
41. Have a tab
42. Light-colored beer
43. Prima donna
44. Presidential middle name
46. Don't share
47. Cosmonaut Gagarin
49. The Producers actor Dick
51. Item for an attempt at hiding
54. Playground apparatus
58. Cabinet dept.
59. Anew
62. ___ Bator
64. Ticked off
65. "Ciao"
66. Tennis score
67. Offspring
68. Part of QED
69. Santa's sackful
70. Entice
71. Famous loch

DOWN

1. Dramatize
2. Curry spice
3. "Let that be ___ to it!"
4. Maine seaport
5. Don't hold back
6. Captain of literature
7. Two of a kind
8. Blew it
9. Company with a Formula One racing team
10. Rank below cpl.
11. Alaskan prospector
12. Pear variety
13. Defeat decisively
21. Poet's muse
22. Presidential monogram
26. New Age singer
28. Slender reed
29. R&B singer Lou
31. Dejected
32. Yale student
33. Sixties counterculture icon
35. Wife of Jacob
37. Sign of summer
38. Work unit
40. Heavy hammer
42. Decrease
44. Pepys, notably
45. Emerging
48. Whistle blower
50. Make tidy
51. Quake causer
52. Domed home
53. Jedi's power
55. Fixed look
56. Play the role of
57. "___ new?"
60. Hurt severely
61. Organ setting
63. Video game letters

❖ Solution on page 265

Dukes   Lane Gutz

❖ Solution on page 266

ACROSS

1. Explode
6. Serves well done
10. Quaker pronoun
14. Get warmer
15. Campus military org.
16. Keyboard key
17. The Ringo Kid
19. ___ eye
20. Costa del ___
21. Vertical spar
22. Toros
24. Sign of music
25. ___ song (cheaply)
26. Pepper sprayers
29. Sheriff John T. Chance
33. Acknowledges
34. Automobile pioneer Karl Friedrich ___
35. Kinglet
36. Psych teacher, e.g.
37. Bandleader Shaw
38. Ventilates
39. City in Belgium
40. Cougar and Jaguar
41. Mescal source
42. Cole Thornton
44. Water ___
45. Gives approval
46. Horse color
47. Van Dyke
50. Space filler
51. All alternative
54. Type of fruit
55. Dusty Rhodes
58. Iguana's milieu
59. Approximation
60. Frighten
61. Nostradamus, e.g.
62. Kin of oxen
63. Compass directions

DOWN

1. Angler's catch
2. "Do ___ others . . . "
3. In existence
4. Droop
5. Kevin Bacon movie (1990)
6. Woke up
7. Paint layer
8. Mail Boxes ___
9. Sweet talk
10. Taw Jackson
11. Borough west of Brighton
12. Islamic prince
13. Congers
18. Jungle carnivores
23. Spherical object
24. Stony Brooke
25. Terminus
26. Syrup flavor
27. "Complicated" singer Lavigne
28. Murmured softly
29. Backward prefix
30. Opera solos
31. Enthusiasm
32. Beginning
34. Small nails
37. Faculty member
41. In fashion
43. Future school?
44. Coconut husk fiber
46. Ostrich kin
47. Fortitude (informal)
48. Fairy tale monster
49. On the calm side
50. Non-intersecting
51. Ostrich kin
52. 1996 Pulitzer Prize winner
53. Red and black
56. Stir
57. Aviation org.

Ring Toss   *Michael Wiesenberg*

ACROSS

1. Police team
5. Old
9. Windblown soil
14. Site of activity
15. Kinks hit
16. Sleep disorder
17. Working
18. Floors
19. Sea birds
20. Scholarly work about the 29th president's personal finances?
23. Bristles
24. Hankering
25. Panaji is its capital
26. Western pal
29. More trite
32. ___ *Lay Dying*
33. By way of
35. "Bien sur"
36. "You take the Jetta tonight, and I'll take the Passat"
42. Legal thing
43. Dedicated poem
44. Say this to a dentist
46. Thwart
49. "Per ardua ___" (Kansas motto)
52. ___ standstill
53. Singer famed for screeching
55. Good deal
56. Dads of college kids?
61. Tease
62. Hold sway
63. Hubbard of sci-fi
65. Wrinkle-resistant synthetic fabric
66. Lost
67. Deceased
68. Checks
69. Pickle
70. Somewhat

DOWN

1. ___ Na Na
2. Coolly
3. Flying female
4. Foursome
5. Jai ___
6. Ball attire
7. Poetic lament
8. Track events
9. Exerciser's concentration
10. Argentina, Venezuela, et al.
11. Anger
12. Motion detector
13. Alexander's nickname
21. Site of iniquity
22. Chanted
23. Patio tub
27. Runaround
28. Start of a film dog's name
30. Eighth in a series: Abbr.
31. Steven Tyler's daughter
34. Past
37. Weep
38. Do a sewing repair job on a skirt
39. Actress Lupino
40. Mole's *Wind in the Willows* friend
41. Site of the Circus Hall of Fame
45. Shakespearean prince
46. England's James I or II or Charles I or II
47. Snarl
48. Memory trace
50. Part of last remains
51. What Stanley yelled in *A Streetcar Named Desire*
52. Dos
54. Worth something
57. Marvel villain Dr. ___
58. Roadside stops
59. Rainier products
60. They might be black or green
64. Homer's neighbor

❖ **Solution on page 266**

Goners *Lane Gutz*

ACROSS

1. IOU
5. Of the least quality
10. Proper partner
14. Optometrist's term
15. A-muse-ing Greek name?
16. Complete a second time
17. This can be happy
18. Suffix for air or ocean
19. Point
20. Karate expert gone Bionic?
23. Stone marker
24. Epoch
25. Psychic ability: Abbr.
28. Owns
29. Dali's devotion
31. Leno's employer: Abbr.
34. Place for Irish Spring cleaning?
36. Big fuss
37. On a cruise
38. Comedian gone golfer?
41. Sound of error
42. Farm female
43. Use persuasion
44. Scholastic org.
45. Item on a Grecian urn?
46. Ring master
47. Your, of yore
48. Batman and Robin, e.g.
50. Anas genus members
52. Director gone shock jock?
58. Hence
59. Hobo in the desert
60. Scoundrel
61. Olympian who enjoyed brotherly love?
62. Home of Minos
63. Once more
64. Simple
65. Rear-___ (Auto accident)
66. "Hey you!"

DOWN

1. Jim Carrey role?
2. At any time
3. Girl's guy
4. Soft minerals
5. Justly merited
6. Bay windows
7. Raja's wife
8. Twist this to change time
9. Shul scroll
10. Erenow
11. Send again
12. Midmonth maker
13. *Mr.* ___
21. Net prefix, in networking
22. Type of engine
25. Deter by law
26. "Darn!"
27. Hairstyles
29. Contribute
30. Obstacle course obstacle
32. Tree with triangular nuts
33. Drew on TV
35. Once existed
36. Belch inducer
37. Keyboard key
39. Be in debt
40. Blue dyes
45. Expression of delight
46. Make livable, as an aquarium
49. Take back, in a way
50. Domesticated
51. Reverse parts?
52. She played Carla
53. "___ upon a time . . . "
54. Eroded
55. Eras
56. Feels sorrow for
57. *Aliens* role
58. ___ *Ten Commandments*

❖ Solution on page 266

Planetarium   *Alan Olschwang*

ACROSS

1. Impulsive
5. Hood
9. Want too much
14. Public exhibition
15. Priest's title
16. It provides a licorice flavor
17. Wealthy ruler
19. Seed cover
20. Cassia family plant
21. Rick's love
23. Vaticinator
24. Former, formerly
26. River of NYC
28. Bounders
31. Backhoe, e.g.
36. Horse show performance
38. Deem
39. Jeb Stuart, for one
40. Italian spice
43. Fr. holy woman
44. Radio station sign
46. Unnerves
48. French seaport
51. Take the plunge
52. Florence's flooder
53. Puerto ___
55. Actress Cheryl
58. ___ problem!
60. Sort of sprawl
64. Jumbles
66. Melancholy
68. Fire starter
69. Australian natives
70. Kett of the comics
71. Bacon product
72. Sleep movements
73. Forest denizen

DOWN

1. 10-percenters
2. Supporting shaft
3. Made yarn
4. It's equatorial
5. PGA event
6. Birthright
7. Russian river
8. Prepare to go
9. Kind of burglar
10. Sort of shopping
11. Clamping device
12. Italian noble name
13. Speed
18. Scull
22. Expression of satisfaction
25. Charcoal
27. Utah Senator Reed ___
28. Disk for reading
29. Bailiwick
30. Exclude
32. Majestic
33. Panorama
34. Sign on a door
35. *Touched by an Angel* star
37. More achy
41. Plant with showy, colorful flowers
42. ___ decree
45. Actress Duncan
47. Embellished
49. Place without room, biblically
50. Less secure
54. Pound regular
55. Finish third
56. High peaks
57. First to round the Cape of Good Hope
59. Broken
61. Zest
62. Pot start
63. Approaching
65. Type of dive
67. Steamship name start

❖ **Solution on page 266**

8

Whirled Leaders   *Jerry Rosman*

ACROSS

1. Transferred image
6. Yews' juice?
10. Shed tears
14. Keep an ___ the ground
15. Other, to Jose
16. ___ breve
17. Newspaper headline about Russian president entering computer data?
20. One of Freud's trilogy
21. Unimagined
22. Chicken/king connector
25. Cartoon caveman's surname?
27. Garcia's uncle
28. Poivre's partner
29. Pens for inkers, not oinkers
31. Boca's state
33. Make a cipher
35. Theme
37. Piece of music to be played slowly
39. Headline about Senate overide of presidential veto?
43. In the interim
44. Sci-fi or romance; to a publisher
46. Accepted propostitions
49. Fix a road
51. A twinkler
52. Pizarro's gold
53. "___ out!" Ump's call
55. Break of day?
57. Yenta's expressions, perhaps
58. Hall you can get to if you practice?
61. Voice vote
63. Headline comparing Syrian living conditions to president's commercial
68. Rain hard
69. Himalayan he-man?
70. *The ___ Mutiny*
71. Perry's creator
72. "Hike!"
73. "Oops" preceder, perhaps

DOWN

1. Airport monitor: Abbr.
2. The Seine's makeup
3. Computer screen, to a tech
4. End in ___
5. Hope has one; hop hasn't
6. Old French coin
7. Westernmost Aleutian island
8. Cursive alternative
9. Padres hometown
10. Opposite of wax
11. Marty Robbins tune
12. Like Yankee Doodle's cap
13. Act the rat
18. It's heard when things disappear
19. Laundry chore
22. Mil. weapon stored in a silo
23. *The ___ King*
24. Play opening
26. Factory
30. Dinnertime, for many
32. Exercise and go on ___ (ways to weigh less)
34. Ice cream holders
36. Raided, to plunder
38. Lumberjack
40. Corsages
41. "___ each life, some rain must fall"
42. Picture of health?
45. Sounds of hesitation
46. Find
47. Pencil end
48. Tidbit
50. Skates
54. Like bread vis-à-vis matzoh
56. Sign of the '60s
59. Type of tag at a convention
60. ". . . hungry, I could ___ horse!"
62. Hebrew month
64. Drink with a straw
65. General's address?
66. Sajak may sell one
67. German article

❖ **Solution on page 266**

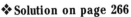

Vehicular   Roy Leban

ACROSS

1. Akebono, for one
5. Tailor
10. Some knowledge
14. Kitchen activity
15. Anna Paquin character in *X-Men*
16. "Excuse me"
17. Page
18. Blintz cousin
19. Computer opening
20. They match?
23. Way to turn?
25. You can buy pants without one
26. Dutch cheese
27. Flat space
32. Temptress in *The Odyssey*
33. Clark's girlfriend
34. They're coins in England
35. Pretty rock?
37. Rocker Billy
41. Acronym for a bad result?
42. Pitcher Gossage
43. Something you don't want to lose?
48. Catnip, for one
49. *Mad About ___*
50. What the British call petrol
51. *The Adventures of Baron von Munchausen* pretended to be one
56. Decaf coffee brand
57. Pepsi color introduced in 1993
58. Double-reeded instrument
61. Half a tropical isle?
62. Smog, for one
63. Farm cries
64. Inspires
65. Large boats may have several
66. Shrek, for one

DOWN

1. Resort
2. Psychic Geller
3. Not so hot
4. British ___
5. Possible eyebrow position
6. *Sound of Music* song
7. Bronze and Iron
8. Inactive insect life stage
9. Swarm
10. Kappa follower
11. John Glenn, for one
12. Identify again
13. Expel
21. Add water, perhaps
22. Some sushi
23. Coin of Fidel's realm
24. The Parthenon, for one
28. Nesman of *WKRP*
29. Remote
30. Way to bid at an auction?
31. Hip or prep suffix
35. Knock follower
36. Freud thought one part was super
37. Debt letters
38. To go?
39. Safety grp.
40. Tennis calls
41. What the Gee in Bee Gees stands for
42. What Horace Greeley would have said to the Chrysler Building
43. Economist Lester
44. Hit the hay
45. Odors
46. King George, to the colonists
47. Prepares for a disaster, perhaps
51. Swedish singing group
52. Star Wars target: Abbr.
53. Gandhi's paper
54. You can pull them in a rocket
55. Rail rider
59. Stick in the water
60. Taiwan or Japan follower

❖ Solution on page 266

Men on Film *Michael Wiesenberg*

ACROSS

1. Natated
5. CEOS, often
9. Too
13. Light
14. COBOL cousin
16. Silver wear
17. Fr. miss
18. It's a bear
19. Sit
20. Star of *Bond 21*
23. Contacts
24. FICA funds it
25. A tuna
28. Before
29. Force
32. Part of O'Neill's best-known title
34. Star of *The Mouse That Roared*
36. Attenuate
39. Speed
40. Colon in a mathematical proposition
41. Star of *Man in the White Suit*
46. Title role portrayer in *Rob Roy*
47. A Python
48. Walt Kelly's "___ Pogo"
51. Familiar name of one of Trump's Atlantic City properties
52. Scouting org.
54. First name in Mideast politics
56. The Man with No Name
60. It's a wind
62. Condor's nest
63. Ye ___ Shoppe
64. Sucker
65. Author of *Age of Reason*
66. Pungent German river?
67. Recedes
68. Stengel's last team
69. Untouchable one

DOWN

1. Graze
2. More cunning
3. Actress Dahl
4. Cat in the Hat portrayer
5. Succeeds
6. *The ___* (Steve McQueen's first big role)
7. Seaweed extract
8. Flies alone
9. Govt. agcy. that developed the Internet
10. 1932's *Murders in the Rue Morgue* was his first major role
11. Bro's sib
12. Lone
15. She played the title role in a TV series that ran from 1954 to 1973
21. Give up
22. It's salt
26. Playwright Moss ___
27. ___ many words
30. Soda of yore
31. Singer Lopez
33. Yalies
34. Trainer's concentration, maybe
35. Submit
36. Gasp
37. "Jacta ___ est" ("the die is cast")
38. His real name was Leo Jacobs
42. Asian desert
43. Click open
44. Champs ___
45. One sells for $1,000,000 on the NYSE
48. Tristan's Wagnerian love
49. Hollow stones
50. They might be marching
53. Mr. T's group
55. Faint
57. Bottle bottom bits
58. Canal town
59. "___ That a Shame"
60. Bauxite, for one
61. Fella

❖ Solution on page 266

Handy   *Alan Olschwang*

ACROSS
1. Has obligations
5. Sort of slicker
9. Anabaptist sect
14. Cold cut seller
15. Neighborhood
16. Me too
17. Enunciated
18. California city
20. Gets one's life back
22. It's on the books
23. Theologian Brunner
24. Sentence subject
26. Scuttlebutt
28. Pitcher's alternative
32. See 34A
33. Cote denizen
34. Allay
39. Civil rights worker Medgar
41. Sis, e.g.
43. Lyric poem
44. Experience, perhaps
46. The bottom line
48. Brings up the rear
49. New York attraction
52. Type of knife
56. Exploit
57. Superstar
58. Small boy
60. At the back of the waterbus
64. They go right down to the wire
67. Fencer's foil
68. Radials
69. Parrot
70. Disburdens
71. Bailiwick
72. Showdown time
73. Dundee denizen

DOWN
1. Stench
2. Existed
3. ___ vital
4. Sidearm accessories
5. Space traveler
6. George's brother
7. William of Uri
8. Motorbike maker
9. Lime drink
10. Scrooge
11. They're on the to-do list
12. Thin, narrow channel
13. In an intense way
19. Expatiate
21. Stir-fry pan
25. It's found in the headlines
27. Not aweather
28. ___ over
29. Wheel hub
30. Takes advantage of
31. Human ___
35. Bedaubs
36. Inundate
37. Head start
38. Cape
40. One palate
42. Complaint
45. Italian prime minister
47. A high crime
50. Unclutter
51. ___ Cruses
52. Santa Maria companion
53. Fire fighter Red
54. France's longest river
55. Sitcom canceled in 1998
59. Art ___
61. Long narrative poem
62. Make over
63. Brooding place
65. GSA counterpart
66. Letter from Greece

❖ **Solution on page 266**

Playing the Game   *Alan Olschwang*

ACROSS

1. Stupefied
6. Top treatment, briefly
9. Dispatched biblical style
14. Drink garnish
15. Expose to the public
16. Long-legged wader
17. Ecclesiastical law
18. Keanu in *The Matrix*
19. Fed the kitty
20. Making trouble
23. Cassowary cousin
24. Pose
25. Handles roughly
28. 41D to François
31. False hope of a sort
36. Chicken/king connector
37. Ninth inning follower
39. Wall hangings
40. Deciding
43. Unfasten is a way
44. Gilbert and Teasdale
45. Tiger's concern
46. Beset
48. Johnson pet
49. Lawyer's levies
50. ___ Moines
52. La la leader
54. Taking the dare
62. Embankment
63. Check out
64. Extent
65. Conceptions
66. Spell spell spel
67. Actor Stu
68. They hold gravy
69. Mr. Leibman
70. Marshal Earp

DOWN

1. Wharf
2. Jai ___
3. Brass component
4. Elicits
5. Jeans material
6. Zest
7. Stead
8. Harvest
9. Suckers' experiences
10. Diner's card
11. Food for Fido
12. Digits
13. Conclude
21. Spirit of a place
22. Part of a ready trio
25. ___ New Guinea
26. Alda and Arkin
27. Hornets
29. Outpatient exams: Abbr.
30. Indian prince
32. Grog ingredient
33. Fred's first dance partner
34. Bottle denizen
35. Colorado state park
37. Lack of flexibility
38. Unadulterated
41. One of the magnificent seven?
42. *Star Wars* name
47. O in Oahu
49. Long way
51. Villain's expression
53. Darn
54. Make over
55. Eye part
56. Pinlike?
57. Pita sandwich
58. Gull cousin
59. Hawkeye's state
60. Narrow point of land
61. Ohio state school
62. Movement word

❖ **Solution on page 266**

Spice Shop   *Merle Baker*

ACROSS

1. *Mad About You* cousin
4. Gives a hand
11. Sound investment
14. Communicate with
15. Sammy Davis autobiography
16. Indignation
17. Connecticut
19. Presidential monogram
20. No turn ___
21. 911 responders
22. Up in arms
23. One-sidedness
24. Salvia family member
27. Puts down roots
29. Article part
30. Med. specialty
31. Cad
33. Heaps
34. Horse grooming tool
38. Alexander III, e. g.
41. Prefix meaning "work"
42. Dipl. official
45. William Allen White's town
49. Judge
51. Baseball warm-up
53. Kind of list
54. World workers agcy.
55. Profess
56. Ancient Greek region
57. Withdrawal syndrome
58. Superfluous embellishment
61. *Malcolm X* director
62. Front to back
63. 95, for one
64. Football stats
65. Lies close
66. D.C. VIP

DOWN

1. Base
2. Family turnout
3. Appeal to
4. Turned red, maybe
5. Alpha wave record: Abbr.
6. Balaam's ride
7. Soda size
8. Rascals
9. Snitch
10. "I'll be right there!"
11. Postal option
12. Nearsighted cartoon character
13. Dangling
18. Arizona city
24. Look searchingly
25. ___ -friendly
26. Try
28. Cal. heading
32. Caustic chemical
34. Soybeans or strawberries
35. Pull an all-nighter
36. Monstrosity
37. Crowd around
38. With indifference
39. Turned out iron
40. Places side-by-side
42. Yom Kippur celebrants
43. Act the 49A
44. Expand
46. *Bedtime for Bonzo* star
47. University of California city
48. Scully and Mulder
50. "Take ___ leave . . . "
52. In-group speech
56. Some PCs
59. Photo-shop order: Abbr.
60. Sandwich choice

❖ **Solution on page 267**

Take Charge — *Mark Milhet*

ACROSS

1. Proofreader's concern
5. Hoglike animal
10. Feudal flunky
14. Swing a scythe
15. Put up with
16. High point at the Met
17. Working diligently
18. Tiny bits
19. Bring bad luck to
20. CHARGE
23. Shed
24. NASA thumbs-up
25. *Mad TV* specialty
28. Kind of loser
30. So-so connection?
33. Salad garnish
34. At this place
35. Tie over, in music
36. CHARGE
39. Wee workers
40. Is human?
41. More severe
42. Fork over
43. A ton
44. Cold season
45. Mata Hari, for one
46. Alleviate
47. CHARGE
54. Bit of a biter
55. Auto maker
56. Margarine
57. Correct text
58. Make into law
59. Bank transaction
60. Kind of list
61. Stadium toppers
62. Take-out order?

DOWN

1. Ore carrier
2. Mythical Himalayan
3. Bucket
4. "Half-full" viewers
5. Hot treat
6. Cancel, à la NASA
7. Compassion
8. Invention beginning
9. Trucker's turnoff
10. Game show host
11. Author Ambler
12. Zamboni site
13. Wired message
21. Body section
22. Cargo measure
25. Discontinue, as a project
26. Sports complex
27. Irritable
28. Amish feature
29. Spheres
30. On one's toes
31. Nightingale, for one
32. Washer companion
34. Mrs. Zeus
35. Needs to be microwaved
37. Used again
38. Checker's move?
43. Curative waters
44. Belt sites
45. Heated argument
46. Bring out
47. Reverse, on a PC
48. Remarked
49. City near Lake Tahoe
50. Final, for one
51. Soothing plant
52. Not a movie
53. Finished
54. Catch on to

❖ **Solution on page 267**

15

Top Notch   *Sylvia Thompson*

ACROSS

1. Blue shade
5. Trio card game
9. Cleans the boat deck
14. Upper hand
15. Masking ___
16. Rock climber's holding device
17. A small buffalo
18. King of comedy
19. Prelude, for short
20. The ___ Ambersons (Booth Tarkenton novel)
23. Spanish river
24. A lustrous fabric
25. Huff and puff
26. Offshoots
29. Etc. stuff
31. Shade trees
32. Go-between
37. Pitcher spout
38. On the q.t.
40. Rhoda's mother
41. Very lucky
43. Mary Kay competitor
44. Famous redhead
45. Leave unexpectedly
47. Telephone line in use
49. Guarantees
53. Winding path
54. An elaborate display
58. Horned beast
60. Take a header
61. General's helper
62. Take delight in
63. Gilded enamel metalware
64. Crossword diagram
65. Hogback's relative
66. Pindar poems
67. Retracts a statement

DOWN

1. Tigers or Mets
2. *Giant* writer's first name
3. In awe
4. Shelters with only one sloped roof
5. Hires office personnel
6. Muhammad's successor
7. At breakneck speed
8. Conviction of truth
9. Kebob holder
10. Be victorious
11. Alluring
12. Karloff of the movies
13. Secretly watch someone
21. McKellen or Holm
22. McKellen and Holm
25. Juliette Low's org.
26. Narcissist's love
27. Erato's sister
28. Stirring
30. Modern nest egg: Abbr.
32. Wharton degree: Abbr.
33. Scrap of food
34. Female rabbit
35. Landfill problem
36. Bombastic declamation
38. A Chinese dynasty
39. Take a lid off
42. Make an effort
43. Appease
45. Coverings for windows
46. International organization
47. Lawrence Peter ___ of baseball
48. Theater guide
50. Melee
51. Young cod or haddock
52. Of some benefit
54. Item underfoot?
55. Early violin
56. Mine passage
57. Half the checkers
59. Web of a spider

❖ **Solution on page 267**

Up and Atom   *Douglas Fink*

❖ Solution on page 267

ACROSS

1. Catches
6. Early pulpit
10. Breathing place
14. Dole out
15. Be ablaze
16. Send out
17. Physicist's containers
19. Poorly thought out
20. Torso-wear
21. A likely story!
22. Carla's portrayer
23. City on the Rio Grande
25. Amusing when told or given to a cat
26. Go next to
30. Elixir
32. Trickster
34. One against what's popular
38. Fall flower
39. Record part with the hot songs
40. Fears
43. Title role for Kathy Bates
45. Used a 10A
47. Capone's rival
48. Hit TV show of the '70s
51. Charlie's brother
53. Middle East veep
54. KFC option
55. Turned skyward
60. Eject
61. Physicist's news show
63. Surface life
64. Premed class
65. 48A role
66. Bit part in *Julius Caesar*
67. Bear's cry
68. 86 or 99

DOWN

1. Moslem tradition
2. Skin cream
3. Not a nice thing to say
4. Washington insiders
5. Tariffed item
6. Bar bloc
7. Goes in the Iditarod
8. Scope
9. Like a beached raft
10. Physicist's TV hero
11. D-Day beach
12. Tread support
13. A Coen brother
18. Blue shades
24. Deteriorate
26. Right now!
27. Poppycock!
28. Until
29. Physicist's upheaval
31. Asian range
33. Eye part
35. Become weary
36. Bad time for Caesar
37. Old levy
41. Earhart and Bloomer
42. Anybody
43. "Runaway" singer's first name
44. Hatred
46. One if by land, or two if by sea
48. Butte's kins
49. More than enough
50. Prolonged attack
52. Nightly place for the Marx Brothers
56. Rugged rock
57. Helper
58. Use an MRI
59. Dessert pastry
62. Part of NATO

Chapter 2

Themes Like
Old Times

I Hear Voices   *Merle Baker*

ACROSS

1. Sap sucker
6. Earth tone
11. Corp. VIP
14. 3D deity
15. New Zealand natives
16. USAF rank
17. Fictional family head
19. Leg. certifiers
20. Kind of product or user
21. Barrel
22. Donation, perhaps
24. Links areas
26. Opposite of a dork
28. Fleecy cloud formation
31. Contradict
34. City of Europe or Texas
35. Knock over
37. Impulse path
38. Target
39. City on the Nile
40. Criticize, slangily
41. First Best Actress Oscar winner Gaynor
42. Dissuade
43. Local news choice, at times
46. Promoted in checkers
47. Polar sight
51. Kind of cuisine
52. Unaccompanied
54. Grassland
55. CPR giver
56. Game fish
60. USN address
61. Occasion
62. New dough
63. Tax ID
64. Cans
65. Hang in folds

DOWN

1. Late bloomer
2. LP player
3. See 14A
4. Northeastern league
5. South Dakota senator
6. Diamond figures
7. A letter may be one
8. Coiler
9. Osprey cousin
10. Hysterical
11. Lacks ability to perform
12. Spotlight
13. Beginning
18. Hops oven
23. Unwell
25. Profit
26. Rector's assistant
27. Leave out
29. Spoke one's mind
30. Beast of burden
31. Harmful
32. Ways off
33. Miss
36. Scorecard figure
38. Swiss river
39. Characteristic determinant
41. They may be kept up with
42. Put in plain text
44. Alba. neighbor
45. Loathsome
46. White hat wearers
48. Barton or Bow
49. Man of fables
50. Not current
52. Swim alternative
53. Chooses
57. Depression-era proj.
58. VCR button
59. Scottish speech characteristic

❖ **Solution on page 267**

Not Out of the Woods Yet
Merle Baker

ACROSS

1. Scan hypertext
7. Candidate of 2000
11. SARS studier
14. Make up for
15. Lots
16. Fictional little hopper
17. John and others
18. Paper precursor
20. People might come out of this
22. Progresses slowly
23. Panchen ___
24. First senator to go into space
26. Word with circle or star
29. Dylan didn't play this
34. " . . . must come to ___"
35. Walk like a stilt
36. Sweetums
37. Be undecided
38. Practices
40. Fabric texture
41. Call letters?
42. Hickam AFB locale
43. ___ Gables
44. Mythological deity
47. Honor, in a way
48. Wee
49. Thin nail
51. Versatile blood
54. *The Long Hot Summer* star
58. Fuel source
61. "You are what you eat," e.g.
62. Bother
63. Unwritten
64. Court position
65. Marshal executed for treason
66. Manage without assistance
67. More likely to win

DOWN

1. Lager, for one
2. Move, in Realtor-speak
3. Numerical prefix
4. Bird habitat
5. Tanning position
6. Derby site
7. Rubberneck
8. Prefix meaning ear
9. Tigger's pal
10. Back
11. Child actor Brandon ___
12. Welfare in Westminster
13. Filches
19. Bridge, over the Seine
21. Like a new recruit
24. Fall guy
25. Tacks on
26. Fruit in a patch
27. " . . . and ___ grow on"
28. Slowly, musically
30. Admit
31. Tara resident
32. Pop choices
33. Got down, in a way
38. Methods
39. " . . . and bears, ___!"
40. Instrument
42. Up-to-date with
43. Held protectively
45. Conked out
46. *Six Feet Under* network
50. Boxer Marciano's first name
51. Duplicate
52. Days past
53. Dawdling
54. Connect securely
55. Play parts
56. Start for stat
57. *Coming Home* actor
59. Indignation
60. Office connection: Abbr.

❖ **Solution on page 267**

Late Affirmations   *Grace Becker*

ACROSS

1. Mater's lead
5. Slight impression
9. Milan's La ___
14. Oil, for the Tin Man
15. Jewish month
16. More out of the sun
17. Hollywood song and dance man
19. " . . . say and not ___"
20. Immigrant's subj.
21. Video game letters
22. Recycled item
24. Sure thing
26. Use "five finger discount"
27. Sarge, perhaps
28. Shaker ___: Abbr.
29. ___ *Good Men*
32. Suited one on a field
35. Part of the eye
37. Downed a meal
38. Mr. Grant portrayer
39. Kind of flush
41. RR stop: Abbr.
42. California wine valley
46. "Dixie" composer
47. Punjabi believer
49. Newhart of *Elf*
50. Smoking alternative
51. Stands for pictures
53. ___ Nixon, Richard's daughter
57. Devoid of germs
59. Bank deposit?
60. "Surprise!"
61. True-blue
62. Movie and TV crew members
65. That is
66. Field of study
67. Take charge
68. Unlike a rolling stone
69. Kind of caterpillar
70. Snack for hikers

DOWN

1. South American mountain range
2. This makes Rover no rover
3. ___ Park (Edison's lab site)
4. Calculator function
5. Be afraid to
6. Sealtest competitor
7. Dundee denial
8. Tabloid talk shows, e.g.
9. It points up in a deck
10. Tapioca plant
11. *Alexander's Ragtime Band* actress
12. "___ and the Swan," Yeats
13. Elvis ___ Presley, entertainer
18. It can be chased by the chaste
23. River through northern France
25. Fairy tale opener
26. Cal. abbr.
30. L' ___, c'est moi
31. Strip of shoe leather
32. Accumulation
33. Wine city near Turin
34. Drama with Gary Sinise
36. Gunsmith
40. All-encompassing beginning
43. Fourth person
44. Ferret relative
45. Workout spot
46. Implore
48. Treat not-so-nicely
52. Like some deltas
54. Engraved pin
55. "___ a Symphony"
56. Supermarket chain
57. ___ pickings
58. Ruckus
59. Handwriting on the wall
63. *Diamonds ___ Forever*
64. Math class, for short

❖ **Solution on page 267**

As Seen on TV   *Lane Gutz*

ACROSS

1. Eve maker
4. Lowlife
8. Secret plan
14. Clothes cleaner
15. Some stereos
16. Ivory Wayans, for one
17. On some TVs
19. Gofer's chore
20. Primate example
21. On some TVs
22. *Who Framed Roger Rabbit* henchman
24. Egg producer
25. Amontillado container
26. Song on vinyl: Var.
27. Dr. Frankenstein's assistant
29. Parallel to
31. Type of wood?
32. Pool shot
33. Small racecars
34. On some TVs
36. Late bloomer
39. Maned beasts with large forequarters
40. Owns
43. Question starter
44. Hive raider
45. Ken, e.g.
46. Homonym of 47A
47. Musical talent
48. Contemptibly small (slang)
50. On some TVs
53. Island south of Sicily
54. East
55. On some TVs
58. Dennis, e.g.
59. Formerly
60. Exclusive word
61. Proofreader, at times
62. Methods
63. Arctic prefix

DOWN

1. They record CDs
2. Hebrew name meaning "watchful"
3. Luggage carrier?
4. NYSE term
5. Nonmilitary person
6. They defy physics, supposedly
7. Use an Oster product
8. Flock of ducks in flight
9. Proof of ins.
10. Rhea's daughter
11. Lawmaker
12. *The Fugitive* plot
13. Conclusions
18. Snoopy
21. Beach in L.A.
22. Doo follower
23. Builder's contract
24. Indiana native
28. Mystery purchase
29. Analogous
30. Banyan sap
32. ICU part
34. MPH part
35. Not unusual
36. "Radical!"
37. Used scissors
38. The ends
40. Church cry
41. Clothes cleaner
42. Sneaky
45. ROM and RAM contain this
47. Key with an arrow on it
49. Toy makers
51. Bench, e.g.
52. Remarkable (Scot.)
53. Tropical Asian starling
55. Pen filler?
56. End of pot or not
57. Wall denizen

❖ **Solution on page 267**

Bridge Tutorial *Alan Olschwang*

ACROSS

1. Doesn't have
6. Masseuses' milieus
10. Make a lasting impression
14. Puerile
15. Not on tape
16. Pith
17. River frolicker
18. Lost
19. Shades
20. American of Japanese descent
21. Jetsetters' needs
23. Expressions of satisfaction
25. Cravat
26. Get
27. Event for the true fan
33. Logan of music
34. Instant greenery
35. Puts up
39. African antelope
41. Gratuity
43. Pretentious person
44. Animosity
46. Uno e due
48. Kazan of films
49. Unsparingly
52. Function
55. Id companion
56. Mrs. Cantor
57. NBA crowd pleasers
60. Part of table setting
65. It might get a run when up
66. Kent's love
67. San Diego player
68. Fencer's foil
69. Culture medium
70. Interoffice communication method
71. What's left over
72. They stand for something
73. Freeway exits

DOWN

1. Serengeti stalker
2. She goes against the grain
3. Top Broadway hit
4. Patella's place
5. Number of your PC
6. One way to achieve a goal
7. Tiltin' tower town
8. Sacred text of Zoroastrianism
9. California city
10. Kind of chamber
11. Sees the sights
12. Greek island
13. German state
22. Equals
24. The males of a species
27. Does, for instance
28. Stew pot
29. ___ Bator
30. A place to keep your money in Mexicali
31. Head of Hollywood
32. Actress Russo
36. Weather word
37. Drudgery
38. Judge's order
40. Figured out
42. They extol
45. Kind of army
47. Finish the coda
50. Minority
51. Like Dan
52. Poe's House?
53. Ski path
54. Mellows
58. Competition
59. Strike sharply
61. Tibetan monk
62. Funnyman Sandler
63. Excursion
64. Snigglers' pursuit

❖ **Solution on page 267**

I Like Candy *Leslie Nicoll*

ACROSS

1. Fleck from flint
6. Whistle blowers
10. Ballet move
14. Brownie or elf
15. Puts two and two together
16. Actress Kudrow of *Friends*
17. Candy for the adventurous
20. Chess piece
21. Barn's upper level
22. Group of eight
23. Jai ___
24. There or where follower
26. In a word, SWEET
33. Recluse
34. Regret
35. Shoppe type
36. Ram's mate
37. A research investigation
39. 56D, south of the border
40. ABA members
42. Prior to, poetically
43. Angled edge
45. Flavorful hard candies
49. Top notch
50. Composer Novello
51. Suspect's story
54. Wineglass part
55. Outcome of 15A
58. Candy to puff or blow
62. Creamy French cheese
63. Mrs. Nick Charles
64. She may be practical
65. Comedian Foxx
66. Put one's foot down
67. Early computer

DOWN

1. Unwanted e-mail
2. Pocket bread
3. Neural transmitter
4. Edge
5. *Prairie Home Companion* host
6. Basket material
7. Mark a manuscript
8. Four-term prez
9. U-turn from NNW
10. Control group medication
11. Pleasant tune
12. Castaway's place
13. New York river
18. Anthracite, e.g.
19. Afghanistan's Tora ___ region
23. Hole in one
24. Hatfield-McCoy affair
25. Follow orders
26. Transparent
27. Manual type
28. ___ a customer
29. More loyal
30. With Lucy, '50s sitcom
31. Old Ford
32. Aquatic mammals
37. Spotted
38. Shade provider
41. Impaled
43. No. 35 on the Periodic Table
44. Make a mistake
46. Poach the pasta?
47. Electronic image
48. With, to Henri
51. 40A, e.g.
52. Tackle box item
53. As before, in footnotes
54. Confident
55. Indian wrap
56. Celestial bear
57. In the blink of an eye?: Abbr.
59. USN officer
60. "I ___ You Babe"
61. Rev up an engine

❖ **Solution on page 268**

25

Cheese All That   *Verna Suit*

ACROSS

1. Jo, Beth, and Amy's sister
4. Water rings?
9. Basketball's Johnson
14. Fuss
15. Allergy season sound
16. Bonaire neighbor
17. Baton Rouge coll.
18. Cheesy Lon Chaney film?
20. Turner or Mack
21. Crustacean with claws
22. Ibsen play
23. Cut, like prices
25. Country quarry
26. ___ all that!
27. Hit dead-on
28. *JAG* network
31. Urged (with on)
33. Good luck symbol
35. Hip
36. Hangout
37. "___ she comes . . ."
38. Old small-value coin
40. Rod ___
41. Uneven
42. Twelve ___: Tara neighbor
43. Mason portrayer
44. Cover up
45. Most delicate, in a way
48. Sufficiently dressed
51. Slime
52. Be beholden
53. Cheese with time to talk?
55. Bagel topper
56. Worship
57. Producer Joshua ___
58. Time
59. Man-goat
60. Brother to Babette
61. Bo Derek movie

DOWN

1. Soda fountain treats
2. Failed Ford
3. Cheese maker's standard?
4. Paired up
5. Earthy pigments
6. In the future
7. Crypt
8. Old French coin
9. Underground access
10. Pyromaniac's crime
11. No ___, no glory
12. Tell me another one
13. Road users
19. Self-absorbed person
24. Book holder
25. Fair folk
27. Subject words
28. Goat-cheese maker's car?
29. Sudden tidal rise
30. Prophet
31. Narcissus admirer
32. Bully
33. Purse item
34. Ventriloquist Lewis
36. Fireside
39. Cat, at times
40. Swiss lake city
43. Church sale
44. Like some drinkers
45. Slopes hangout
46. Used strong language
47. First lady, for one
48. Cape of Good Hope explorer
49. Icelandic poem
50. Cream lump
51. Skunk giveaway
54. Tiny person

❖ **Solution on page 268**

'50s Pop Music — Michael Wiesenberg

ACROSS

1. Approximately
6. Burden
10. Angers
14. Place to sweat it out
15. Keenan or Ed
16. Horiz. counterpart
17. Directed against a thing, legally
18. Coin of France
19. Biblical measure, one-tenth of an epha
20. "Davy Crockett" singer
22. Singer McEntire
23. "___ Anyone Explain?" (Ames Brothers)
24. Ricky Nelson hit
26. Folk's Kingston ___
29. Police team
32. Bottomless pit
33. ___ Tafari (Haile Selassie)
34. Trade
35. ESP relative
36. Marty Robbins hit of 1957
42. Old space station
43. Hawaiian garlands
44. Ash repository, sometimes
45. "No it isn't very pretty/What ___ without pity/Can do"
48. "___ not gonna take it"
49. First word of Fats Domino's biggest hit
50. "Young at Heart" singer
52. "___ River Rock" (Johnny & the Hurricanes)
54. ___-mell
55. Dean Martin hit of 1954
61. Composer Satie
62. Seat of Hawaii County
63. Lhasa is its capital
64. Rice-a-___
65. "___ You"
66. Eat away
67. Middle East Gulf
68. Chief Untouchable
69. Certain woodwinds

DOWN

1. "Riiiiiiiight"
2. Ruination
3. Not theirs
4. Paris-based world org.
5. Buccaneers' home
6. He's in debt
7. Curly's laugh
8. Turmoil
9. Quick shot
10. Singer of 1959's "Morgen"
11. Cure
12. Darkness personified
13. NYC's subway cars no longer have these
21. Response
25. Brewers' ovens
26. Lala preceder
27. Like sushi
28. Kinda
30. Existed
31. Jobs company
34. Tour of duty
35. Nosey Parkers
37. Fats Domino hit of 1957
38. "___ the ramparts . . . "
39. Nice yes
40. Prince Valiant's older son
41. Explosive initials
45. "Ad astra per ___" (Kansas motto)
46. Steering system component
47. Connected to the Web
48. Dispenser of 43A
49. Look up to
51. Prefixed title accorded supreme judges of England: Abbr.
53. Restaurant patron
56. Start of a Shakespearean title
57. "___ in the Attic"
58. One of 69A
59. Comic Foxx
60. Summers in France

❖ **Solution on page 268**

Nonsense   *Roy Leban*

ACROSS

1. Stockholm quartet
5. The top
9. Plays alone
14. A rare day
15. Long, for short
16. Show
17. Julie Andrews film role?
20. Tide replacement?
21. Signs
22. Tearjerkers?
23. Sprite, for one
24. ERA, for one
25. Petty officers
28. Wonka author
29. Sky org.
32. Computer char. code
33. A Spelling
34. Land's end?
35. Answer to this clue, if you're not sure?
38. Camera component
39. Cow kin
40. Rook or bishop
41. Posed
42. Dessert treats
43. *The French Lieutenant's Woman* screenwriter
44. Proposes, perhaps
45. Competitor to 1D
46. Horse headgear
49. Toledo's most famous actor?
50. Roll opening
53. *The King and I*'s "et cetera . . . ," today
56. Happening
57. Eat to lose
58. "Hike" follower
59. Bobby of the Black Panthers
60. One of the back forty
61. Makes good

DOWN

1. Romeo opening
2. Book and candle companion
3. Empty a boat, perhaps
4. PD's alert
5. Attaches a rider, perhaps
6. Winter gear
7. Some phone no. endings
8. Top of a clock
9. ___ Tap (fictitious rock group)
10. Sputnik did it
11. NY Liberty's Rebecca
12. Hot spot
13. Tennis units
18. Like Steve Austin
19. Architecture style
23. Bridge divisions
24. It's a wrap
25. Cries
26. Actor Milo of *Barbarella*
27. Short amount, in cooking
28. Fuller houses
29. Choice cut
30. Friend of the White Rabbit
31. Change
33. It's said they're unavoidable
34. Coburn spy role
36. Gretzky's game
37. Bee home
42. Emulates the White Rabbit
43. Harry Morgan, for one
44. More, briefly
45. Car stereo control
46. Free wins
47. Rant alternative
48. Inkling
49. Bank agcy.
50. Dame who's a man
51. Outback greeting
52. Spaces
54. Smile protectors?
55. Cleopatra's cold-blooded killer

❖ **Solution on page 268**

28

A Little Rearranging *Alan Olschwang*

ACROSS

1. Cozy
5. Pack down firmly
9. Proofreader's mark
14. Soft drink
15. Battle souvenir
16. *Dunes and Sea II* painter
17. Hokkaido native
18. Post-game show in Indiana?
20. Land buy
22. Window attachment
23. Take advantage of
24. Second-place finisher of note
26. Stated
28. Astronomer's surprising find?
32. Id companion
33. Enterprise rival
34. Grab
38. Salve
40. Jefferson Davis's domain, briefly
42. Farm outbuilding
43. Hull House cofounder Jane
46. QED part
49. Thai language
50. Skill yet to be identified?
53. Party giver
56. Sported
57. Harem room
58. Speed
60. Green
64. Record of milk production?
67. March Madness org.
68. Sort of management
69. Greek victory goddess
70. Exam
71. Daytime TV fare
72. She was born free
73. Pindar works

DOWN

1. Ella's forte
2. Bordeaux black
3. Radius neighbor
4. Pampas horseman
5. Recipe meas.
6. Kind of freedom
7. Medieval war club
8. Shaped in advance
9. Nottingham suburb
10. Farewell
11. Happen more than once
12. Obliterate
13. Worked the keyboard
19. Evaluates
21. Soho so long
25. Gun the engine
27. Meaningful times
28. First name in country
29. Mild expletive
30. Aspic creation
31. German industrial city
35. Roofer's supply item
36. Extended family
37. Night call
39. Stag attendee
41. Museum assets
44. They suffer severely
45. Proud mount
47. Where the speedometer rests
48. Mountain lake
51. Weasel
52. Crude shelter
53. Concluding passages
54. Hersey's bell town
55. Subarctic Eurasian forest
59. Beach toy
61. Type of tea
62. Roses' place
63. Raids the fridge
65. 10-percenter
66. Indeed

❖ **Solution on page 268**

Aviary Authors *Lane Gutz*

ACROSS

1. Small cobra
4. Rising in elevation
10. Attention getter
14. Sanders's rank: Abbr.
15. Place for a bamboo umbrella, maybe
16. This and that
17. Andrew M. Greeley novel
20. Jet along
21. Watch over
22. Executive's assistants
23. *Beowolf* or *Iliad*
25. Incision
27. One-one?
30. Rob Roy's group
31. PC alternative
34. ___ acid
35. Lecture hall platform
36. *Beowulf* or *Iliad*
37. Michael F. Duke novel
40. Otherwise
41. Amorous look
42. Expiate
43. Load with woad
44. Dixie Chicks, e.g.
45. Frasier and Lilith, in *Cheers*
46. Isn't bad
47. Educator Horace ___
48. Not right or obtuse
51. Port in Yemen
53. Man or Wight
57. Margaret Coel novel
60. Beams
61. Noise reduction tool
62. Green card org.
63. D.A. aide
64. Not level
65. Not, to a Scot

DOWN

1. Play parts
2. This is next to TriBeCa
3. Insanity, e.g.
4. Thurman of filmdom
5. Rhodes in *Nine to Five*
6. Stows
7. "Get ___ writing!"
8. Way to win the election
9. Debussy's "Air de ___"
10. Suggest
11. Lost traction
12. Triangle ratio
13. Determine heads or tails
18. Fissure
19. Kicked back
24. Hen follower
26. Sweetheart
27. Receded
28. Type of gag?
29. Wipe out
30. Monte ___
31. TV attorney
32. In the past, to Bunyan
33. Walking sticks
35. Foxglove genus
36. Devilish
38. Put on earth
39. Merit
44. "___ yellow ribbon . . . "
45. Land promised to Abraham
46. "This is only ___"
47. Religious goal, for some
48. It doesn't need a strop
49. Addams who made the Addams Family
50. 180s
52. Gateway competitor
54. Ankle-knee connection
55. Olin or Horne
56. Gaelic tongue
58. State in India
59. Cable TV channel

❖ **Solution on page 268**

You Can Say That Again   *Dave Fisher*

ACROSS

1. With 1D, chocolate bar
4. Arroyo in Arabia
8. Fish hawk
14. Kerfuffle
15. Verily
16. Light sleeper's complaint
17. Evasive language?
19. Morissette
20. Spotted
21. Henry's Ann
23. Half man, half goat
25. Wapiti
26. Season
29. Betray?
32. Gasoline additive, once
33. Frosted
34. Party veep
35. Sergeant ___
37. End of something hanging in a cave
38. Sinewy
39. Thrown into ecstasy
42. Nemesis
43. Name on a specimen
46. Yucky stuff
47. Mole?
50. Woodwinds
52. Opposite of fast
53. Flues
54. Some are false
56. Otherwise
57. Comprehension
59. Quick march?
63. Stole a glance
64. Sacred bird of Egypt
65. ___ Dolorosa
66. Emphasize
67. Ambulance crew
68. URL ending, maybe

DOWN

1. See 1A
2. Ore. neighbor
3. Novelist Leo
4. ___ *Down*
5. Start of a famous palindrome
6. Singer Shannon
7. Pattern for Rorschach
8. Roundish
9. Cobbler's inventory
10. Good baseball action?
11. Not as thick
12. Major record label
13. "Owner of a Lonely Heart" group
18. Openers
22. Approves
23. High school subj.
24. A rainbow, for example
25. Highlander's tongue
27. Overhead item
28. Newspaper VIPs
30. Terra ___
31. Louis or Paul
36. Bald, in a way
37. Delayed reaction?
38. Desire
39. It could be inflated
40. Hob___
41. Early riser
42. ___ Boys
43. Hoodwink
44. Canadian prov.
45. Aliens, briefly
48. Come down with
49. Sudden blow
51. Japanese wines
55. Cincinnati players
56. Give out
57. "Brown" company
58. Stroke
60. Co. in Armonk, NY
61. Day or night opening
62. Huguenot's H_2O

❖ **Solution on page 268**

No Three-ums 1   *Douglas Fink*

ACROSS

1. Emcee
5. They're vile near the Nile
9. Charm school skill
14. Not fooled by
15. Room activity?
16. Adams of photos
17. Mortgage papers holdup
18. Asta's owner
19. Amazingly low price
20. A "Bye Bye Love" singer
22. That place!
23. Saw wood
24. Artificial topper
26. Pipsqueaks
28. Cyrano feature
32. Militia
36. *Battlestar Galactica* role
38. They grow on trees
39. ___ on (get close to)
40. Ham it up
41. Comfy chair features
42. Chichi's coin
43. Most extreme
45. Feeds the plants
47. Title role for Madonna and LuPone
52. Shankar's strings
55. Classic film by Dennis Hopper
57. Full of wonder
58. Dog with a big tongue
59. Airport maneuver
60. Spin doctor, perhaps
61. Sawyer's pal
62. Eurekas
63. Ciao
64. Airport problems
65. Sole

DOWN

1. Cargo spaces
2. It might make you cry
3. Taker of notes, or anagram of notes
4. Copier need
5. Facial feature
6. Abbreviates
7. Sitting rooms
8. Avoid hitting the hay
9. Like the necklace in "The Necklace"
10. Precisely
11. "Understood"
12. Cooking verb
13. First name in modeling
21. Gave the kibosh to
25. Biblical book
27. Was victorious
29. Victorious cries
30. Narrow cut
31. Too long a wait
32. Kerplunk
33. TV studio sign
34. Old pros
35. Toss
37. Train aide
39. Place for a guard
41. One source for news
44. Begin at the links
46. Combat site
48. Very important
49. Spud state
50. Stetson wearer, often
51. Come up
52. Samples sake
53. About
54. Not too wild
56. Passions

❖ **Solution on page 268**

Just In Time *Mark Milhet*

ACROSS

1. Lecture focus
6. Golden Fleece craft
10. Drops in the air
14. Sister of Polyhymnia
15. Average
16. Dilly-dallying
17. Timely military facility?
19. Light gas?
20. Wee one
21. Stuff
22. Quartered
24. Pandora's Box remnant
25. Hay there?
26. Amber and umber
29. "Just right!"
33. Intense hatred
34. Seats for sermons
35. Beaver's dad
36. Warm, in a search
37. Count in jazz
38. Dry as dust
39. Cymbal relative
40. Sciences partner
41. Home at a park
42. Laboratory task
44. Shred
45. Sets a price at
46. Hotel or cracker's name
47. Give a hard time to
50. Losing proposition?
51. Time and again
54. '40s foes
55. Timely visionary?
58. Cameo, e.g.
59. ___ fixe (obsession)
60. Poker ploy
61. Son of Seth
62. Signals at Christie's
63. Kooky

DOWN

1. Bubble sheet event
2. Hydrox rival
3. Treaty
4. "Am ___ understand . . . "
5. Comply
6. Don't hurry
7. Not a movie
8. 19A is one
9. Like a tiny town
10. Timely dance?
11. Midmonth day
12. Gin flavoring
13. Watch over
18. Pool visits
23. In error
24. Timely vision aids?
25. Clark's partner
26. Line dance
27. Classic theater name
28. Jungle vine
29. Vermin
30. Weight of a stone
31. Hackneyed
32. More peculiar
34. City of Light
37. Enjoyed the feel of
41. Sewer's guide
43. Fashion monogram
44. Wedding cake layer
46. Park attractions
47. Long-eared racer
48. Neuron arm
49. Missile site
50. Changed 26A
51. Forget about
52. Hootenanny
53. Deuce beater
56. Hubbub
57. Amateur-sports gp.

❖ **Solution on page 268**

Metallic *Alan Olschwang*

ACROSS

1. One bear
5. Pike's and its ilk
10. What gets marked up
14. Renee's friends
15. Initiation
16. Sea World attraction
17. Tad's toy
19. Lowest high tide
20. Go in
21. Yemen's capital
22. Corn holders
23. Where speakers spoke at the Forum
25. Continental currency
27. Idols' realm
33. Hoover, for one
36. Faux pas
37. Sort of sore
38. Fence the diamonds
40. King of Judea
42. Little ledge
43. Jean fabrics
46. Food for Fido
49. Chess champ
50. Common wrap
53. Old French coins
54. Keeps up with the Joneses +
58. Depot filler
61. Flowers of the future
64. Type of lily
65. Stead
66. Honor for valor
68. Black fly
69. Unworldly
70. Cube maker Rubik
71. Foots the column
72. Hangover?
73. Talk back

DOWN

1. Brit's father
2. ___ acid
3. Quart parts
4. They're on the left side of the balance sheet
5. Alderman, for one
6. Closes out
7. Katmandu's place
8. More acute
9. Waltz king
10. Agreements
11. Lunchtime favorite
12. Wound wall
13. Emulates Hines
18. Species of iris
24. Clear start?
26. Initials in electronics
28. By way of
29. Sort of salts
30. Refine the rhetoric
31. Singer Fitzgerald
32. Jody Foster film
33. Baby's first word, maybe
34. Seth's bro
35. Bill of fare
39. Umps calls
41. Call from the kennel
44. Tax form of old Rome?
45. Rebuffed
47. Also
48. Yet
51. He overcharges
52. Takes the loft
55. Extremist
56. Blueprints
57. Turkish gulf
58. Seaweed
59. Do you ___?
60. Anthropologist Margaret
62. Copperfield's wife
63. Cut short
67. Zuider ___

❖ **Solution on page 269**

No Three-ums 2 — *Douglas Fink*

ACROSS

1. Nail shaper
5. Disney villain
9. Sine site
14. It's struck when hot
15. Brouhaha
16. Actor with a voice like Ren
17. Family affair?
18. *Guys and Dolls* Tony winner
19. Intended role for Clooney to repeat
20. Casts, often
22. Validates
23. Far from regal
24. Before the drop-dead date
26. Ann-Margret's birthplace
28. Yuletide starter
32. It's bashed at a bash
36. It's offensive
38. Do away
40. Treeless field
41. Staccato
43. Blaze beginner
44. Agitate
45. Split to join
47. Like mermaids and sirens
49. It has many roots
54. Like some ends
57. Playbook play or phone option
59. Unregulated
60. Where 2003's big blackout started
61. Play the wolf
62. What it does is heartfelt
63. More than a suggestion
64. Listen to
65. Made holy
66. Gal for a (fictional) tec
67. With a certain style

DOWN

1. Items for marchers of yore
2. Castle of dancing
3. Unadmirable one
4. Hit a sunset date
5. Dark behavior?
6. Timmy had one
7. Afterthoughts
8. Some fowl
9. Depresser of sorts
10. Elton John classic
11. Bed or patch
12. Do consulting work?
13. Layers
21. Pizzeria of film
25. Sentence finisher
27. Screwy thing?
29. Make one's way
30. Rice of fiction
31. 16A or 18A
32. Places to be at home
33. Yeah, right!
34. Denier's response
35. Red flag raisers
37. With fervor
39. Accident scene in *Superman* or *ER*
42. He walked and talked
46. Asteroid belts, in sci-fi
48. Annoyed
50. Yo, Ho!
51. Lady's alternative
52. Fjord
53. Lacking yen?
54. Prop for Quincy
55. Combine
56. It's handed down
58. Nail holders

❖ **Solution on page 269**

E

Chapter 3

Unthemely
Behavior

Too Clumsy *Alan Olschwang*

ACROSS

1. ___ apparent
5. Vino region
9. Tic
14. Swit costar
15. Writer Daudet
16. ___ Mesa
17. It takes extra room in the closet
19. Helicopter assembly
20. Sand, e.g.
21. Brave's ax
23. Roy's love
25. Emulate Hines
26. Shriver of tennis
29. They're foolish
35. Sir Guinness
37. Old French coin
38. Enticement
39. Kind of dish
41. Indian address
43. Socialite Peggy
44. Chefs' protections
46. Chill the bubbly
48. Three-piece suit piece
49. They're likely to lead the assault
52. Actor Stephen ___
53. Meadowland
54. Cairo's river
56. Italian island
61. Dieters' picks
65. Prepare for the match
66. Crowd pleaser on the hard court
68. Maturing
69. Ms. Bagnold
70. Actress Skye
71. Augurs
72. Mark for removal
73. Checks out

DOWN

1. Expressions of false levity
2. *Time Machine* race
3. Big screen star
4. Type of transit
5. Soluble mineral salts
6. Uno, due, and tre
7. Wrong
8. Entirely
9. Pork and cornmeal product
10. Milne character
11. Movie friend of the Thin Man
12. Put on cargo
13. X, e.g.
18. Peruse
22. Member of a '60s singing group
24. Seth's son
26. They accompanied 22D
27. First of a series
28. Subway system
30. Bric-a-brac piece
31. Norway's patron saint
32. Sort of space
33. Novel writing?
34. Actress Berger
36. Hook follower
40. Hints
42. Representation
45. Brit's gun
47. Scene
50. Hefted
51. Sort of shot
55. TV bovine
56. Wild guess
57. Jason's ship
58. It kills bugs dead (the best way to kill 'em!)
59. Break bread
60. Problem spots
62. Nautical greeting
63. Like a fait accompli
64. Fr. holy women
67. Wall hanging

❖ **Solution on page 269**

Homophony   *Merle Baker*

ACROSS

1. Brewski
5. Home or bed attachment
10. Cracked
14. Nebraska native
15. Sequence
16. Cook book
17. Take on cargo
18. Shield
19. Dull sound
20. Revolutionary figure
23. Super-secret org.
24. Walkingstick, for one
25. Ice remover
27. Trivial matter
30. Traditional Romanian dance
31. Cornfield sound
34. Burst forth
36. Arrange, as hair
39. Molokai neighbor
41. Fair amount of time
43. Fit of pique
44. Drink heartily
46. Suit material
48. Watershed assessment org.
49. Let slip
51. Link
53. In some way
56. Form alliances
60. Kind of code
61. Strip of stamps, perhaps
64. Devotion
66. Jonathan Pryce role
67. Pre-adult stage
68. Bjorn contemporary
69. Happening
70. Theological concern
71. Author Ferber
72. Netherlands necessity
73. TV rooms

DOWN

1. Conductor Sir Georg ___
2. Hatch, for one
3. Extinct birds
4. Looked like
5. Maudlin plea
6. Links hazard
7. Work of Norse mythology
8. Sponsorship
9. Sop
10. Pretense
11. Maureen O'Hara costar
12. Entertain
13. *M*A*S*H* character
21. Lot measurement
22. Son of Aphrodite
26. Crafts companion
28. Mincemeat constituent
29. Give rise to
31. ___ au vin
32. Junior Olympic Games org.
33. "I hate this!"
35. Genealogy display
37. Sass
38. Greek letter
40. Roswell sightings
42. Nautical collectibles
45. Washout
47. Hamilton-Burr encounter
50. Like a dashiki
52. Devitalized
53. Harriet's mate
54. Area
55. *Three Coins in the Fountain* fountain
57. Purple shade
58. Remove from the lapel
59. Sounds of laughter
62. Arduous journey
63. Actress Skye
65. *Back to the Future* actress Thompson

❖ **Solution on page 269**

Who in the Dickens?   *Michael Wiesenberg*

ACROSS

1. Washer cycle
6. Lost
10. Mideast Gulf
14. Got into the pot
15. Roam
16. Aura
17. Certain Tanzanians
18. Level
19. Smell
20. David Copperfield's first name
23. Houston affirmation
24. Ivan of trading malfeasance
25. Principal's offspring in *Hard Times*
31. Graduate exams
32. Clunker
33. Word for one of Dickens's best-known characters
36. Storm of "Dark Moon"
37. Mends
38. Capital of Moravia
39. Adam of pop
40. Her dad's last name is Voight
41. Sourish
42. It's set in an English debtors' prison
44. Skedaddles
47. Goddess of the dawn
48. Whom the speaker wanted informed that "Barkis is willin'"
53. Indian princess
54. First name in jazz singing
55. Old truth
58. "Puppy Love" singer
59. Exam for prospective atty.
60. Location of Troy
61. "Hey, you!"
62. Fabric that might be gold
63. Tribal leader

DOWN

1. Measurement of PC capacity
2. "___ New York minute!"
3. Hwy. safety org.
4. Tern
5. Newspaper functionaries
6. Pretentious
7. Second word in the motto of the Order of the Knights of the Garter
8. Any time
9. Good exercise
10. Sworn
11. Caprices
12. Electronic attempt to subvert our reading habits
13. Like someone who has 12D
21. Reggae kin
22. Rummy game in which players try to get less than 15 or more than 49
25. Greek garb
26. Venue for Camus's *The Plague*
27. Shake additive
28. Lived
29. Quest of *Indiana Jones and the Last Crusade*
30. CSA leader
33. "It's c-c-c-cold!"
34. Counter
35. Songwriter Axton ("Greenback Dollar")
37. Change in the weather
38. What a tippler might fall off
40. Iwo ___
41. 1982 Dustin Hoffman role
42. Will Rogers usually carried one
43. ___ gratias
44. Deep-six
45. MacGregors and MacDougals
46. Orders
49. Lanchester who was Frankenstein's bride
50. Glitz
51. Concert receipts
52. Word preceding "Cassius" in Caesar's Shakespearean description
56. Fasten
57. Half a laugh

❖ **Solution on page 269**

In Position   Roy Leban

ACROSS

1. Classic violin
6. Home run record holder
11. Big wheels, for short?
14. Corsican hero
15. How tuna may be packed
16. Biblical name suffix
17. Pinnacles
18. Prefix for four
19. Animal associated with Linux
20. First in line
22. Orange or peach
23. "Hike" preceder
24. Took care of
26. Pen follower
29. Opening for a boy?
32. Italian soup pasta
33. All thumbs
35. The moon
37. Does in
40. Living-room piece
41. Beat
42. Romulus, to Remus
43. "No" voter
44. Frost
45. Lamb Chop lady
46. In the know about
48. "It's Only ___" (Beatles song)
50. "Is it soup ___?"
51. Trumpet blare
54. Hot blood
56. Crystal ball
57. What you might not go below
63. Source of the Rio
64. Fisherman, at times
65. Go onstage
66. "Absolutely!"
67. Lithe
68. Japanese-American
69. ___ Miss
70. "We ___ Overcome"
71. Comb, in a way

DOWN

1. Tiff
2. Shell you can eat
3. Cakewalk
4. Hebrew opening
5. Break up
6. ___-Honey (candy bar)
7. Standout
8. Untagged, in tag
9. Country lane, perhaps
10. Buffy, for one
11. Privilege
12. Legal locale
13. Turned on an axis
21. NASDAQ debut
25. Quicksilver
26. Leaning locale?
27. By and by
28. Homeless?
30. A hodgepodge
31. Agricultural
34. A stripper takes it off
36. Famous fiddler
38. What not to shout in a theater
39. Peeved mood
41. Exhaustive
45. Garden tempter
47. Parsi percussion
49. Vigor's partner
51. Ultraman's home
52. The Little Mermaid
53. Some building lobbies
55. "Rubber Duckie" singer
58. Apple shooter?
59. Baseball's Hershiser
60. "___ girl!"
61. Mediocre marks
62. Old railroad name

❖ **Solution on page 269**

Ask Away   *Lane Gutz*

ACROSS

1. Mess maker
5. La ___
10. National ___
14. One might see *Cats* here
15. Small (Fr.)
16. Hose hue perhaps
17. Rod's area?
18. Don't want (to)
19. In that case
20. Culver City, California
23. JFK lander
24. Circa: ___ about
25. Part of RSVP
28. Actor Omar
31. King in *The Tempest*
35. Didn't miss any
37. "I could ___ horse"
39. Nin from Neuilly
40. Noted game show host
43. Nice heavyweight?
44. Dramatic introduction
45. Lisbon lady
46. Welles and Bean
48. This stinks
50. Lawyer's association
51. '74 Peace Prize winner Eisaku
53. Scottish beret
55. The theme
62. Place
63. Dijon honey
64. Quaker's pronoun
65. Rich Little, e.g.
66. Some are glass
67. D or AA
68. Joins with a ring
69. Hindu apology?
70. He gets a whooping

DOWN

1. Cabbage, carrots, and mayo
2. Ness for one
3. Legendary monster
4. Miller and Molson
5. Type of soup
6. Gates and Eisner, e.g.
7. Rat ___
8. Piece of art, for short
9. Odysseus guardian
10. Got off the pot?
11. Sound rebound
12. Create suds
13. Port packaging
21. Beverly Glen to Culver City dir.
22. Type of panel
25. Handled
26. Olympic blood
27. Uris and Trotsky
29. Hide, to Houdini
30. Boil in a bag
32. Gates or Eisner, e.g.
33. Tuscan town
34. Schindler of *Schindler's List*
36. They were huge, once
38. Roll with it
41. Nice body?
42. It comes in a shell
47. Remote areas
49. Disneyland freebie
52. Milo of *The Verdict*
54. Its head lights
55. Reformat, slangily
56. Mind
57. Mock
58. Author/lawyer Gardner
59. Mother of Zeus
60. Farmer's PC?
61. Way to get attention
62. TV's *L.A.* ___

❖ Solution on page 269

Fill the Bill   *Merle Baker*

ACROSS

1. Soda insert
6. West of Hollywood
9. Extent of view
14. Mrs. Bush
15. Uncommon
16. Teared up
17. Facing Martinez
18. Word with end or line
19. Boat bodies
20. BILL
23. Southern resort city
24. Last: Abbr.
25. "___ Be the Day"
29. Expert
31. *The Three Faces of* ___
34. Kind of amplifier
35. Put away
36. Put away
37. BILL
40. Drops the ball
41. "___ bien!"
42. Comic book cowboy Red ___
43. Deli selection
44. Ruffles
45. Go-betweens
46. Oxlike antelope
47. Timber dresser
48. BILL
56. Emulate Bing Crosby
57. Sock section
58. Great-grandmother of David
59. Multitude
60. Blackguard
61. Another time
62. Kind of circle
63. "___, Good Lookin'"
64. Identified

DOWN

1. High-five, essentially
2. "See ya"
3. Red shade
4. Composer Khachaturian
5. Crushing defeat
6. Words to live by
7. Purim's month
8. Brim
9. Snoopy creator
10. Dressing holder
11. Stops a squeak
12. Throw snowballs at
13. Mag. big wheels
21. Nothing
22. Bee product?
25. Come to a point
26. Make haste
27. More than like
28. They may be left on the table
29. Walks through water
30. Greet the villain
31. Chopin piece
32. Senator, at times
33. Washstand pitchers
35. Tug
36. Achilles was dipped into it
38. Swagger
39. Barry Goldwater, for one
44. Less sensible
45. Depression pres.
46. Glittery rock
47. Mimicking
48. Jeff Bridges sci-fi movie
49. Shofar, for one
50. Engrave with acid
51. Libertine
52. Totally smitten
53. Wander
54. Lady friend in France
55. Object to
56. Fraternity letter

❖ **Solution on page 269**

Br-r-r! *Merle Baker*

ACROSS

1. Gives in
6. " . . . gyre and gimble in the ___"
10. Greedy
14. Graceful
15. Syr Darya feeds it
16. Many a computer program feature
17. "Et tu," e.g.
18. Financially secure
20. It's inaccessible
22. Afore
23. It's nonreturnable
24. Checks
26. Kingston Trio hit
29. Barley bristles
32. Hebrew day
33. Corn belt state
35. ___ Linda, CA
37. Moves like the Blob
41. A party crasher may get one
44. Squalor
45. *Duck Soup* actor
46. Sicilian spewer
47. Military weapons: Abbr.
49. Military option
51. AOL, for one
52. Caustic criticism
56. Putdown
58. "It's Alright" singer
59. Not at all romantic
65. Salt cellar and such
67. Kinshasa's country, once
68. Olympian's sword
69. Afghan Mullah ___
70. Having pizzazz
71. Eye problem
72. Yields
73. Some saxes

DOWN

1. Baby elephant
2. Ice cream thickener
3. Don Corleone
4. Role for Audrey
5. Largest of the Finger Lakes
6. Guitarist's pedal
7. Son of Zeus
8. Hobbyist's wood
9. Queen of fiction
10. "Who ___ to argue?"
11. Nettles
12. Quiescent
13. Teen chums
19. Ken Berry series
21. Not long ago
25. Feign feeling
26. Rub the wrong way
27. Doughnut shapes
28. MP's quarry
30. Crosby or MacDonald
31. Sling mud at
34. *The Maltese Falcon* star
36. Back forty section
38. Tubular pasta
39. Long periods
40. Break
42. " . . . thou shalt deny me ___" (Matt.)
43. Give off
48. Fifties musical genre
50. Public square
52. Yeas and nays
53. Not fit
54. *Pleasantville* star Maguire
55. Beast of burden
57. Parsifal's quest
60. It carries a heavy load
61. "Nor shall ever see that face of ___ again" (King Lear)
62. Hue
63. Accordingly
64. Former rulers of Tripoli
66. Grant or Remick

❖ **Solution on page 269**

Cooked Books   *Verna Suit*

ACROSS

1. Shoo!
6. 50 percent
10. Lip
14. Showing emotion
15. Where your eye color is
16. Stagger
17. Nom de plume
18. Waiflike Kate
19. Entry
20. James Joyce's pastry how-to?
23. Photogenic Weimaraner
24. Linked computers, briefly
25. Cologne count start
26. Pi follower
29. Guys' guide to pilaf?
32. In case
35. Fashion monogram
36. Diva showpieces
37. Promise
38. Refine ore
41. ___ meridiem
42. Monsters
44. Swiss river
45. Make a home
46. Sautéing for fat phobes?
50. Skill
51. Lode load
52. Air quality org.
53. Ms. Lupino
56. Ovid's tricks with goat cheese?
60. Wait a minute!
62. Niger neighbor
63. " . . . o'clock and ___ well"
64. Hearers
65. Dash
66. Female relative
67. Whirlpool
68. C-H fill
69. Bags

DOWN

1. Music score lines
2. Jonson's "To ___"
3. Like Oregon's winter
4. Irish knit sweater
5. Me
6. People-centered thought
7. English river
8. Lease holder
9. Architectural band
10. Ponch on "CHiPs"
11. Ascertain
12. Golly
13. Nightmarish street
21. Burghoff and Cooper
22. O'Neill's Christie
27. Warms
28. Start
29. Alternative
30. Declutter
31. Sturm und ___
32. Dishcloth gourd
33. Keen
34. Town on 7D
39. Dressing strategy
40. Lewinsky cohort
43. Lampblack
47. Set up (sl.)
48. Cow or sow
49. Boston suburb
53. Small key
54. Clear the windshield
55. Fools
57. A cinch
58. Norwegian king
59. Miscellany
60. Tiny
61. Past perfect part

❖ **Solution on page 270**

Prepare to Act   *Matthew Skoczen*

ACROSS

1. King who sounds like he has a mean look
5. Comic Quinn
10. Stern counterpart
14. Car bar
15. Exxon rival
16. Pot holder, perhaps
17. It's left to you, but not to others
19. It isn't much
20. Show your humanness
21. Apollo's mom
22. Dr. Lizardo of *Buckaroo Banzai*
24. Kid Ory's "Muskrat ___"
26. Type of tire damage
28. Rather red
30. One who has served
31. Maid's mini-mop
34. Good guy with a saber
37. Peaceful
39. Buckeyes' sch.
40. Mechanic's need
42. John K's creation
43. "Robert's ___"
45. Little singer
46. Pulls up
49. Splinter group
50. Masterpiece
51. St., or prayer to a saint
52. Skinflint's verb
54. Sportscasting Marv
57. *TV Guide* topic
61. Like shows during sweeps
63. She, in Salerno
65. Day-___
66. Calif. campus
67. Doting parent's camcorder time
70. It's meant to offend
71. Refrain from farming
72. It isn't much
73. Places for rings
74. Forever, far in the past
75. Piggies

DOWN

1. Weapon for Dr. Evil
2. Non-celeb cameo
3. Upset terribly
4. *Max Headroom* role
5. They're more than just jobs
6. Leave out
7. They stand for things
8. Start of a Kennedy quote
9. ___ if you paid me!
10. Part of a flight
11. Lead
12. 37A race
13. A secretary might take one
18. First name in scat
23. Kind of maid
25. He doesn't mind getting a flat
27. Current ___
29. More like an X-File
32. Just ___
33. It blows
34. Digital picture type
35. Gutter site
36. Where a star might first appear
38. Legal thing
41. Mold
44. Word pro
47. Manage
48. Vidal ___
53. Tender meat
55. Tellers of tales
56. Li'l giggle
58. Nome dome home
59. Draw away the sorrow
60. Tofu legumes
61. Horizon spoiler, perhaps
62. Legal gp.
64. Nice night
68. Camp asst.
69. Poe's place

❖ **Solution on page 270**

What's Missing? *Michael Wiesenberg*

ACROSS

1. Lip
5. In front of
10. Actor Ian
14. Gallop
15. MTM spinoff
16. Arab pooh-bah
17. Rights org.
18. ___ a limb
19. Dodos
20. Humanitarians
23. Prosodic foot
24. Droop
25. Capital by Gulf of Tonkin
28. Band aid
31. ___ Nova
35. Roughly
37. PC company
39. MSNBC rival
40. Nursing spot
44. Thanksgiving bird
45. "Jumpin' Jack Flash, It's a ___"
46. Dawn
47. Pangs
50. Shasta and Hood: Abbr.
52. Long, angry complaints
53. ___ Lobos
55. First man
57. Lion location
64. ___ avail
65. Scot with a lot
66. John in Russia
67. Grad
68. Story of Troy
69. Taboo
70. Physics calculation
71. Quotidian
72. Biting bug

DOWN

1. Buck
2. Gas station brand
3. Han of *Star Wars*
4. Bookish
5. Golf tour championship classification
6. Cuban rug cutting
7. Jot
8. Olfactory stimulus
9. Sari-clad royals
10. Takes a stab at
11. Gulf kingdom
12. Pouting parts
13. Virginia Woolf's ___ *Dalloway*
21. Mark or John
22. Bar bill
25. Sword grips
26. Running wild
27. Marilyn, at birth
29. Thick
30. *NOVA* spot
32. Offspring
33. Shot
34. Paquin and Pavlova
36. UN's Hammarskjold
38. Kingston Trio train
41. "___ Sam. Sam . . . "
42. Acoustic
43. On a trail
48. Blossoms
49. Our sun
51. Holy or spinal
54. Hardly flimsy
56. Papa
57. Author of *Nana*
58. Load
59. Blowout
60. Sundial hour
61. "___ calling!"
62. 9D's music
63. Half hitch, say
64. Scottish cap

❖ Solution on page 270

Family Films   *Verna Suit*

ACROSS

1. Turkish title
5. Western pals
10. Peace symbol
14. Paraphernalia
15. Give tools to
16. Tel ___
17. Take on
18. 1958 Rosalind Russell film
20. Cobra
21. Decks
22. Clip
24. Fused
28. Uncle Remus character
31. Slug's trail
32. Aruba neighbor
36. Well-used eraser
37. 1955 Fred Astaire film
41. Distant
42. Irked
43. Missouri county
46. Jonathan Livingston ___
50. Constructs again
54. Assad's country
55. Most pricey
58. Partner word
59. 1938 Ronald Reagan film
62. Bagnold or Markey
63. Gal Friday
64. Christopher ___
65. Bike or bus starter
66. Like wine
67. Trapshooting target
68. Stuffing herb

DOWN

1. Appalled
2. Japanese entertainer
3. TV's Morgenstern
4. Live and breathe
5. Ringing
6. Pale teal
7. Pip-squeaks
8. Likewise
9. Sales pitch
10. Maiden
11. Roman eggs
12. Pep
13. First lady
19. Tips
21. Trickery
23. Opening run?
25. Bathtub problem
26. Ostrich cousins
27. Ledger col.
29. ___ Mawr
30. New Haven school
33. Folding bed
34. Picnic pests
35. Make eyes at
37. Stupor
38. Saudi or Omani
39. Smallest amount
40. Nervous
41. Not against
44. Oxidized
45. Kin partner
47. Muse of astronomy
48. Coat insulation
49. Little Scot
51. Looks lasciviously
52. John or Bo
53. Binge
56. Overhang
57. Leave as is
59. Sheep's comment
60. Set up
61. Emotional poem
62. Wide-open spaces

❖ **Solution on page 270**

Double Duty   *Dave Fisher*

ACROSS

1. Span's partner
5. Prefix with body or freeze
9. Pearl or peridot
14. Broke
15. What a litigant does
16. Spanish birthplace of St. Theresa
17. Choir section
18. Con's game
19. Flax fabric
20. Like a stunned beachcomber?
23. ___ loser
24. Choose
25. Mar's follower
28. Part of SUV
31. Flavor enhancer
34. Fleece
36. It could be white
37. Salmon type
38. Anxious cigarette consumer?
42. Go ___ (nag)
43. Use 52D
44. Speeds
45. ___-Mex
46. Black and white
49. ___ for the money
50. See 51A
51. Uses 50A
53. Soviet actors take a bow?
61. Nasty necktie?
62. Seed coat
63. Popular cookie
64. Market opener
65. Takeout place?
66. Await judgment
67. Acid and litmus
68. Put up
69. Lessen

DOWN

1. Ems et al.
2. Vault necessity
3. Tiny Greek letter
4. Ticked off
5. State categorically
6. Cell centers
7. Colorful duck
8. Doctrines
9. Hillbilly's car
10. Turn out
11. "Just kidding" signal
12. Robert ___
13. Bring down
21. Mythical Muslim maiden
22. Roomy place?
25. Cravat
26. Booth item
27. Send a document again
29. "Camel" of the Andes
30. Jr.'s kid
31. Slogan
32. Martin ___ in *Apocalypse Now*
33. Furze
35. Buccaneer's back
37. KGB adversary
39. S. Pacific island with important phosphate deposits
40. Goose egg
41. Providence, R.I., university
46. Riot cops at times
47. Schools
48. Daily preparation
50. Early stage
52. It magnifies the game
53. MIT, for example: Abbr.
54. Cad
55. Trip taker's exclamation
56. Parking garage feature
57. 30D, for example
58. W × H
59. Eye part
60. It makes a prospector prosperous

❖ **Solution on page 270**

❖ Solution on page 270

From Broadway
Alan Olschwang

ACROSS

1. Metric measure
5. Portuguese president
10. Card game
14. Hard to locate
15. Name in Dolphin football
16. Roofer's supply item
17. Foots
18. Intricate pattern
20. Religious holiday
22. It's south of the Sahara
23. Won's follower?
24. Police transmission, briefly
26. South Carolina river
30. Mechanic
33. They're 35D
36. Blanket
37. Lode load
38. Sort of shop
40. Krazy ___
41. His number 15 was retired
43. Pub potable
44. One making amends
47. Seine sights
48. Landlords' restraints
51. *Lie Down in Darkness* author
52. ___ Paolo
53. Unit of electric current, shortly
56. Organic compound
59. Less pointed
61. Perennial also-ran
65. Too
66. Extended family member
67. One-on-one game
68. Sign for a theme word
69. Lairs
70. Squared
71. Unit of force

DOWN

1. Payola
2. Call
3. Sacramento suburb
4. Sort of hall
5. He's on the lam
6. Expression of discovery
7. They're zany
8. She was born free
9. Native American chiefs
10. Russian ruler
11. Glove material
12. Lion's share
13. Driver's aid
19. Makes over
21. Road worker's material
25. Trust in
27. Drinker's shout
28. Haute head?
29. Court hearings
30. BSA counterpart
31. Meager
32. They consume
33. Russian despots
34. Night hunter of the future
35. Very small
39. Washington city
42. Sit, differently
45. Tony and Maria sang it in *West Side Story*
46. Railroad requirement
49. Land buys
50. Brock of baseball
53. Oop in cartoons
54. Subatomic particle
55. Lying down
57. Rood reversal?
58. Hosiery shade
60. Come down
61. Bounder
62. Cry partner
63. A place to stay the night
64. Take advantage of

❖ **Solution on page 270**

Getting Around   *Alan Olschwang*

ACROSS

1. Aromatic herb
5. Marked by shallow depressions
10. Biblical preposition
14. Invention start
15. Toledo's 71A
16. Pizarro captured it in the 16th century
17. Woe is me!
18. Lien
19. Ridicule
20. Extreme position
22. Fleece
23. Casa component
24. Actress Parsons
26. Enthusiast
29. Diversion
31. All over again
33. The NRC replaced it
34. Pass
38. Right triangle reciprocal
40. Medic
42. Choose from the slate
43. Store fodder
45. Fall behind
47. Act like the banker
48. Gizmos
51. Iverson's playground
52. Exhibit passion
55. Appear
57. Puts on cargo
58. Rectify
63. Gray wolf
64. Ceiling
65. Bacon buy
66. Sufficient, formerly
67. Old-womanish
68. Food fish
69. Sea swallow
70. Brandish
71. Calendar confines

DOWN

1. Place a call in the old-fashioned way
2. Wait for the green
3. Turn the pages
4. Shoe forms
5. Music's patron saint
6. Kind of petrol
7. Ring
8. Lion families
9. ___ Kippur
10. Extremely frustrated
11. Staircase support
12. Kind of run
13. Bizarre
21. Fourths of a series
22. Took a base on the pitcher
25. Haggard heroine
26. It may be worth saving
27. Soon
28. Capone's nemesis
30. Elève's place
32. Overburden
35. Low man on the totem pole
36. Replacement worker
37. Sicilian volcano
39. Flemish sculptor Sluter
41. ___ Mountains (*Dirty Dancing* site)
44. Begley and Begley
46. Said hi
49. Third zodiac sign
50. "___ out!"
52. Bridge engineer Charles ___
53. Herman's Hermits lead singer
54. Fife accompaniment
56. Lachrymose
59. René's friend
60. Affix, in a way
61. Nurse in *The English Patient*
62. Ski lift
64. It's on the books

❖ **Solution on page 270**

Going Down   *Alan Olschwang*

ACROSS

1. ___ lively
5. Room partner
10. Diving birds
14. Kind of chest
15. Sign on a door
16. Player's bio entry
17. Dictator Idi
18. Jim Carrey character
20. Metric units of area
22. Deck out
23. Circle part
24. They're learned
26. Game fish
31. Aoki of the PGA
32. See the world
33. Major network
36. Sort of shot
38. Yorkshire river
39. Comic ___
41. French seasoning
42. Not so long ago
45. Evaluate
46. Bedroom option
48. Fills the tank
51. Lair
52. Typeface type
53. Fidgets
58. Relating to the presidency of "Old Hickory"
61. Jot
62. Tennis great
63. Borneo ape, briefly
64. Sea eagles
65. Pay attention
66. Some are kept secret
67. Showy rugs

DOWN

1. Former Iranian ruler
2. Heavy reading
3. Long narrative poem
4. Arlington landmark
5. Cincinnati athlete
6. Less than occasionally
7. Old-time actor Roscoe
8. Gun the engine
9. Rap entertainer
10. Sidereal
11. It's a no-no in some places
12. Gold fineness measure
13. Judge's orders
19. Some oranges
21. Sea extension
24. Vegas winners
25. Exist
26. Buss
27. It has lots of waterfront property
28. Brad
29. Las ___
30. Actress Black
33. Sidestepper
34. Zestiness
35. Raced
37. Thin porridges
40. More faddish
43. Snakelike fish
44. Good ___
46. Trembled
47. Brit's list ender
48. Indian leader
49. Obliterate
50. Film used for storage, shortly
53. Barcelona aunts
54. Crave
55. Australasian parrot
56. Sicilian volcano
57. Back talk
59. Alley in a 39A
60. Powerful D.C. lobby

❖ **Solution on page 270**

Heeeeeere's Johnny   Mark Milhet

ACROSS

1. Defense org.
5. A prince not yet kissed?
9. Puts on the brakes
14. Neighborhood
15. Wight or Avalon
16. To the left, to sailors
17. Inclination
18. On the level?
19. Shopaholic's binge
20. This Johnny is right on time
22. Catch some z's
23. Long-eared hound
24. One and only
26. Hangs back
29. Grant
33. Bobby Fischer's game
37. "Not to mention . . . "
39. Lessen the load
40. Rodgers's songwriting collaborator
41. Minoan's island
42. Tuneful Fitzgerald
43. Pelvic bones
44. The third man
45. Classic theater name
46. Latin-American dances
48. Boys, Boom, or Bean
50. Off-the-wall answer?
52. Connect
57. Guiding principle
60. This Johnny was in *MIB 2*
63. Shaving need
64. *Clue* weapon
65. Car follower
66. Canton neighbor
67. State firmly
68. Pillow covering
69. It followed "Da" when Ditka was dere
70. Word preceding souci or serif
71. Blabs

DOWN

1. Wealthy man
2. Basketball hall
3. Revival sites
4. "Drats!" and "Rats!"
5. Party, south of the border
6. Party request
7. Stick in the fridge
8. Chaps
9. Give a hard time to
10. This Johnny bears fruit
11. Handed-down history
12. December purchase
13. Dance move
21. Slithery swimmers
25. Clarinet cousin
27. What's donned
28. Rain-snow mix
30. Yarn
31. Munch Museum city
32. Give up by degrees
33. Stylish
34. Good sign?
35. Julia role
36. Johnny's Broadway hangout?
38. Town in Normandy
41. Carry's cohort
45. "As seen ___" (ad phrase)
47. They get squirreled away
49. Polishers
51. Gumbo pods
53. Feeling no pain
54. HI hi
55. Dagger's partner
56. Wheel sites
57. Zodiac scuttler
58. Do a fall chore
59. Pound of poetry
61. Old Chevy
62. Bid one club, e.g.

❖ **Solution on page 270**

53

E

Chapter 4

My Country 'Tis of Theme

All the Same   *Roy Leban*

ACROSS

1. Heaven's door
6. Vegetable fuel
10. Star reporter at *The Daily Planet*
14. As ___
15. Barney and Gomer's boss
16. Mexican bears
17. On a leash, perhaps
18. Initial request
19. Ads tout them
20. 1963 Kingsmen recording
22. Suffix meaning "collective"
23. Film parts
24. *I Am Woman* singer
25. Slap follower, perhaps
29. Confound
31. Sign
33. Movie where the credits scrolled down
37. Dance in a suite
38. Reporter's contact
39. More sedate
41. Vehicle in several James Bond movies
42. Weaving, perhaps
44. *Ghostbusters* prefix
45. With aloofness
48. Hoods' dames
50. Olympic speed skater
51. 1957 Richard Berry song
56. Half of Mork's signoff
57. Going follower
58. Hood's ammo
59. Four on a watch
60. Sweetheart
61. English Channel river
62. Saskatchewan native
63. IDs introduced in 1935
64. Fire fighters?

DOWN

1. Runner Devers
2. Cartoonist Peter ___
3. Bishop Desmond ___
4. Morlock victims
5. Betsy Ross, for one
6. Ex-con, perhaps
7. Followed
8. Iches or Atwater
9. E for a Jaguar
10. Song played for Guinness record of most simultaneous guitar players
11. Syria's president
12. "There's ___ in sight!"
13. Swift work
21. What Maine used to feed prisoners
24. Where the Republican Party was born
25. Reps.' rivals
26. Stone, for one
27. Dame who's a man
28. Song investigated by the FBI in 1964
30. Anatomical sac
32. Wipe again
34. Fonzie addressee
35. ___ above the rest
36. Mountain where Moses saw the Promised Land
40. *Rock 'n' Roll High School* band
41. Environments
43. Sam of cereal
45. Classical architectural style
46. Run, as a meeting
47. Bellybutton, perhaps
49. Web address separator
51. Some returns
52. Black and white treat
53. *QB VII* author
54. Actress Skye
55. Baa belles

❖ **Solution on page 271**

One Good Turn Deserves Another   Alan Olschwang

ACROSS

1. Green veggie
6. Caboose's place
10. Highlands miss
14. Evangelist McPherson
15. Teen's trouble
16. Fair
17. POTS
19. Norway's patron saint
20. Hosiery shade
21. Set the pace
22. Breeds
24. Harbor
26. Leslie Caron role
27. ROOD
32. Response to a knock
35. Chang's twin
36. See 56A
37. Cook meat
38. TV waitress
39. Boa
41. Test response: Abbr.
42. Taro dish
43. Meager
44. PETS
48. Bridge position
49. Locks
53. Corrects
56. Curaçao cocktail, with 36A
57. Convex moldings
58. Expression of grief
59. PEEK
62. Church part
63. List ender
64. Astronomer Jump
65. Command to a friend
66. Eli's realm
67. Members of an ancient Iranian people

DOWN

1. Assignments for the social worker
2. Unexpected obstacle
3. Rome's love
4. Fights off
5. Like Gore: Abbr.
6. See 8D
7. It turns litmus red
8. Hostelry
9. Gam protector
10. Soviet Brezhnev
11. Type of tree?
12. Prepare for the bout
13. Chesterfield
18. It's found in fat
23. Type of roll
25. Gibe
26. Cappelletti of football
28. Icy
29. Tent tycoon
30. Sculls
31. Abundant
32. Fiddler
33. A Mrs. Chaplin
34. Like some foreign words, for short
38. A New Jersey Lee
39. Graf ___
40. Zenith
42. Super's need
43. Long, narrow groove
45. 24A for a friend
46. Billfold filler
47. 42D, to some
50. Intact
51. Banks of baseball
52. The offense and the defense
53. Indian nursemaid
54. Brood
55. Let off pressure
56. Blue/green color
60. Letter from Patrai
61. St. Louis pro

❖ **Solution on page 271**

Cookie Attachments   *Verna Suit*

ACROSS

1. Indonesian island
5. Northern native
9. Bonzo, briefly
14. Tartan signification
15. Farm measure
16. Movie component
17. Three cookie attachments
20. On the way
21. Disobey, as a law
22. Acts of daring
23. Closed up
24. Eye rudely
27. Little girl's toy
32. Portuguese saint
35. Jungle vine
37. Hasty
38. Three cookie attachments
42. Sutherland solo
43. Charlie's employee
44. Color
45. Croaked
48. Writer of secret message
50. Slim win margin
52. MTV fare
56. Ocean condiment
60. Leaking slowly
62. Three cookie attachments
64. Invalidate
65. Doctorow's ___ *Lake*
66. Summit
67. ___ Midler
68. Work units
69. Child's questions

DOWN

1. A trailer
2. Unaccompanied
3. Dern or Ashley
4. Metal bars
5. Ultimate
6. Heart or back problem
7. Post- opposite
8. Irk
9. *In Cold Blood* author
10. Toss
11. Think tank product
12. Fine rain
13. Work for an artist
18. Sell aggressively
19. Light dye
23. Religious punishment
25. Tune
26. Indian prince
28. Electricity bridge
29. Port ___, Egypt
30. Cyber mole?
31. "I do not love ___, Doctor Fell"
32. Sign of damage
33. Pervasive quality
34. ___ Redding
36. Jason's craft
39. Dance variety
40. Primary color
41. Football team
46. Make possible
47. Numbskull
49. Lumber mill fixture
51. Steps over a fence
53. Get rid of
54. Adversary
55. Monstrous people
56. Strike breaker
57. Sea eagle
58. Em or Bee
59. Dirty stuff
60. Air problem
61. Centuries
63. Neither companion

❖ **Solution on page 271**

A Dose of 5 cc's   *Merle Baker*

ACROSS

1. Rated PG-13, maybe
5. Player inserts
9. Naysayers
14. Workplace watchdog
15. "___ Kleine Nachtmusik"
16. Heart connectors
17. Warp
18. 1965 Mustang, perhaps
20. Hammer in obliquely
22. Emulate Ella
23. Fin. neighbor
24. Minn. neighbor
26. Makes into law
30. Relaxing
32. Fish eater
34. She played Carla
35. Org. Bush headed
36. Kind of cocktail
38. Ens. org.
39. Adversaries might be
   on this
43. Bustle
44. "Peanuts" kid
45. Buddy
46. Yogi wore one
48. "Cry ___ River"
49. Drive-in server
52. Separation into factions
54. It might be in a pot
56. Number cruncher: Abbr.
57. Yuletide tune
59. Different from the first
61. Kurt Vonnegut Jr. book
65. Primo
66. "Eight Days ___"
67. ___ Pilot
68. Fishing spot
69. Prepares to play
70. Queens stadium
71. Slips up

DOWN

1. Places for speakers
2. Try to date
3. Coarse cotton gauze
4. Sign of boredom
5. Come to a conclusion
6. Country residence
7. Genetic material
8. Mtg. of Congress
9. Birdlike
10. Hummingbird food
11. One X of XXX
12. Tempest-teapot connection
13. Ukr., formerly
19. Word with trail or railway
21. Bombard
25. *On the Road* writer
27. Sopranos' place
28. Hardy heroine
29. Reasonable
31. Trouble
33. Operates
36. Result of haste?
37. Salad morsel
39. Engine parts
40. Like Pindar's works
41. Seethe
42. Onetime Mideast alliance:
   Abbr.
47. Dec. decoration
49. Filmmaking
50. Kitchen device
51. Kitchen utensils
53. Punches
55. Berry of film
58. Passes on the track
60. End of a dash
61. Bounder
62. Admiration
63. Kind of towel
64. Morse code syllable

❖ **Solution on page 271**

M&M's   *Merle Baker*

ACROSS

1. Gross
5. Lower in Mexico
9. Shape a plant
14. Reunion attendee
15. Riyadh native
16. ___ the Riveter
17. *A Clockwork Orange* star
20. Go around
21. Withdraws
22. Roman writer
25. *Fantasia* artwork
26. "Method" educator
34. Loud, as a crowd
35. Radar's orders
36. Favorite
37. Disheartened
38. Drawback opposite
39. Distinctive times
40. Letters in some church names
41. More sardonic
42. Cremona craftsman
43. *The Medium Is the Message* writer
46. Tractor part
47. ___ song (cheaply)
48. Dead Sea find
52. Pond denizen
57. "The Morning After" singer
60. Not as new
61. Awestruck
62. Like some cheese
63. Daly costar
64. Chicken, to a hawk
65. Normandy landers

DOWN

1. Two-syllable poetic unit
2. Orator Henry
3. *The Beverly Hillbillies* actress Nancy
4. Community pool site
5. Aromatic fir
6. Chair part
7. Traffic tie-up
8. Kindergarten lesson
9. Homogenization, e.g.
10. Spur wheels
11. Not new
12. Thebes river
13. Some are electric
18. *Sesame Street* grouch
19. Double-dealing
23. Throat feature
24. Exert ___ (struggle)
26. Sir alternative
27. Bouquet
28. Crew member
29. Mott the Hoople singer Hunter
30. Dynamic start?
31. First name in TV talk
32. *Giant* ranch
33. "___ the bag!"
38. Not barren, as land
39. Flightless bird
41. Pequod crew
42. Battle site of 1836
44. Music stand items
45. Rugged, as a coastline
48. Urban pollution
49. Bird sound
50. Inconsiderate
51. Cinch
53. Circus Maximus shape
54. Brain tests, briefly
55. Bart's brother
56. Common connectors
58. Clerk's boss: Abbr.
59. Runner Sebastian ___

❖ **Solution on page 271**

Three F's for Effort   *Douglas Fink*

ACROSS

1. Short time units
6. Hemsley coworker, once
11. Local theater, briefly
14. Awry, to Burns
15. Really upset
16. TV role for Marilu
17. Wordless "yeah, right!"
18. Star of TV's *The Marshal*
20. Product made in *Boogie Nights*
22. Actor who said, "Bueller? Anyone?"
23. Time of note
24. Fuddy-duddy
26. Wee one
30. Relaxing
32. Recipe phrase
33. Burning
36. Computer component, often
38. Student of Socrates
41. Vivacity
42. Really wants
43. Sushi chef supplier
44. Type of dancer
46. She played Mrs. Garrett
47. Least sensible
51. Open
54. Household holder
56. Recurrent role for Keanu
57. Leading man
59. Figurehead
61. Bad taste
65. Fight verbally
66. What one might say on a lea
67. Like the *Home Alone* thieves
68. Attendee
69. MENSA stats
70. Not much for words
71. Sworn oaths

DOWN

1. Painter Johns
2. Alternative to retry and abort
3. Local plant groups
4. *Charlotte's Web* gal
5. Head toward
6. Gandhi opposition
7. Spilling over
8. Like a bluff
9. Game or magazine
10. Like Keebler magic
11. Good cheer
12. Title role for Woodward, Baxter, or Smollett
13. Put in your two cents' worth?
19. One among several
21. Motown music
25. Trial-by-fire result?
27. Uncle Martin's home
28. Good spot for a bed
29. *American Idol* rejects, often
31. Looker's London locale
34. Socialize at a party
35. Lyrical poem
36. Scaler's challenge
37. Escape route in many a movie
38. Llama land
39. Slant
40. Actor Baldwin or Guinness
45. It's spun
48. A big question mark
49. Transitioned well
50. Tinkerers
52. Pound sound
53. Bush arena, briefly
54. Split
55. Basketball
58. Lion's pride
60. One who croaks
61. It's binding in Japan
62. Web site info
63. About halfway between dos
64. 66, for one

❖ **Solution on page 271**

Urban Jungle *Lane Gutz*

ACROSS

1. Fast aircraft: Abbr.
5. Chaste, as a virgin
11. Org. in *The Freshman*
14. University in North Carolina
15. English Channel swimmer Gertrude
16. Salt, in Saint-Etienne
17. City in Iowa
19. Golf expert
20. Place for pekoe
21. They reject laws
23. High-tech project
24. Can material of old
25. Strands of genetics
26. Supreme Egyptian god
28. "Fudge!"
29. "___ personality . . . "
32. Car window sticker, maybe
33. Frustrating
36. RVs park here
37. Use a stage?
39. Elton John's john
40. Mayor who wrote "Mayor"
42. Extra, in Encinada
43. Sax prefix
44. Game opponent
45. Not currently active
47. All letters
49. Some appliances
50. Dr. of fiction
54. Some Asians
56. Some beat it
57. Poetic "pre"
58. City in California
60. There are four in Monopoly: Abbr.
61. With a melody
62. Otherwise
63. Ready
64. Witty
65. Way down the hill

DOWN

1. Quakers, etc.
2. Like a Lamborghini
3. USA follower
4. Dogs might do it
5. Florida city
6. Made up?
7. . . . Aug-___-Oct . . .
8. Trebek specialty
9. Pilgrim at Plymouth
10. For fear that
11. City in Maryland
12. Word with cotta or firma
13. Dentist's direction
18. Lack a map, maybe
22. Kind of exam
24. Severe injuries
27. King Cole, e.g.
28. Infamous middle name
29. 50-cent piece figure
30. Dollar word
31. City in Illinois
33. Scented liquid
34. "I'm ___ crazy!"
35. Moo ___ gai pan
37. Type of bandage
38. SNL character
41. Seep
43. Wardrobes
45. Aviator Nielsen?
46. Cop helper
47. Soccer star Michelle
48. Joe the Yankee
49. Knot in the tree
51. Odor
52. Fat
53. Bare ___ Ladies
55. Plane attachment: Abbr.
56. Erato, e.g.
59. Cold month: Abbr.

❖ **Solution on page 271**

Leaders and Counts   *Alan Olschwang*

ACROSS
1. Small opening
5. Model wood
10. Type of team
14. Hummus go-with
15. Argot
16. Patent origination
17. 19th-century Russian tsar
19. Pusher pursuer
20. Emma of the soaps
21. Sought redress
22. Chills and fever
23. Raided the fridge
25. Barkin and Burstyn
27. 18th-century Polish king
33. Hebrew letter
34. Infield protector
35. Senator Kefauver
39. Supervising
42. Towel word
43. Steps for crossing a fence
44. Potential jurors
45. Abound
47. Thanksgiving victim
48. 16th-century Norway and Denmark king
52. Part of a formal outfit
55. Where the speedometer rests
56. Mimic
57. St. Louis skyline feature
61. Insurance center
65. Rats' reversal?
66. 17th-century Ottoman Empire sultan
68. Yarn
69. Ano opener
70. Mischievous prank
71. It goes downhill
72. Overhaul
73. Olla output

DOWN
1. Some resorts
2. Lee, in 1922 *Blood and Sand*
3. Thing
4. IRS agent
5. Coal holder
6. Foots the column
7. Place
8. Achy
9. Some organic compounds
10. She's still going for the gold
11. Catchphrase
12. Summer TV fare
13. Medieval war clubs
18. Sparkling wine production locale
24. Body shop's quote: Abbr.
26. Stretches the truth
27. Go over the edge
28. Sousaphone cousin
29. In a short time
30. Finnish city
31. First zodiac sign
32. Unexpected triumph
36. South American monkey
37. *Time Machine* victim
38. Big rig
40. Guided the pilot
41. Much of one's school life
46. Player Hamm
49. Hole shaping tool
50. Crumb
51. Wanderers
52. Fastest times
53. Relating to eight
54. Type of shark
58. Ancient alphabet character
59. He may own the restaurant
60. Spy Mata ___
62. Mine entrance
63. Play a child's game
64. Declare
67. Incisive remark

❖ **Solution on page 271**

63

Dances We'd Like to See   *Michael Wiesenberg*

ACROSS

1. Right now
5. 65A problem
9. Begin
14. First name in country
15. Where doves cry
16. It's a pig
17. Thrown
18. Cupid
19. Irregularly worn
20. Aerobic dance to work off extra pub pounds?
23. 1,000 kilos
24. Mauna ___
25. Tennis fault
26. X-ray kin
29. Attempt
32. Spoon bender Geller
33. Yak
35. Coroner's term
36. Ball at the home of David Copperfield's landlord?
42. Je ne sais ___
43. Track
44. Tenth Hebrew letter
46. Something to pick up at the pub
49. What one might turn to something one doesn't want to hear
52. Before
53. Astronaut Grissom
55. Hot drink
56. Togetherness tango?
61. Old Testament abode of the dead
62. One might do this to a slot machine
63. Memorized
65. Where to find the most 5A
66. Novelist Bagnold
67. Copies
68. Items found in a shoe repair shop
69. Churchill, for one
70. Sticker price

DOWN

1. (
2. Coastal region
3. Someone might be tried in this
4. Typewriter rollers
5. One who crosses a picket line
6. Apple, say
7. Eniwetok, e.g.
8. Fine red wine
9. Part of AA's program
10. Poi source
11. Brother of Diana
12. One who gambles
13. Trick's alternative
21. It's a room
22. What football teams gain
23. Ft. Worth college
27. Long past
28. '60s and '70s destination for many young men, familiarly
30. "Ouch!"
31. Part of a sobriquet for the Beatles
34. Bridge maneuver
37. Where to find "Car Talk"
38. Held court
39. Not prepaid
40. Ophthalmologist's recommendation
41. Convertible
45. Hang on a line
46. It's bull
47. Leader of Trojans after destruction of Troy
48. Casino meal
50. ___ Z
51. Middle of graveyard shift
52. Failed Ford
54. Pool member
57. Tower atop San Francisco's Telegraph Hill
58. Home sections
59. He might get the throne
60. Whirlpool
64. Sixth sense

❖ Solution on page 271

Board Members *Douglas Fink*

ACROSS

1. Like a little nubby bit
8. Minnesota twins
11. He has a beat
14. Whistling instrument
15. D&D doohickey
16. Rue Morgue figure
17. He tends to play slimeballs
19. Tommy Chong's daughter
20. Part of a slalom path
21. Cash for cannolis, once
22. Bridge player?
24. Honkers
26. Pitiful one, to Mr. T
27. *Fall Guy* actor
30. New start
32. Tape of yore
35. Abrade
36. Pickle pusher
37. Understanding
38. They're in the middle of the curve
39. Diet-conscious adjective
40. Aileron holder
41. Little isle
42. King of comedy
43. They're nice, in some ads
44. *Honey* star
46. Monty Python opener
47. Properly
48. Tiger trap springer?
50. Card where opportunity knocks?
52. Like Popeye's voice
54. Outlet item
55. Second letter of frat?
58. Tree, or log remains
59. Fictional detective
63. Grace hubby, in *Will & Grace*
64. Pre-school?
65. Radcliffe grads
66. Need for reading Zener cards
67. A place to get into hot water
68. Sam Beckett and others

DOWN

1. Former *West Wing* star
2. Wood sorrels
3. Responds to the moon
4. Caterer's vessel
5. Golfer's concern
6. Capri pants show 'em
7. Sari sorts
8. Brink
9. D.C. med. gp.
10. Bout
11. *Tapestry* artist
12. Milky gem
13. Film role for Thurman
18. Ginger Rogers role
23. First name of 1D
24. *The ___ Must Be Crazy*
25. Bard's before
26. Item for a fencer
27. Muslim's magnet
28. It's been ___ pleasure
29. Rat Packer
31. Joie de vivre
33. Metric fraction
34. Teen's tension
36. Lamebrain
39. Reclined
40. "There's more!"
43. Tem head
45. Couples' cruise ship?
47. Diamonds around one's ankles
49. Criminal trials
51. Of the ear
52. Skipper star
53. Employs
54. Say it to the judge
55. Lacoste of the court
56. Try, as in a case
57. Tiller filler
60. Prune
61. Sine ___ non
62. Diamond specialist

❖ **Solution on page 272**

The Play's the Thing   *Michael Wiesenberg*

ACROSS

1. "Voila!"
5. Center
10. Et ___
14. Niche
15. Cooling
16. Author Morrison
17. Someone who lacks a horse
20. "Much ___ . . . "
21. Response to "Am not!"
22. Troy locale
23. French girlfriend
24. Some Fords
26. Noted Elizabethan
30. Coal carrier
33. Caravan stop
34. Rocky Lane spoke for him
35. Reverence
36. Hubbard of Dianetics
37. Like Falstaff
39. Seat of Allen County, Kansas
40. Son of Prince Valiant
41. Fox, Rabbit, or Bear title
42. Dot in the ocean
43. Redeye
44. She urged her husband to murder Duncan
47. It's a monster
48. Flair
49. Has the lead
52. Miller of sing-along
54. "Against my power; thrice from the banks of ___" (*Henry IV*, Part 1)
57. First tragedy of 26A
60. Actress Sommer
61. Spartan serf
62. Postal units: Abbr.
63. Ring out
64. That is
65. Minstrel's instrument

DOWN

1. O'Hara's estate
2. Dry
3. Art ___
4. Say this to your dentist
5. 9Lives cat
6. Debt-ridden
7. Telegraphic clicks
8. "As you are friends, ___, and soldiers" (*Hamlet*, Act I, Scene V, line 157)
9. Golf aid
10. A Musketeer
11. Pork cut
12. Cross letters
13. Verdi heroine
18. Willie of *Eight Is Enough*
19. Helped through difficulty, with "over"
23. Related
25. It grows in Brooklyn
26. Sunny
27. He met Sally
28. Synchronized
29. File material
30. Non-Hawaiian
31. Nestling
32. Passing
37. Kind of exam
38. "Thou mayst ___ for that wicked deed!" (17A, Act I, Scene II, line 108)
39. Library ID
41. Ecstasy
42. Trump rival
45. Rapid transits
46. Author of *Little Men*
47. Twist's meal
49. Beginning of a long journey
50. Arrange PC windows
51. An Aleutian
53. A Python
54. Carrie Nation's org.
55. Mongolian tent
56. Sum, ___, fui
58. Sushi tuna
59. Sick

❖ Solution on page 272

Blood Type   *Merle Baker*

ACROSS

1. File type
5. Soften in feeling
9. Pages
14. Area measurement
15. "I concur!"
16. Immature seed
17. "As if I care!"
20. Renters
21. Waiting, perhaps
22. ER figures
23. Fisherman's aid
25. Change direction
26. Without warning
31. Declare openly
32. "Absolutely!"
33. Hubbub
36. Popular houseplants
38. Numerical prefix
39. Prod
41. ___ Quentin
42. Attachments
45. Former mayor Giuliani
46. Herculean
48. Voguish
51. Mitchell, Reno, et al.
52. Sharpton, for one: Abbr.
53. State tree of New Jersey
55. Pooh-pooh
59. Second chance
62. Fish feature
63. Bread unit
64. USPS items
65. *Siddhartha* author
66. Gang territory
67. *Crouching Tiger, Hidden Dragon* star Michelle

DOWN

1. Part of NFL
2. Long
3. Investment options, briefly
4. Disappoints
5. Grandeur
6. Birds raised for meat
7. French article
8. USA alternative
9. Blessing
10. Develop gradually
11. Musical featuring Gregory Hines
12. Geometric surface
13. Haggadah reading time
18. Vassal
19. 52A, e.g.
23. Ganglia components
24. Receding
26. Blockheads
27. Iris site
28. Of two minds
29. Show-off
30. Western native
33. Son-of-___
34. Extinct bird
35. Black quartz
37. Cal. column
40. Like Andy Devine's voice
43. 16th-century circumnavigator
44. Broadcasting pioneer David ___
46. Mean looks
47. Observed
48. Shattering sound
49. From now on
50. Suggestions
54. Sheltered, at sea
55. Scorch
56. ___ of passage
57. Hendrix hairdo
58. New Age musician John ___
60. Computer key
61. Trifling amount

❖ **Solution on page 272**

Warning Signs · *Dave Fisher*

ACROSS

1. Usage fee
5. Ponders
10. Nursery items
14. Nabisco product
15. Son of Cain
16. Halo
17. Keep out of . . .
20. Hawkeye State
21. Supervise
22. Wireless operator
25. It stretched from Germany to China
27. Map abbreviation
28. Turkish title
30. The first of a famous trio
32. Religion founded 5th century A.D.
36. Treated mercilessly
37. A meal
39. Beer type
40. Do not puncture . . .
43. Janis ___ (singer)
44. Overthrows
45. Fog
46. Part of a brooch
48. Actress Winger, to friends
49. A swindle
50. Globe
52. Il ___ (Mussolini)
54. Needlefish
55. Fatigues
59. Mechanical repetition
61. . . . are closer than they appear
66. Not written
67. Concur
68. Small amount
69. Rowboat
70. Commence
71. Night light

DOWN

1. Rocky hill
2. Pay dirt
3. Field
4. Places
5. Catcalls?
6. Let loose
7. Interest group: Abbr.
8. Nymph who missed Narcissus
9. Hindu god, "The Destroyer"
10. San Diego players
11. Smokey to Simone
12. Family ___
13. Perfectly understandable
18. Happy ___
19. Actor Joseph Gordon-___
22. Like Horatio Alger lead roles
23. Unlike Horatio Alger lead roles
24. Saudi city
26. Matured
29. Gloaming
31. '60s draft dodger, perhaps
33. Performing punchbowl hijinks
34. U.S. acquisition of 1867
35. Trusted guide
37. Tear
38. Stockholm's airline
41. Containing copper
42. Flightless bird
47. To a great degree
49. You ___ would! (Sure!)
51. Greek letters
53. One is Halley's
55. Ash, for instance
56. Longest river in Spain
57. Open a crack
58. High-ranking NCO
60. ___ Brockovich
62. A Gershwin
63. Future flounder
64. Ear-ly Native American?
65. Sought election

❖ **Solution on page 272**

Deserving an A–   *Michael Wiesenberg*

ACROSS

1. Type of music
5. Moon trip?
10. Truck
14. Wise to
15. Under
16. Double
17. '50s TV comic Ernie's wife
18. Infection in the intestine
19. Philly Ivy
20. Witnesses in court
23. Insecticide ingredient
24. Short old king of Egypt
25. Comforter stuffing
28. Big inits. in the record business
31. Poetic exploit
35. Record holder
37. Corn holder
39. Slop recipient
40. Whodunit's objective
44. Finish
45. Born
46. Memory improvement supplement
47. The defense does this
50. "Sure thing"
52. Senior member
53. Not well
55. "Just missed me!"
57. "To heck with the cost!"
65. See previous, in footnotes
66. Hobbit home
67. Smell
68. Burt's ex
69. Toughie
70. Detention victim of 1977
71. Very sensitive
72. Knifelike?
73. English gun of WWII

DOWN

1. Mini-kingdom
2. Word processor function
3. Film genre
4. Mired
5. Not very thin
6. Reel off
7. Group of countries
8. Princess loved by Hercules
9. 'Mid
10. Southern resort city, briefly
11. Jug
12. Pillow topper, sometimes
13. Overnight stops
21. Bold
22. Boxer or dog
25. Icy ridge
26. Kristen of *One Life to Live*
27. Scouts try to do good ones
29. Fibber, to Mollie, in old comedy
30. My debt
32. Like punks' tresses
33. Color
34. Incite
36. Very long time
38. Do this on bended knees
41. You might do one in the middle of the block
42. Hit's flip
43. Cons
48. Linked (with)
49. Stone of '60s rock
51. Germs
54. Speech problems
56. Ones weeding
57. Exploit
58. One of the reeds
59. Cubs or Orioles
60. Come in third
61. "De mortuis nil ___ bonum"
62. Modify writing
63. One-time employer of Rockwell plus Wyeth
64. 1982 Disney sci-fi flick

❖ **Solution on page 272**

It's a Laugh   *Douglas Fink*

ACROSS

1. Reality show host, at times
6. Do secretarial work
10. Coin-flipping gangster portrayer
14. "Maria ___"
15. "Jabberwocky" opener
16. Pod in a pot
17. They're funny but scary
20. It falls when firing
21. Lab burner
22. They might be drawn
23. Bush league?
24. Varnish need
25. Li'l one
26. Funny money?
31. Unexpected
32. *Twilight Zone* host, to friends
33. Trio in Rome
34. Nasty ones
37. Horde member
38. Bridge sections
40. What's mined is yours
41. "Minnie the Moocher" man
42. Some questionnaire answers
43. Funny cop show
50. Not working
51. Genetics initials
52. A Gabor
53. Faint traces
54. Speed
56. Safety device
57. Be funny but firm
61. Applications
62. Extra in an Indiana Jones movie
63. Less ornery
64. Ask, like a question
65. Pleasant things to say
66. Movie town-goer

DOWN

1. Separate
2. What Miss Daisy's driver had
3. Bring a case back to court
4. Hell hath this ending
5. Arctic explorer
6. Timely nonet saver?
7. Meany of prayer
8. Indian VIP
9. Half a fly?
10. Signs of spring
11. Motion stopper
12. Total control
13. They had red letter days
18. Evil Spock feature
19. Exile isle
24. Juliet portrayers, originally
25. Throw in
27. Work the land
28. Isle near Venezuela
29. Opie portrayer
30. They precede dos
34. How pretty!
35. Spanish source of comic relief
36. Goes over again
37. Hem's mate
38. Remote location?
39. Trident-shaped symbol
41. Hatted Seuss menace
42. Last inning, often
44. Place side by side
45. Don't wake the baby!
46. Eye malady
47. City with canals
48. Squared up
49. Mix flicks
53. Trounce
54. Smiling
55. Wood tool
58. Beatle wife
59. Finale
60. Nasal expander?

❖ **Solution on page 272**

Mouth Pieces   *Merle Baker*

ACROSS

1. Star of stage and screen
6. Not us
10. Boost
14. Bounty captain
15. Runner's goal
16. "Now it's clear"
17. ___ bird
18. Baseball stats
19. Ache
20. Craving, of a sort
22. Desert sight
23. "___ about that!"
24. Fixes upon
26. Mulching material
31. Sun. talk
32. 1952 Winter Olympics site
33. Chicago district
35. Like Wrigley Field's walls
39. Put on
40. Largest country in Africa
42. Man, for one
43. Expenditures
45. "Toodles"
46. Geometric solid
47. Tiny Tim's ax
49. Bridge need
51. Accumulates
55. Coverage provider
56. Med. school subj.
57. Confectioner's assortment
63. Shankar of the sitar
64. Brand symbol
65. Coeur d'___, ID
66. Nastase of the court
67. "Are you ___ out?"
68. Hawaiian feasts
69. Iditarod vehicle
70. Cubicle staple
71. Skin layer

DOWN

1. Lincoln and Vigoda
2. Kind of hammer
3. Grow weary
4. Gawk at
5. Backbeat
6. Scraps
7. Vagabond
8. Pours forth
9. Fits together
10. Concordance without conviction
11. Son of Abraham
12. Deceptive action
13. Is disposed
21. Screwdrivers
25. Circle of life
26. Funny pages possum
27. Son of Rebekah
28. Came down
29. Speechless
30. Fountain selections
34. Grab bag
36. "The jig ___!"
37. Corsica neighbor
38. Title
41. Singing Judd
44. Approves of
48. Greek mathematician
50. George's predecessor
51. Continental capital
52. Considering everything
53. C'est ___
54. Kind of tag
58. They may be inflated
59. Fasten, in a way
60. Landing ___
61. Word on a penny
62. City east of Phoenix

❖ **Solution on page 272**

Chapter 5

It Themes to Me

Changelings   *Michael Wiesenberg*

ACROSS

1. Place for 14A
5. Where to find Qom
9. Get-go
14. She taught the King's children
15. Lawyer's concern
16. Superman portrayer
17. Personal trainer's focus, maybe
18. Henri's follower
19. Reagan used to hawk it
20. Fly the warm skies?
23. Boil down
24. Consume
25. Moral code for geeks?
32. *Alice* role
35. Rowers
36. Mistakes
37. It's kept in a chest
39. Thanksgiving dish
41. YSL part
42. Endowers, often
45. Lacunae
48. *ER* extra
49. Batman portrayer nabbed?
52. Princess annoyer
53. Where Arcturus is
57. "Okay, cooking class, let's prep our fowl"
62. Type of daisy
63. ___ good example
64. *Peter and the Wolf* duck
65. Modernize
66. Got off
67. Manage
68. Elegance
69. Addressees
70. Tos and ___

DOWN

1. It's toast
2. Silly
3. Caprice
4. The Stanford Tree, e.g.
5. Summer drink
6. Pro ___
7. California wine country town named for an Italian town
8. Start of a hymn
9. Columbia is the oldest in the shuttle fleet
10. Small Dodge
11. Parched
12. Gabor and Marie Saint
13. John Ritter's father
21. Admirer of Narcissus
22. Tahoe or Titicaca
26. Parched
27. Largest tributary of the Missouri
28. Attempt
29. Possess
30. Thing
31. Staff a movie
32. Hangover, of sorts
33. Doozie
34. It weighs you down
38. Daybreak determiner?
40. Sheepish sound
43. Huey and Dewey, to Donald
44. Thought
46. Small wartime naval attack craft
47. Shortly
50. Home, to Dorothy
51. Seek sheep?
54. Veggie staple
55. Lodge lead-in
56. TV lineups
57. *Beverly Hills Cop* lead role
58. Olin or Horne of film
59. Caustic compounds
60. Place with a rye sense of humor
61. Use a spoon
62. D&D "red shirt"

❖ **Solution on page 272**

Four-Footed Friends *Lane Gutz*

ACROSS

1. Enron tactic
5. Nukes
10. Inside informer
14. 1970 Kinks hit
15. Juno's message
16. Astronaut hostage takers, in film
17. "Your turn" on the radio
18. Haile Selassie follower
19. Avis asset
20. Four-footed foreigner?
23. Larry and friends
24. Dead-doornail connection
25. Church address, for short
26. Got off one's high horse?
29. Show stoppers
32. Taint a quaff
35. Tumbler's contents, perhaps
36. Way to get tipsy
37. Four-footed foreigner?
41. JFK info
42. ABC show
43. Let loose
44. Massive unit
45. *Friends* character
46. Decompose
48. Short sandwich?
50. Larry Holmes's home state
54. Four-footed foreigner?
58. Date gone awry for Caesar?
59. Parking meter patent owner
60. Discovery
61. Ball balancer, perhaps
62. Edmonton rink lubricator?
63. Some frames
64. Forced to
65. Some contain smoke
66. Geog.

DOWN

1. Toils ardently
2. Commandment no-no
3. Oldsmobile automobile
4. Miniature monkey in Mozambique
5. Actor Klemperer
6. Form a party
7. Quick to act
8. Teensy weensy spider
9. NHL shot
10. Stud's mates
11. La Scala solo
12. Let use
13. Long Island time, for short
21. Minor determinant
22. Racist
26. Titles in Turkey
27. Bodybuilder's term
28. Ending for Israel
30. Makes Easter eggs
31. All dried up
32. Pass this to sue: Abbr.
33. Bat beginner
34. Soul food loaf
35. Used car sign
38. Floozies
39. 1969 Peace Prize winner (org.)
40. Upgrade, to a techie
46. Cites
47. Reaction to fireworks
49. Naperville neighbor
50. Canine cleaner
51. Cover
52. Sanctum starter
53. One who counts or bites
54. Just a thought
55. Some MDs get paid by them
56. Watch a watch
57. Look at a looker
58. Capital ending

❖ **Solution on page 272**

Air Force   Viv Collins

ACROSS

1. Dressed
5. Fashionable dance of the 1840s
10. Meager, as pickings
14. Non-PC Halloween costume
15. Pertaining to space
16. Pulled apart
17. Like some drinks
18. Happy as a lark
19. Evangelist Roberts
20. Oscar-winning song from *Pocahontas*
23. Fisherman's catch
24. Washington's number?
25. Official permission to do something
29. Son on *Father Knows Best*
30. CIA predecessor
33. Diminish
34. Give in the middle
35. Andy Taylor's son
36. Margaret Mitchell's novel
40. "Chestnuts roasting ___ open fire"
41. Declare
42. Pound parts
43. Nine-digit ID
44. Accepted standard
45. Inventor, in a way
47. Metered vehicle
48. E-mail option
49. Elton John's tribute to Diana
57. Comment ender
58. River at Orleans
59. Word with coat or shoe
60. Jackson 5 member
61. Steady runner
62. An avatar of Vishnu
63. Point skis inward
64. Usher's beat
65. Radio control

DOWN

1. In vogue
2. Crazy, to Desi
3. Soviet spy Rudolf
4. It's extinct, for being too naive
5. Analyzes a sentence
6. Baltimore bird
7. Folios
8. *Critique of Judgment* author
9. Despite the fact that
10. Harriet Beecher ___
11. Loughlin of *Full House*
12. Persia, since 1935
13. Card combo
21. Subscription choice
22. Conclusion
25. Toy building blocks
26. *Reversal of Fortune* star
27. First name in talk TV
28. First garden
29. Flying mammal
30. State a view
31. From then on
32. Passover supper
34. Withdrawn
35. Actor Reginald ___
37. Sponsor of Columbus
38. Fix a leaky roof, maybe
39. Lyric poem
44. Buddy
45. Low-flying seabird
46. Reply to "Where are you?"
47. Electronic info source
48. Small cuts
49. "Memory" musical
50. Busy
51. It might be held or delivered
52. ___ *Arabian Nights*
53. Toil or labor
54. Lendl of tennis
55. *Nautilus* captain
56. Dull and boring

❖ **Solution on page 273**

76

Multiple Choice *Mark Milhet*

❖ Solution on page 273

ACROSS

1. Area for an arrival
5. Bayou feature
10. Town of Normandy
14. Dry as dust
15. Unified
16. Tom, Dick, and Harry, e.g.
17. Pickup spot?
19. Hotel or cracker
20. Cash, often
21. Before of yore
22. Pointless Olympic event?
23. Walkie-talkie word
26. Nearby
28. Asked
32. '86 World Series champs
35. One-sided win
36. The 411
38. Jellied garnish
39. Lab eggs
40. Gives a hand
42. Sheep's milieu
43. The pits
45. Placed down
46. Novelist Bellow
47. Homily
49. Fax forefather
51. ___ the ante
53. Bring up
54. Sing the blues
56. Historic time
58. Rope fiber
62. Lot measurement
63. Two guys, two girls, dinner and a movie, perhaps
66. Current choice
67. Nocturnal primate
68. Fifty-fifty
69. Hit show with three stars?
70. Kenyan grazer
71. Tourney rank

DOWN

1. Omigosh!
2. Diva's solo
3. Like Ho's bubbles
4. Win by a nose
5. Wild, wild West
6. Pompous sort
7. Garb for Rehnquist
8. Rover's warning
9. Now and forever
10. Places for waders
11. Diamond rarity
12. Dieter's word
13. Move like the Blob
18. Denim name
24. One of the Great ones
25. Of the kidneys
27. Printer's primary color
28. Does pressing work
29. Super stars?
30. Cats and dogs, e.g.
31. First of the black pair
33. Keep busy
34. Piano exercise
37. Willow wood
40. Release
41. Dilly-dallying
44. Remove from office
46. Progress
48. Pine product
50. Lessen the load
52. Run at the mouth
54. Sir alternative
55. Whale of a film?
57. Heavenly glow
59. Success for a closer
60. To ___ (precisely)
61. Front the money
64. Recycling ___
65. Timothy Leary's turn-on

Oxtail Soup *Merle Baker*

ACROSS

1. Egyptian dam site
6. Church plate
11. Broadcast-regulating org.
14. River of Germany
15. Likeness
16. ___ Alamos
17. Source of unforeseen troubles
19. Cycle starter
20. ___ Ivory Wayans
21. List entries
23. Tableland
24. Ways out
27. Hook helper
29. Former Spanish dictator
31. Pecan, for one
32. Some offspring
33. Nile biter
34. Tears
36. Schoolbooks
37. Rommel's nickname
39. Pepe ___
42. Attended
43. D.C. big shot
46. Islamic cleric
47. Whistle blower
48. Cut application
50. River of Spain
51. Some saxes
53. To boot
54. Company div.
56. Cease to exist
58. "Far out"
59. Former Eurythmics singer
63. Environmental prefix
64. Have a craving
65. Cubic meter
66. Annoy
67. Mex. misses
68. Rolls rollers

DOWN

1. Dada pioneer
2. Movers partners
3. Apple type
4. Like llamas
5. Sign gas
6. Ellington's instrument
7. Mornings, briefly
8. Can feature
9. Self-centered person
10. Barbershop call
11. Bewilder
12. Approval
13. ___: Miami
18. Changes the style of
22. County of England or New Jersey
23. Juilliard deg.
25. Like some beer
26. Corrodes
28. Road curve
30. A racing sport
35. Post with stairs
36. Movie pooch
37. Energetic worker
38. Former Saudi king
39. Stretch out
40. Accept
41. Seeming absurdity
43. Pale beer
44. No longer at sea
45. Baseball's Durocher
47. Costar of Curtin and Chase
49. Certainly not gross
52. Hot spots
55. Calendrical units
57. Tree house
58. Gun
60. Cole or Turner
61. Lyricist Gershwin
62. Crosses (out)

❖ Solution on page 273

When in . . . *Merle Baker*

ACROSS

1. *Cheers* serving
5. To any extent
10. 2004 candidate
14. As well
15. Chutzpah
16. Erupter of 1169
17. Theater where Houdini made an elephant disappear
19. Marker
20. Office purchase
21. Bar cry
23. Pipe cleaner
26. Managed
27. Sport for big guys
30. Film monster
33. NFL scores
36. Since
37. Accrue
38. ___ room
39. By a substantial amount
41. Influential journalist with a "Weekly"
43. Pizarro's quest
44. Exasperate
46. "You said it!"
47. Defense advisory org.
48. Err on the court
49. Nice noggin
50. SHO alternative
52. Put up
54. World's tallest building in 1930
58. Ancient moralist
62. Detroit player
63. One starts with a man
66. Admiral Zumwalt
67. Serious
68. German river
69. Took off
70. Up to this time
71. Clammy

DOWN

1. Coin of Thailand
2. Italian director Petri
3. Armchair quarterback's channel
4. Reserved, in a way
5. Intel competitor
6. Rocky peak
7. Mexican salamander
8. South American capital
9. Wine sediment
10. Bing Crosby's record label
11. Wharton work
12. Source of indigo
13. Part of NAACP
18. Legendary Bruin
22. Green adjuncts
24. More copious
25. "Beats me!"
27. Suppressed
28. Software buyers
29. Color alternative
31. Young cow
32. Perturb
34. *The Maids* playwright
35. Play part
40. Bismarck and Graham
42. Like Emmett Kelly's costume
45. Blanket
51. Already
53. Bounder
54. Musical symbol
55. *The Music Man* professor
56. Annika Sörenstam's gp.
57. Corn units
59. Fountain order
60. Harbinger
61. Fringe benefit
64. "___ had it!"
65. Court divider

❖ **Solution on page 273**

Tri-State Region   *Merle Baker*

ACROSS

1. Baker's meas.
5. "There!"
10. River in a 1957 film
14. Field
15. Early Mexican civilization
16. Realize
17. Surf sound
18. Soul singer Hayes
19. Graph line
20. Recliner furnishing
23. Citrus drink
24. Nightfall, poetically
25. Unsophisticated
29. Like a ballad
31. Carving material
33. Cholesterol letters
34. Trattoria serving
37. Corona
38. Like most SUVs
42. Jack Sprat's preference
43. Jim Bowie's rank
44. Moon shape
45. Clinks
46. Slip by
50. Nesting places
52. Current unit
54. ___'easter
55. They are readily
    convertible
59. *The Sicilian* author
62. Randall role
63. Movie pooch
64. Large land
65. Vote to accept
66. *Law & Order: SVU* actor
67. Engrossed
68. Like Elwood P. Dowd
69. City of Poland

DOWN

1. Foot bone
2. Dwelling on one's troubles
3. Driveway application
4. ___-mutuel
5. Express
6. *Sunset Boulevard* actress
   Nancy
7. Priest of a mosque
8. Table extension
9. Instrument for Weird Al or
   his dad
10. "Endymion" poet
11. The whole ball of ___
12. *Exodus* protagonist
13. Elected ones
21. Transfer
22. Wish undone
26. Whaler's direction
27. Not working
28. Lump of earth
30. Heavy metal
31. Grey and McCrea
32. Dog dish filler
35. Police division
36. Part of, as a conspiracy
37. Hot spot
38. Portion of whipped cream
39. Aviation prefix
40. *Jungle Book* star
41. Bewails
45. Key letter
47. Paris-based intl. agcy.
48. Like some lines
49. Not natural
51. Be overly pleased
52. Proficient
53. Best Picture of 1955
56. Word processing command
57. "___ Rhythm"
58. Go to sea
59. Equality
60. Mex. neighbor
61. Nothing

❖ **Solution on page 273**

The Old Corral   *Verna Suit*

ACROSS
1. Hammett heroine
5. Lessened
11. Basketball pos.
14. Victor's cry
15. Albanian capital
16. "You ___ There"
17. Irish New Age artist
18. Charismatic cowboy star, also rodeo world champion
20. Mongrel
21. Aria
22. Coffeehouse order
23. Person's name used for a thing
25. Noblewoman
27. The Singing Cowboy
30. ___ but for fortune . . .
32. Exile island
33. 6/6/44
37. North of Paris
38. "To be" separator
39. Steak order
40. Dick Tracy's wife
41. Weather service agcy.
42. Nuts companion
43. Cowboy star, also Trooper Duffy in *F Troop*
45. Paint type
49. Knack
52. Mongol
53. Oaf
55. Promise
56. Cowboy star of 1930s serials with wonder horse Tarzan
59. Legal scholar Guinier
60. Palindromic preposition
61. Darning need
62. Seth's son
63. Edward, sometimes
64. Battery terminals
65. Dep.

DOWN
1. Bridget to Jane
2. Admit
3. King of the Cowboys
4. Santa ___
5. In
6. High school subj.
7. End of a buck?
8. Use a lace shuttle
9. NZ language
10. Dancer Dan
11. Social class
12. Participates in harness races
13. Magritte and Russo
19. Saloon
21. Auld lang ___
24. Non-jocks
25. JFK's 109
26. Quod ___ demonstrandum
28. Needer of oxygen
29. Arm bones
30. Explosive letters
31. Bladed tool
33. Amusing
34. Queen of the West
35. Gallery object
36. No alternative
38. Yoko's family
42. Rhythm
43. Ice cream parlor fruit
44. Musical studies
45. "The Old ___ Bucket"
46. French river
47. Like worried brows
48. Slam sound
50. Prohibited things
51. Drink garnish
53. Alan or Cheryl
54. Heraldic border
57. Osaka money
58. Classical prefix
59. Meadow

❖ **Solution on page 273**

Spare Change   *Dave Fisher*

ACROSS

1. Wound remnant
5. Purse pros
10. Tell on
14. ___ mater
15. Athens, to Sparta
16. Napoleon's prison, e.g.
17. Mary's follower
18. Some tourneys
19. Garfield's foil
20. Cheap hams?
23. Wrath
24. Earlier in time than
25. Words of relief
28. John Fowles novel
33. Windbreaker
35. Eggs
36. Find a cheap place to park?
38. ___ qua non
40. "Brown" co.
41. Simpleton
42. Beach bum's wages?
47. Word on a wine bottle
48. More desertlike
49. Canine
51. Salon supply
52. Weeks in a Roman year
54. Chicken or small
55. Inexpensive footwear?
61. Proscribe
64. Spreads
65. It has a creamy filling
66. Highly excited
67. Quit
68. Iranian money
69. Dorothy's doggy
70. Option on a form, perhaps
71. Musician's submission

DOWN

1. Like Lot's love later
2. Scratch
3. Shells and such
4. Thumper, for one
5. Use passive resistance
6. Philbin's cohost
7. Parisian plus
8. Infernal writer
9. Horse that doesn't even show
10. Accounts of a lifetime
11. '60s psychedelic
12. "The Greatest"
13. Kind of line
21. Diaphragm
22. Supermodel Mero (aka Sable)
25. Musical recitative
26. Small community
27. Brief description
28. Israeli spy group
29. Bird sanctuary
30. Mary Poppins, for example
31. Spirit
32. Beatles' record label
34. Strange
37. Key's famous first words
39. Leno's announcer Hall
43. Mark for omission
44. South American river
45. One at rest
46. Covered walk or colonnade
50. Dress shoe
53. Cove
55. Kind of stick
56. Okie-dokie
57. Come second
58. Pennsylvania city
59. 20 quires
60. Stag
61. Container
62. It may be bruised
63. Kid

❖ Solution on page 273

Frequencies *Grace Becker*

ACROSS

1. Comedy's Wilson
5. Taken ___ (surprised)
10. Excess
14. Parks in the bus
15. Scoundrel
16. Superman's mother
17. Inventor of Cordite
18. Writer ___ Booth Luce
19. Sister of Ares
20. Swarm
21. Occasionally
23. Female deer
25. City south of Gainesville
26. Neighbors of Europeans
29. Take issue with
32. Kind of page or role
33. Small bird
34. Letters for Bill Gates?
37. Occasionally
41. Book before Esth.
42. RPI's locale
43. Finger, in a way
44. The wild blue yonder
46. Tree with pink blossoms found in the South
47. '50s pop hit "Maria ___"
50. Famous Lisa
51. Occasionally
55. L.A. phenomenon
59. Word with per or carpe
60. Thumb-raising film critic
61. Actress Anderson
62. Agatha contemporary
63. Mercury product
64. Cassini of fashion
65. Farmer's place
66. Fisherman's basket
67. ___ Ma

DOWN

1. *Animal House* house
2. Leaf division
3. What video means
4. Los Angeles neighbor
5. McDonald's trademark
6. Weighted ropes used for catching cattle
7. Ice cream thickener
8. Muffet tidbit
9. Underwater projection
10. Jacket lining
11. Polliwog, for one
12. Spirit in *The Tempest*
13. Iraq city
22. "___ don't say!"
24. R.E.M.'s "The ___ Love"
26. Heaps
27. Math term
28. *The Seven Year* ___
29. Shady garden bower
30. Bank (on)
31. Animal that sounds new
33. Marketable merchandise
34. Fictional detective Mr. ___
35. Words on Halloween
36. Grandma Moses
38. Unspecified power
39. 2000 role for Julia
40. Elvis, for one
44. Part of a tooth
45. Summer goal?
46. Talk show host Williams
47. "Our revels now are ___" (Shakespeare)
48. River at Orleans
49. Tom ___, a *Baretta* regular
50. Reagle of crosswords
52. Offspring: Abbr.
53. Lift for a skier
54. Greek goddess of youth
56. *Bloom County* regular
57. Follow orders
58. You get what you start with, for short

❖ Solution on page 273

No Three-ums 3   *Douglas Fink*

ACROSS

1. Takes notice
7. They come back for more
15. It's what's for dinner
16. Popular hymn
17. When leaves leave
18. Type of factor
19. They're a real pain
20. They're not much to go on
21. After-dinner beverages
23. Agricultural product ingredient
31. Process a passport again
37. Unmoved
38. Dark rings
39. Cassandra, for one
40. Where someone might wear a barrel
41. Go deeply into
42. Staff leader
44. Wee playful ones
51. Reduces to ashes
58. Olympic skater Yagudin
59. One way to go
60. Where your wrist tunnels are
61. Like this puzzle
62. Still
63. Lap dog
64. Teen on the Enterprise

DOWN

1. Contact
2. Accustom
3. Perfume from petals
4. Bio film of '94
5. Lure
6. One of our five
7. Red salad item
8. Level
9. Ascot locale
10. Actor Jannings
11. Arroyo
12. Oscar-winning title role for Julia
13. Tolkien concern
14. Goes down in the middle
22. Advertiser's concern
24. What Gilderoy Lockhart failed to do to Harry's arm
25. Parsley feature
26. ABBA item
27. Bring on
28. Computer maker
29. Soviet informer of old
30. Or ___!
31. Loud tirade
32. Iroquois Indian
33. Yoko's son
34. Like some pizzas
35. Apple spray
36. General Antony
43. Work on the farm
45. Flying talker
46. Part of a service
47. Bach and Wagner
48. Get rid of
49. Ad with a hook
50. Like delta water
51. Lamb serving
52. Infrequent
53. Ponch portrayer
54. Gift givers
55. Related
56. It's got a point
57. Timely times

❖ **Solution on page 273**

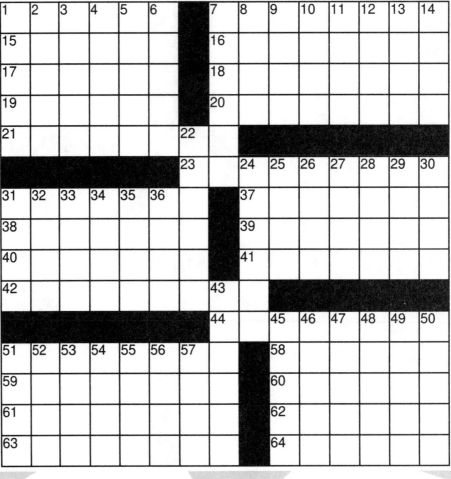

Just Say It *Alan Olschwang*

ACROSS

1. Sandwich side
5. Some singers
10. Pack down
14. ___ Doc Duvalier
15. Noose
16. Flightless bird of South America
17. Farewells
18. Teeth protector
20. Wind instruments
22. Wool source
23. Before, before
24. Musical syllable
25. Dapper one
26. It beats the locals
32. Exist
33. Stop, look, and look?
34. Divine
38. TLC part
40. Start of a shot?
42. Command to a team
43. Psalms
45. I give up!
47. 19th of series
48. It may have four lanes
51. Expression of discovery
54. Holiday forerunner
55. Extinct New Zealand bird
56. The world's third largest island
58. Purse item
63. Total pandemonium
65. Teheran's place
66. Skirt feature
67. Inventor Berliner
68. Tiny victory margin
69. Checks out
70. ___ down
71. Emulate a busy beaver

DOWN

1. Masseuses' milieus
2. Etna effluvium
3. Summit
4. Nut holder
5. Car interior features
6. MGM icon
7. Greek letters
8. Ed ___ of baseball
9. It's north of the Sahel
10. Stumble
11. Leading
12. Center of activity
13. A 43A
19. Tartan-patterned cloth
21. Lode loads
24. Sapper's creation
26. Per pop
27. Lead stops it
28. Salon offering
29. Greeting for the brass
30. Peter, Paul, and Mary, e.g.
31. Rights org.
35. Expression of relief
36. Windy City slugger
37. What pie may stand for
39. Printer's measure
41. Espies
44. Bum chaser
46. Ids' companions
49. Long-legged shore bird
50. Despising
51. Corrupt practice
52. ___ contested
53. Bandleader Shaw
57. Kidd's team
58. Reclined
59. Hercules' captive
60. One age
61. Sala holder
62. Understood
64. Health care provider, briefly

❖ **Solution on page 274**

This Bud's for You   *Mark Milhet*

ACROSS

1. The lion's share
5. Wing it
10. Starting from
14. Golden rule word
15. Royal topper
16. Crater, for one
17. Sore loser's remarks
19. Pelvic bones
20. 1997 U.S. Open winner
21. Lent ender
23. Knucklehead
24. Gill openings
25. Tasmania's capital
29. LSD, slangily
30. Party attire
33. Apartments
34. Niles or Frasier
35. Buccaneer's affirmative
36. Tiny parasite
37. High scout
38. Creole vegetable
39. Play the part
40. Pancake topper
41. Kilmer opus
42. Born, in bridal bios
43. Response to "Shall we?"
44. Opposed (to)
45. Way to go
47. Dashed-off plea?
48. In
50. Emphasizes
55. Bistro sign word
56. Sugar pine?
58. Scale starter
59. Latin land?
60. Taboo
61. Sosa's squad
62. Paradigm of strength
63. Eat like a mouse

DOWN

1. Clio, for one
2. ___ about (roughly)
3. Kind of gun
4. Pop singer Amos
5. Chilling out
6. Indicators
7. Swimmer's regimen
8. Tick off
9. Tennis boundary
10. Select group
11. Item with holes in its head
12. Dust Bowl migrant
13. Trepidation
18. Bike features
22. Assistant
24. Hair holder
25. Mortal
26. Chilling
27. Aloe
28. Had a cow?
29. 100-eyed giant
31. Lew ___ of *Johnny Belinda*
32. Act the coquette
34. Bistro menu
37. Useful in making contacts
38. Smeltery input
40. Milieu for rats, maybe
41. Cable outlet
44. Pertaining to a main line
46. Flows like lava
47. One cubic meter
48. Current abbr.
49. Intro to art?
50. Like a dustbowl
51. Dance partner?
52. Any time now
53. Smoker in Sicily
54. Come in third
57. In need of changing

❖ **Solution on page 274**

Who Do We Appreciate   *Alan Olschwang*

ACROSS

1. Indian nurses
6. Lion's pride
10. Greek portico
14. Wooden shoe
15. Jet black
16. Couch potato aid
17. They had rumble seats
19. Ceremony
20. Backslid
21. Stable sounds
23. A nice thing to say
24. WWII command
25. Pitcher's faux pas
26. Evils from the New Testament
31. Psyche
34. Conception
35. Mrs. Cantor
36. Type of tube
37. Held title
39. Ado
40. Bikini part
41. Eager
42. Simple song
43. HBO hit
47. Behave humanly
48. James's creator
49. Southern Hemisphere constellation
52. Some computer instructions
55. Skinflints
57. Olfactory offense
58. '70s car accessory
60. Man in a box, perhaps
61. Art deco designer
62. Upper crust
63. ERA, e.g.
64. Impudence
65. Church assembly

DOWN

1. Jetsons' dog
2. Swerved
3. Supervising
4. Gardener's need
5. Hi-fis
6. Night sky sight
7. Down for the night
8. Start of a way?
9. Trapped
10. Ump's call
11. Math course
12. Office entry requirement
13. Some votes
18. Westernmost of the Aleutians
22. She was born free
25. Augur
26. Watch pocket
27. Northern India native
28. Catcher's need
29. Improve the content
30. Not one
31. Flows out
32. Convex moldings
33. Counterfeit
37. Monitors
38. Intelligence
39. Knight's address
41. Dynamic leader
42. Marks
44. Delve into
45. Wall recesses
46. Flit
49. Once more
50. Right-hand page
51. Queried
52. May celebrants
53. Ore door
54. Unconscious state
55. Some NCOs
56. Paris airport locale
59. Saver's device

❖ Solution on page 274

Joint Venture   *Lane Gutz*

ACROSS

1. Biodegrade
4. Charge beginning
9. 20th president's middle name
14. In existence
15. Soap suffix
16. Actress Kelly
17. Change on the beach
18. Bit of gridiron gear
20. Italian time bomb?
22. Lengthwise of yore
23. Caught minnows
25. "___ better not cry . . . "
26. Create a date
29. Beginning or ending for "up"
31. Contaminate
33. Mad cow disease, for short
35. Speak up, long ago
38. Rolls
39. Needing a tenant
41. How Rocky liked eggs
42. Motion with "Ouch!"
43. Ito's cover
44. Like some spores
46. Entertainment center room
47. ASAP
49. Part of TMC
51. Use a Singer
52. Door leading to ore
55. Melt the fat
58. Mel Blanc film?
60. Actress Ione ___
61. Slow pitch
65. French born
66. Studio tripod
67. Grass raisers?
68. Hyperion's daughter
69. They often honk
70. All filled up
71. LAX to O'Hare direction

DOWN

1. Taxi sign
2. Spout a speech
3. Woe for 10D
4. MS-___
5. Dangerous dieter's option
6. Bean picker, e.g.
7. Jerry Marcus comic strip
8. Fox hunter's shout
9. ___ honorable (Fr.)
10. He serves 58D
11. Cord starter
12. Telescope's focus, possibly
13. Lost it
19. Rock band with "No"
21. Rocker Adam ___
24. "___ Coker" (T. S. Eliot)
26. Chief Bigfoot was killed here
27. Scale marking
28. Ashley or Mary-Kate
30. Not a pro
32. ATF cohorts
33. Pats a back
34. Noise in the night
36. Stuff the gullet
37. Crawl in the water
40. Dusk, to Donne
42. "___ Only Just Begun" (The Carpenters)
44. Runway denizen
45. Peril on the Rhine
48. Line, hook, and sinker
50. Type of agt.
53. Bullet points
54. Heretical
56. ___ *America* with Dan Rather
57. Witherspoon of *Legally Blonde*
58. These are served by 10D
59. Big's partner
61. This usually requires a deposit
62. Rob Roy's refusal
63. Deplete with "up"
64. Timothy Leary's elixir

❖ **Solution on page 274**

T Squares   *Michael Wiesenberg*

ACROSS

1. Battle groups
8. Moves a picture
15. Substance having chemical activity
16. Stuff
17. Content
18. Fanfare
19. Huck's old man
20. ___ de los Muertos (Mexican Holiday)
21. Spike TV, once
22. Copy
23. French season
24. Not one goes unpunished
28. One of LBJ's dogs
29. Dash lengths
30. Eastern province of Cuba or Ecuador
31. "Wild Bill" Donovan's gp.
32. Describing an irresistable force encountering an immovable object
34. Half of a pet food co. name
35. The Pope
43. Violinist Shaham
46. Chants
47. Fink
48. Victrola maker
49. Springsteen
50. He's no amateur
51. Brainwaves
52. Luxury locus
53. Vietnam's My ___
54. Legal gp.
55. Se habla ___
60. Charges
62. Supreme Court Justice John Paul
63. Certain parlay bets offered by casinos
64. Drugged
65. Blow up

DOWN

1. Algonquian language
2. Does the whole episode again
3. Lewis and Clark, e.g.
4. Get old
5. Where to find Masada
6. Fossilized
7. Makes an advance of a sort
8. Bosh!
9. Zsa Zsa's sister
10. Layer
11. 1998 Tony winner
12. Tidies
13. January birthstones
14. Rush hour subway rider, often
24. Formulaic
25. Adjustable loan
26. Dance or skating move
27. Druggists?
33. Bert's Bobbsey sister
35. Like a 0-0 baseball game
36. How one acts before repenting at leisure
37. Performed, as a minuet
38. Fireplace warming area
39. Lennon's widow
40. First name in guitars
41. Crusade foe
42. Resigned
43. Young tough, particularly of the '50s
44. It's cold
45. Emeril of the Food Network
56. Actress Gardner
57. Clear
58. Single
59. Acid
61. Chevy's bailiwick, in old ads

❖ **Solution on page 274**

Chapter 6

Theme of
Little Faith

Actresses   *Matthew Skoczen*

ACROSS

1. Metal detector
6. Speechify
11. Crane part
14. French river
15. *Gates of Hell* sculptor
16. Address on the Web
17. Comedienne with a bounce?
19. Not noche
20. ASEAN member since 1997
21. Some may be lost in one
23. They have fitting behavior
27. " . . . looking backward with a wise ___ " (J. Dryden)
29. St. Sebastian's near-demise
30. Mystery
31. Pub quaffs
32. Actress Hasso
33. Butt
36. Basketball court area
37. All but gone
38. Chimney place
39. Place for a pupil
40. Tarman
41. Cheats
42. Some seas, comparatively
44. Heavenly offerings
45. The Panthers, Coyotes, and Predators have them
47. Done to exhaustion
48. Puzzled
49. Gunshot
50. Received
51. Actress with some bark?
58. A slick one
59. Unpleasant task
60. It's a mess to work in
61. Vane dir.
62. They may come with stretches
63. Not so nice

DOWN

1. Total
2. Old French coin
3. Better left alone?
4. Jackie's second
5. Shows its age
6. They're usually pulled apart
7. Cheats
8. City Hall off.
9. Poetic adverb
10. Intensify
11. Singer with Christmas decor?
12. Sean or Patrick, say
13. Dagnabbit!
18. Unseen husband on *Phyllis*
22. "___, Bam, Boom," 1956 song by the El Dorados
23. Put on the back burner
24. Matrix
25. Dancer who's always at home?
26. One of the Brat Pack
27. Provoke
28. Recover
30. Duck
32. What 45A are good at
34. Heard
35. Not so neat
37. It's often sought
38. "Swell!"
40. Reason for a good fit
41. Generosity
43. Possible order for 12D
44. Skirt style
45. Plums
46. Siouan people
47. Maupin's ___ *of the City*
49. Lofty place?
52. Exclamation
53. Hemp fibers
54. Word heard from 12D, maybe
55. Create red ink
56. Ref. book
57. Martini option

❖ **Solution on page 274**

He Fell for It . . . *Merle Baker*

ACROSS

1. Café additive
5. Jordan's brand
10. Planting places
14. *Sweet Liberty* star
15. Monteverdi opera
16. Blue hue
17. Maneuvers on ice
19. Former Georgia senator
20. Preclude
21. Pump number
23. Approached angrily
26. More robust
27. Slacken
30. Girder
32. German river
33. Rainy times
35. Pickle
38. Place to hike
41. Nevertheless
42. Stockpiles
43. Invention germination
44. ___ blanche
45. Make use of
46. *Enigma Variations* composer
49. Turn aside
52. Island capital
54. Planter purpose
58. Best Actress of 1997
59. It's easy to miss
62. Rice-shaped pasta
63. 5A product
64. *Night of the Hunter* screenwriter
65. Rhineland neighbor
66. Comes close to
67. R rating reason

DOWN

1. Garland's "catty" costar
2. 1994 NL Manager of the Year
3. Teen ___
4. Be on the alert
5. Blah
6. Rugged ridge
7. Bears play in it
8. "A mouse!"
9. Blah
10. Diminutive
11. Evenly matched
12. *My Favorite Wife* star Irene
13. More reasonable
18. Sweet-talk
22. Deep cleft
24. Flying group
25. Car in a Beach Boys song
27. Count (on)
28. Adams of old TV
29. Contributed, as support
31. Whitney and Terry
33. Get an ___ effort
34. Exams for jrs.
35. Green shade
36. Golden follower
37. Essence
39. Second busiest U.S. airport
40. Gallimaufry
44. Chessman, at times
45. Unceasingly
46. Cultural values
47. Otto Preminger film noir classic
48. Tokyo district
50. Glacial ridge
51. Nautical hazards
53. Book ID
55. Shakespearean schemer
56. Expo, for one
57. Kind of club
60. Eng. neighbor
61. Vardalos of *My Big Fat Greek Wedding*

❖ Solution on page 274

It's a Guy Thing   *Michael Wiesenberg*

❖ Solution on page 274

ACROSS

1. Hammer in soda
5. Spat
9. Chocolate source
14. Fuller enhancement
15. Freezer add-on
16. California governor's middle name
17. James Allen's ___ *Thinketh*
18. Short note
19. 1988 Best Picture
20. Second echelon in business
23. Vacillate
24. It might come from heaven
25. '80s ghost gobbler
28. Giraffe cousins
33. It's east of the Urals
37. Lithuanian actress Lee
39. Author Jong
40. Special shows for a ruler
43. "If ___ Hammer"
44. Dang
45. "Mm hmm . . ."
46. Realm
48. A something to put in it
50. Where to go in England
52. Bandleader Les or Larry
57. You might find this around a doctor's neck
62. Algonquian concept of magical force pervading the natural world
63. 1999 Ron Howard film
64. ___ avis
65. Invitations to duels
66. World's longest river
67. Dada artist/photographer
68. Elmer's female counterpart
69. Fortune teller
70. ___, zwei, drei, . . .

DOWN

1. Kovacs' wife
2. '50s pop group ___ and the Originals
3. Unnatural?
4. Insists
5. *Rocky Horror Picture Show* song
6. O'Neill title character
7. Disaster relief org.
8. '50s singer Clarence "___" Henry
9. Ford or GMC
10. Wings
11. Something of the realm
12. "It ___ Necessarily So"
13. Ottoman Empire founder
21. Luxury site
22. Brian ___ of electronic rock
26. Got ready for play
27. Watchwords
29. Big name in suits
30. Fotos
31. Slurpee rival
32. What publishers expect with a submitted ms.
33. Tart
34. TriBeCa neighbor
35. Mosque leader
36. Rolling Stones hit "Miss ___ Jones"
38. Do
41. What vitamins might be for
42. Glance
47. Xmas drink
49. Dutch airline
51. Portents
53. Pertinent
54. Company founded by Nolan Bushnell
55. Showed over
56. Waiter props
57. It's under the window
58. School groups
59. Pueblo dweller
60. Garfield's foil
61. Monroe ex
62. Parsonage

Take It Off! Dave Fisher

ACROSS

1. Brown ermine
6. *Ben-Hur*, for example
10. Kid
14. ___charged (engine type)
15. Puerto ___
16. Willy was one
17. Greek theater
18. Eddie in *Beverly Hills Cop*
19. Boys in the hood
20. Romantic nudist's preferred reading?
22. Where a nudist keeps contact info?
24. While opening?
25. What 20A took off
28. Puppy prattle
29. Poetic palindrome
31. Doh! nut?
33. Hidden cartoon character
36. Ambiance
37. Exceeded the limit
41. Actor/director Lupino
42. Nudist with a wolfhound?
45. ___ de vie
46. What 42A took off
48. Cincinnati players
49. U.S. airport named after a war hero
51. Senseless
53. Serengeti roamer
54. Because
57. Prune
59. Spoils
63. Crooked nudist's possessions?
65. Flasher at a nudist nightclub?
67. Subs.
68. River dividing Europe and Asia
71. Gallic goodbye
72. Asian desert
73. What 65A took off
74. Hall-of-famer ___ Ryan
75. Sauce type
76. They're walked on
77. What 22A took off

DOWN

1. What 63A took off
2. Henry VIII's family name
3. Nabisco product since 1912
4. Canceled a mission
5. Nobel Prize–winning author Morrison
6. Press the backspace key, perhaps
7. Photos
8. Unusual hotel type
9. Popular drink
10. Pieceworkers
11. Actor Flynn
12. Cone unit
13. Chores
21. Early fruit picker
23. Color
26. Quake
27. They run in Pamplona
30. Purloin
32. Oda ___ Brown (Whoopi in *Ghost*)
33. Head topper
34. Fuss
35. It can be civil
36. Helper
38. It gave a princess discomfort
39. A hole in the head
40. Deserved
43. Grp. involved in "the Troubles"
44. Director Howard
47. Capital of Cyprus
50. Tobacco container
52. ___ Kelly (Jagger role)
53. EST+5
54. Hitches
55. Dome home
56. ___ a long shot (way off)
58. Setting for *Cast Away*
60. Nimble
61. Big birds
62. Floors
64. Catch a wave
66. Touch down
69. Future fish
70. Honest guy

❖ **Solution on page 274**

Look Both Ways Alan Olschwang

ACROSS
1. Mama ___ Elliot
5. Drops heavily
10. Arrestee's need
14. Sometimes it's stashed
15. Unworldly
16. Countercurrent
17. Florence's flooder
18. R follower
19. Show
20. First day of the new business?
23. Anorak
24. Gasteyer of SNL
25. Raises
28. Future DA's hurdle
32. Element type
34. One from the retailer's catalog?
39. Disney sci-fi flick
40. Choir part
41. Type of tea
42. Numero uno Green Bay fan?
45. Change the color of the pumps
46. Hector Hugh Munro
47. Us in Essen
48. Name in electronics
51. Sort of roof
56. A smaller fish?
60. Leer
63. Ghana river
64. Young shoot
65. Egocentric
66. Fencer's foil
67. Hibernia
68. Ripened
69. Arrests
70. Buy by Benny

DOWN
1. Hold tightly
2. Main trunk
3. Detection device
4. Large wading bird
5. Trujillo's nation
6. Bound
7. Table scraps
8. Religious painting
9. Family car
10. Slug
11. Pother
12. Egos' companions
13. Caustic substance
21. Medicine cabinet item
22. It goes up or down
25. New York city
26. Evidenced anxiety, in a way
27. Rosebud, e.g.
29. Cain's other brother
30. Sheltered
31. Fork features
33. Cleveland's lake
34. Primp
35. Highways and byways
36. Race moniker
37. Windy City slugger
38. Odyssey
39. Poetic contraction
43. Uno forerunner
44. Type of tide
49. They're 30D
50. Embrace
52. Nursery rhyme ender
53. Kind of knife
54. France's longest river
55. Beat, but just barely
56. Ward off
57. Run away
58. News piece
59. Talk back
60. What Nero needed for an omelet
61. Judge's order
62. Tiger's concern

❖ Solution on page 275

Recipe for Success   *Leslie Nicoll*

ACROSS

1. Hair lines
6. Pricey theater section
10. Wild guess
14. Anticipate
15. Use a red pencil
16. Skin opening
17. For dinner at eight, first step
20. Needle hole
21. Corn units
22. Fiery felony
23. Cousin of the Atlantic cod
24. Skier's souvenir?
26. Step two
32. Mock words of understanding
33. Uncommon
34. Prom attire, for short
35. Derisive laugh
36. *The Bells of* ___
39. Glass of *This American Life*
40. I love: Lat.
41. Letters of debt
42. Con game
43. Step three
48. *A Death in the Family* author
49. Simon and Garfunkel, reunited
50. Easy ___
53. It may be compact
54. Hosp. areas
57. Last step, don't forget!
61. Muscle quality
62. Em, to Dorothy
63. With ball, a type of pen
64. Caraway or mustard
65. Volleyball dividers
66. Certain drapes

DOWN

1. Type of India ale
2. Up, up and ___!
3. Comedienne Martha ___
4. Neckwear
5. Mill site
6. MacNeil's longtime news partner
7. Poetic tributes
8. Minnesota congressman Gutknecht
9. JFK info
10. Greek city-state
11. Clothing
12. Florence's river
13. Kidney or pinto
18. Give's partner
19. Talks back to
23. Managed care grp.
24. Burn slightly
25. Eagle's home: Var.
26. Sea World whale
27. Strike while the iron ___
28. Refuse
29. City near Rome, New York
30. Adhesive bandage brand
31. It may be physical
32. *Moby Dick* captain
36. Gangster Bugsy
37. Ripped
38. Trombone accessory
42. Tennis match
44. Followed
45. Royal commands
46. Shrub
47. Summaries
50. Play segments
51. Loafer, for one
52. Long for
53. Sign of a fender bender
54. Director Kazan
55. Encircle
56. Fast jets, for short
58. Sunbather's goal
59. Palette selection
60. Type of 4D

❖ **Solution on page 275**

Law & Order Times 3   *Merle Baker*

ACROSS

1. Kristen of *Lost in Space*
6. Ness, for one
10. Afternoon staple
14. Hockey teams
15. Wrapped hay
16. *The Kids in the* ___
17. Detective Benson on *Law & Order: SVU*
20. "Ya got me"
21. Finish
22. Elliott's *Just Shoot Me* coworker
23. More than mega-
25. Hawkeye's tent
29. Product with a tiger in the ad
30. Pilot's announcement
31. *High Rollers* hostess Lee
32. Magician's word
35. ___ good example
36. Detective Briscoe on *Law & Order*
38. Young and Hale
40. ___ *of the Killer Tomatoes*
41. Office communication
42. Elevations: Abbr.
43. ___ favor
46. Start of Fred's phrase
48. H.S. class
50. *Covington Cross* actress Skye
51. Mrs. Peel's partner
53. *Green Acres* pig
55. Detective Goren on *Law & Order: Criminal Intent*
59. Logical beginning?
60. Put ___ writing
61. *Frasier* name
62. *Gunsmoke*'s Marshal Dillon
63. Coloring stuff
64. Jackson and Mulgrew

DOWN

1. Competing on *Stump the Stars*
2. Maine national park
3. Summer fare
4. Actress McGee-Davis of *Boy Meets World*
5. Org.
6. *TV Guide* abbreviation
7. *Politically Incorrect* host
8. *The George and* ___ *Show*
9. Social inept
10. Gilligan's disaster
11. Morsel for Mr. Ed
12. Words on a menu
13. Engage in
18. *Welcome Back,* ___
19. Jamie's *Mad About You* father
24. Snap course
26. Twain, for one: Abbr.
27. Atlas abbreviation
28. John's job on *NYPD Blue*
30. Slips up
32. Houlihan's husband
33. *Romper Room* watcher
34. Big name in gardening products
35. Anatomical pouches
36. Side of a door
37. Adam West series
38. Actress Irving of *Alias*
39. Caroline portrayer
43. Not skilled in
44. Surfing the Web
45. Makes over
47. Dined
48. *The Golden Girls* actress
49. Brandon Cruz role
50. Prefix with red
52. Novelist Bagnold
54. *American Bandstand* music
55. Ebullient energy
56. Rhoda's mother
57. Profit margin
58. Switch positions

❖ **Solution on page 275**

All Ears   *Viv Collins*

ACROSS

1. Flame attractee
5. Butcher's offer
10. Biggers's detective
14. What's more
15. Plus item
16. Mrs. Chaplin
17. Posterior
18. Gaze fixedly
19. College mil. unit
20. Horn of plenty
22. At no time, to bards
23. Put bread in gravy
24. Dr. Jekyll's alter ego
26. Jazz enthusiast
30. Mississippi marsh
32. "___ Me" (1931 song)
33. Kind of band
34. Politician's topic
38. Villain's expression
39. Drop the ball
40. Small barrels
41. Tilts or slants
43. King of Judah
44. Great Britain, to Victoria
45. Railroad switch
47. Magazine choice
48. ___ to the core
51. Baseball's Ripken
52. A 60A probably has one
53. Garden plant
60. Hollywood success
61. Nonchalant
62. Vocalist Jerry ___
63. Red one
64. Sticky stuff
65. Actor Richard
66. Green actor
67. Curl one's lip
68. Verne hero

DOWN

1. Artist Chagall
2. Bread spread
3. Russian ruler
4. Turnpike warning
5. The San Diego chicken, e.g.
6. Bar at the bar
7. Pronto
8. She had a *Tootsie* role
9. Like summer days
10. Nebraska native
11. Nonsense
12. Fed the kitty
13. Mother of pearl
21. Mil. org
25. King of France
26. Connecting room
27. Robert of the CSA
28. Court request
29. Thickener
30. Popped
31. Mogul Empire capital; 1566
33. Actress Harlow
35. Stamp of authority
36. Jamaican citrus fruit
37. Salinger title name
42. Seashell seller
44. Small brook
46. Opens a bottle
47. Movie worker
48. Clears away: Var.
49. Altogether kooky
50. Mendel concern
51. Place to see Franklin
54. Character in *The Good Earth*
55. Pasadena bloom
56. Microwave or kiln
57. Paycheck figure
58. Kingdom east of Babylonia
59. Gambling mecca

❖ Solution on page 275

The Other Red Meat   *Jerry Rosman*

ACROSS

1. Funny Foxx
5. Biblical brother
9. Ex-SNLer Quinn
14. It's pointless
15. About
16. Observe Yom Kippur
17. Lazy cut of beef?
20. Sonata's last movement, often
21. Avoid risk
22. Religion of Japan
24. Puppy, perhaps
25. Word from a bear?
26. Stiff hairs
27. It may be staked
29. It's just passing
30. Member of the lepton family
32. Syrup source
34. Fastest cut of beef to cook?
37. Junior generally
38. Works on a sentence?
41. George Gershwin's brother
44. Allotted
46. Floor fixer
47. Teasing tool
49. Caesar of comedy
50. Southern cooking style
51. Adopt, as a philosophy
53. Tag ___
54. Cut of beef for the West Coast?
58. "Keep ___ to the ground"
59. Pull in
60. Word with Lover's or Lois
61. Blue books?
62. "From the ___ of"; memo heading
63. Village People hit

DOWN

1. Apt. usually
2. Prefix for demic or dermis
3. Rubble
4. Sets off
5. Apt.
6. Jason's ship
7. Syr.'s neighbor
8. What a clueless one has
9. Vikki ___, "It Must Be Him" singer
10. Native Nebraskans
11. Advanced
12. Part of a boot
13. Irritate
18. Way to be heard in the next room
19. Cotton fabric
22. Govt. ID
23. Haw leader
24. Walked with difficulty
27. Turner's first TV sta.
28. Consummate artists
31. *Rhinoceros* playwright
33. Best way to wait
35. Sheet of grass
36. 2.2 pounds
39. Brooks or Blanc
40. Before, to the Bard
41. Alpine sight
42. Loveable Ray?
43. Stroller
45. Like a wedding cake
48. NBC anchor Williams
50. Metallic sound
52. Do, rarely done now
53. They may be put on
55. Burns's negative
56. Business mag.
57. Pod occupant

❖ **Solution on page 275**

Patriot Game *Merle Baker*

ACROSS

1. ___ Nova
6. Gallup undertaking
10. Compensation
14. Medieval calculators
15. Scotland island
16. Slings and arrows
17. Legendary city founders
20. Hull structure
21. Charon's river
22. Cheer up
23. Board leader?
25. Cinephile's purchase
26. Was perfect
35. "See ya"
36. Tread heavily
37. Salmon ___
38. Close
39. Steak option
40. Not keen
41. ___ es Salaam
42. It might be close
43. Early in the Civil War?
44. Daisylike flowers
47. Pacific ___
48. Giant of note
49. State of India
52. Window pulldown
55. Moved, as a sofa
59. "The Stars and Stripes
    Forever" composer
62. One way to run
63. One of the Waltons
64. Bid
65. Agents, briefly
66. Arizona city
67. Repeatedly

DOWN

1. Tree part
2. Slender reed
3. Bar order (with "the")
4. Michelangelo, for one
5. Give trouble to
6. "Over here!"
7. Acceptable
8. Big cat
9. Was ahead
10. Handles
11. Diva Gluck
12. Overabundance
13. Latin being
18. Hand-me-down
19. Increase in strength
24. Scale notes
25. Capitol feature
26. Brief accommodations
27. "You've got ___!"
28. Pageant headgear
29. Cornered
30. Valuable collection
31. Perfected
32. Caribbean tourist
    destination
33. *A Tree Grows in Brooklyn*
    actor Lloyd
34. Small wooded valleys
39. The others
40. Restores to use
42. Be parsimonious
43. Protrude
45. Soreheads
46. Wonton, for one
49. Open slightly
50. Certain persons
51. Kind of steward
52. Bog down
53. Yale team
54. One of a famous trio
56. *Grease 2* actress Lorna
57. Words of understanding
58. Repair, in a way
60. Dress line
61. *Barney Miller* actor Jack

❖ **Solution on page 275**

Whatsitz? *Merle Baker*

ACROSS
1. Hurries
5. The gamut
9. Frank ___ of rock
14. Monthly pmt.
15. Killer whale of film
16. Decorators, of a sort
17. Emerald isle
18. Where Farsi is spoken
19. Group of species
20. 1948 Winter Olympics site
23. Summer cooler
24. Airline once owned by Howard Hughes
25. Whistle-stop
27. Israeli weapon
30. Hyde, to Jekyll
34. Spring sign
36. Till fillers
37. Andy's TV son
41. Conking out
44. Different
45. Like desert vegetation
46. Fall flower
47. Culinary convenience
50. GP's grp.
51. Unkempt
54. PBS benefactor
56. UK label letters
57. Pomeranian ancestor
64. Venice sight
66. First-class
67. Rio contents
68. Nelson of '50s TV
69. Defense system
70. Univ. marchers
71. Approaches
72. Mild oath
73. WWII Japanese naval base island

DOWN
1. There are ten in this puzzle
2. Hip bones
3. Gilpin of *Frasier*
4. Hound's trail
5. Bull or bear
6. Tropical tuber
7. Barbra's *Funny Girl* costar
8. Southwest natives
9. Kind of course
10. Expert
11. Kind of code
12. Definitely not a free spirit
13. Benefit
21. Banjo sound
22. "___ Foolish Things"
26. Eighth-century invaders of Spain
27. Desire
28. Biol. branch
29. Heron cousin
31. In good shape
32. Contest mailing
33. Shorten, in a way
35. Motionless
38. Falafel wrapper
39. Newspaper piece
40. Philanthropist Cornell
42. Plains Indian
43. Electronic communication
48. High fliers
49. Hard up
51. Scout's mission, briefly
52. Stun
53. Tokyo district
55. Not together
58. Level
59. Synthesizer inventor
60. Tolstoy's Karenina
61. *Young Frankenstein* role
62. 1984 Peace Nobelist
63. Drummer Starkey
65. Broadcast

❖ **Solution on page 275**

No Three-ums 4 *Douglas Fink*

ACROSS

1. Mexican, not Spanish, coin
5. Splinter group
9. Winner's attire
14. Bedouin
15. General Bradley
16. Rage
17. Aswan Dam river
18. Father
19. "___ Heat"
20. Buys for Baiul
22. Victoria's Secret purchase
23. Sopwith ___
24. String
26. Justly divided
28. Elder, perhaps
32. Like photos or hair
36. Ambitious title
38. Make bubbly
39. Drink of the gods
40. Bring back
42. Artist's supplies
43. Muchly
44. Part of an Angela Bassett film title
46. At risk for one's involvement
48. Shell food
53. One of the Seven Dwarves
56. Bread spread
58. Customary
59. Strait-laced
60. Bough bearer
61. Start
62. Lad
63. Those you think little of
64. Consumed
65. Sir Connery
66. Puppy pleas

DOWN

1. ___ *Room*
2. Writer Jong
3. Setting for *The Crucible*
4. Needing to lose
5. Slammin' Sammy
6. Sent out
7. Drive wildly
8. Train bridge
9. Sample food
10. Collide with
11. Getting on in years
12. Enjoy a book
13. Military group
21. He has a way of getting things
25. Book by a kneeler
27. Swerved
29. Museo offering
30. Where you'd like to be
31. Mistypes
32. *Fame* star
33. Projectionist's item
34. -ish
35. Singer born Clara Ann Fowler
37. Spanish, not Mexican, coin
41. Frees
42. Deviled-egg spice
45. Town crier's opening
47. Hosiery fabric
49. Pretentious
50. Around
51. Best, slightly
52. Appears
53. Jumbo
54. Out of port
55. Green verb
57. Agents

❖ **Solution on page 275**

G Men *Verna Suit*

ACROSS

1. Trudge
5. Turkish honorific
9. Start in
14. Man Friday
15. Jester
16. Get around
17. Buzz's roomie in space
18. Watusi cousin
19. Hills' opposites
20. Famous German satirist
23. Take in or up
24. Soothing succulent
25. Barely making
27. OAS part
30. String tie?
32. ___ *Delight*: 1939 Clark Gable movie
35. India ale type
37. It sometimes has claw feet
38. College goal
39. Lengthen, in a way
41. Soak
43. Enclosed vehicle
44. Doorway top
46. Edward, informally
48. Diana follower or Perot preceder
49. Playwright of *Medea*
50. Abridge
52. Born in Bruges
53. Understand
55. Terrible tsar
57. Portuguese saint
59. '50s low-key comedian
64. It's in Cape Cod or Nova Scotia
66. Royal widow Catherine
67. Short-tailed mouse
68. Poe's middle name
69. Pizzas, e.g.
70. Della and Hamilton's creator
71. Signifies
72. Calm side
73. Political worry

DOWN

1. Sudden sensation
2. Stead
3. Head Norse god
4. *Designing Women*'s Suzanne
5. Provocation
6. Like wrestler George
7. Cuckoo time
8. Aquatic plants
9. Doctor places
10. Braun or Peron
11. The last Mr. Wilson
12. Original thought
13. Cozy home
21. Lodge member
22. An unfortunate row
26. Country named for a river
27. Some Australian silicas
28. Bast fiber popular in Asia
29. Canadian musical prodigy
31. Porterhouse alt.
33. Make hair full
34. Have a feeling
36. Command awaited on threshold
40. East Caribbean dollars, e.g.
42. Ancestry
45. Use a certain ray
47. Motley
51. Graffiti artist's logo
54. Momma's mate
56. Piece of fiction
57. Knife
58. Woody's boy
60. Track
61. Drill
62. Ms. Fitzgerald
63. Howard Keel's real last name
65. Pole person

❖ **Solution on page 275**

Advanced Alchemy — Dave Fisher

ACROSS

1. Sock
5. Yiddish "trash"
9. Less
14. Lycanthropic prefix
15. Van Morrison's homeland
16. Make the innocent look guilty
17. Like poultry allowed to forage
19. Most populous English-speaking country
20. Alchemist rewrites Charles Dickens classic
22. Wane
23. Nice summer
24. Snake
27. City in the Evergreen State
31. School grp.
34. Decorated
36. 4,840 square yards
37. Art supporter?
39. Alchemist rewrites Alexandre Dumas classic (with *The*)
42. Mission San Antonio de Valero
43. Merit
44. Friend
45. Abbreviation in an ad
46. Withhold
49. Humor magazine
50. ___-mo
51. Me in Montreal
53. Alchemist rewrites Ian Fleming classic
61. Seventh month for Moslems
62. Fine china
64. Saudi's neighbor
65. Draft status
66. SAS is based here
67. Parking spot and corner office, perhaps
68. Part of NASA
69. Enthusiastic exclamation

DOWN

1. Nature conservancy gp., not a fighters' org.
2. Cowboy's concern
3. ___ code
4. Irritate
5. Like some dads
6. Peal
7. Hence
8. Sailboat stabilizer
9. Desert Storm aircraft
10. Bert's buddy
11. Roe vs. ___
12. Author Ludwig
13. Scan
18. BBQ favorite
21. ___ Shannon
24. Draw a bead on
25. Climb
26. ___ colony
28. Pains' partner
29. Doctor
30. Four: Prefix
31. Sacred song
32. Inventor Nikola
33. Synthetic resin used in paint
35. Like a night-light
38. Doctors' org.
40. Lacking certain defenses
41. Unfriendly
47. ___ voyage
48. Zilch
50. Was offensive, in a way
52. Nome dome
53. Something onstage
54. Feeble
55. Not open, not closed
56. Stratford-Avon connector
57. *Who's the Boss?* mom
58. Guitar part
59. ___ does it
60. Stir up
63. Negatives

❖ **Solution on page 276**

Gotta Dance!   *Merle Baker*

ACROSS

1. Long, laborious work
5. South American capital
10. Sea of Antarctica
14. Like paraffin
15. Reversed
16. Quechua speaker
17. Maintain
18. Pictures on a screen
19. Blue-winged duck
20. He danced in Paris
22. "Sheik Yerbouti" rocker
23. No. on a map
24. Bordered
25. State of equilibrium
29. Richard's Veep
31. "___ Bulba"
32. Bummed out
36. Per ___
37. Outdoor feasts
38. Dollar alternative
39. Sure things
41. No voters
42. *Fiddler on the Roof* matchmaker
43. Superficially stylish
44. Lumber
47. Billy or billy's son
48. Best of its kind
49. He danced in Oz
55. Mountaintop sign abbr.
56. Esau's brother
57. Sea World attraction
58. It's a wrap
59. Hogback
60. Diamond cover
61. Rail supports
62. Fix the lawn
63. Grain disease

DOWN

1. Spoils
2. Wash
3. Yoked set
4. " . . . did ___ and gimble in the wabe"
5. Makes still
6. Family member
7. Mammon, e.g.
8. Hardly titanic
9. Takes too much
10. She danced on the West Side
11. Lunch time for some
12. City or moon ending
13. Lunch, for some
21. Barbra's *A Star Is Born* costar
22. Calibrate, perhaps
24. Baseball stat
25. Criteria: Abbr.
26. Word with fin or end
27. Sphere
28. He danced for Charity
29. Quench
30. And
32. Family member
33. "Phooey!"
34. *Topaz* author
35. Bouquet
37. Crescent-shaped figure
40. Farmer's place?
41. Ray of Hollywood
43. Wasn't straight
44. *Parenthood* actress Dianne
45. Dwight's opponent
46. Steel plowshare inventor
47. City on Honshu
49. Few and far between
50. Honors in bridge
51. A great deal
52. Metric unit
53. Undyed wool hue
54. Absorbed
56. Preserves holder

❖ **Solution on page 276**

Better Said Than Read   *Jerry Rosman*

ACROSS

1. City on the Big Island
5. Type of TV screen
11. Inc. in England
14. "___ Brutus"
15. Sea by Greece
16. ___ Jima
17. Graduate's cap
19. Coal or corn container
20. VCR maker
21. Executive spy grp.?
22. Plant with spores
23. Start of a riddle
27. Where things disappear?
28. Bismarck's st.
29. Small cyst
30. Dagger of yore
32. A British isle
36. Pond growth
38. One who runs for the office?
41. Raise
42. Period of time
44. Banjo's bar
46. "Never" in Nuremberg
47. Puts on clothes
50. "Lite" dessert
52. End of riddle
56. Capital of Norway
57. " . . . the grace of God ___"
58. One to Juan
59. Spat conclusion?
60. Marinara stirrer, often
65. Race an engine
66. Most sick
67. "___ first you don't . . . "
68. Shaker ___, OH: Abbr.
69. Prepares a salad
70. Answer to the riddle

DOWN

1. Do some tailoring
2. Am ___ believe . . . ?
3. Env. filler
4. Beat to the tape
5. Emulating a mummer, perhaps
6. Syr.'s neighbor
7. Ecstasy's partner
8. Salt
9. Pillage
10. Ampersand essentially
11. Publisher's concern
12. Make a quick about-face
13. Summer of songs
18. Play the role of
22. One walks on hot coals, perhaps
23. Pup
24. Door joint
25. Sweet treat
26. Call from a crow's nest
27. "___ the night before . . . "
31. French leader?
33. Lamp occupant?
34. Flags, as a cab
35. Hard journey
37. Even if, in brief
39. Ms. Brockovich
40. Tells a story
43. Dispirited
45. Cold temps
48. *Deuce Bigalow* for one
49. High chairs in a bar
51. Nearsightedness
52. ___ Club
53. Land in water
54. Croats et al.
55. Pelts
60. Sense of humor
61. Japan add-on
62. On vacation
63. W. Hemisphere assn.
64. High degree

❖ **Solution on page 276**

Chapter 7

Get Theme to
a Nunnery

Body Language   *Alan Olschwang*

ACROSS

1. Sculptor's subject
6. Male deer
10. Chicken ___
14. Love affair
15. Hebrew month
16. Eye part
17. Beluga caviar source
19. ___ off
20. Cricket sides
21. Type of lamp
22. He's nasty
24. You see it when landing at Ronald Reagan National
27. Weather phenomenon
30. Sit up for
31. Scoters
32. Rick ___ of racing
33. Initials used in mathematical proofs
36. Pollyanna-ish
37. Banned imports
38. Island feast
39. Take advantage of
40. Try out
41. Aplomb
42. Rhino cousin
43. Row, row, row your boat
44. Marianas Trench milieu
48. Crude abode
49. Jackie's number two
50. Romaine
53. Coffee servers
54. It's North America's second deepest
58. Child's assertion
59. Intern
60. Region of ancient Greece
61. Ring
62. Mast
63. Organic compound

DOWN

1. Fast food choice
2. Middle Eastern sultanate
3. Flag fabricator
4. Have a light dinner
5. Prayers
6. Carthaginian leader
7. Madison Avenue offerings
8. ___ Dawn Chong
9. British commuters' alternatives
10. Middle Eastern sheikdom
11. 17th-century tsar
12. Unworldly
13. Darth of *Star Wars* notoriety
18. Start of a motive?
23. Goddess of discord
24. Empathy
25. Conductor of renown
26. Rouse
27. Beige
28. Brits' johns
29. Smallest victory margin
32. What 25D conducts
33. Jape
34. Let off pressure
35. Burr's victory in one ended his political life
37. Beady starches
38. Diving bird
40. Ohio political name
41. Kind of chicken
42. Decorative material
43. ___ David's deer
44. Chubby
45. High home
46. Perennial tropical herb
47. Put on a party
50. Jargon
51. Migratory worker of the '30s
52. Barbecue
55. Actor Torn
56. Oklahoma town
57. ___ Gatos

❖ **Solution on page 276**

Not Brand X   *Dave Fisher*

ACROSS

1. See 69A
7. Rapid transit in France
10. Big part
14. Type of maid
15. Color
16. Color
17. Black Sea port
18. Corrode
19. Contented sound
20. Slip
21. Tiger Woods, ethnically
23. Like a hideaway
25. Serpentine sound
28. Carpet type
29. Comfort
34. This little piggy et al.
36. Author Blyton
38. Spoons and spinners
39. Vehicle for 69A
42. Paint ingredient
43. Dam's opposite
44. Unilever deodorant brand
45. Wears
47. Intangible quality
49. Frank McCourt memoir
50. Applicable
53. Tanner's concern
57. Auto style
61. Libra's birthstone
62. Richard haunted by Anne's ghost
63. Jointed at right angles
64. Attend
65. Name for a famous rag doll
66. Anxiety
67. Was aware
68. '60s psychedelic
69. With 1A, name for this puzzle

DOWN

1. Scary stuff in a B-movie
2. Hitchhiker's quest
3. Swear
4. Egg holders
5. China
6. Belle in *Gone with the Wind*
7. Vehicle for 69A
8. Protect
9. Disallows
10. Only seated people have them
11. Distant start
12. Halo, e.g.
13. Shucks
21. Myles and Davis
22. German name now out of favor
24. Munch
25. Did a bank job
26. Ping thing
27. Spat
30. Bear in Bordeaux
31. Vonnegut's Kilgore
32. ___ Matisse
33. ___ Park, Colorado
35. Lose fur
37. Get by reasoning
40. Wield
41. Singer McEntire
46. Consecutive
48. California live oak
51. Gird one's ___
52. Carrier
53. Punch
54. Informed
55. Identify
56. Seattle ___, Triple Crown winner
58. Caspian Sea feeder
59. 100 centavos
60. First nudist colony
63. Speechless

❖ **Solution on page 276**

Fruit Stand   *Alan Olschwang*

ACROSS

1. Lea lows
5. Bees ready for business?
11. Unit of electric current, shortly
14. Summit
15. Outcast
16. Shad delicacy
17. Type of clam
19. Wine cask
20. Transition
21. Sicilian volcano
22. Coop denizen
23. Open porch
26. Aleutian island
28. Shallow water predators
33. What this answer is
37. Flight school culmination
38. George who was Mary
39. Tommy of the Miracle Mets
40. Praise
42. Hardy cabbage
43. Uncle of fable
45. Brooding place
46. Sort of shot
47. Atlanta thoroughfare
50. Harvest
51. Marginal consciousness
55. Bobby of the NHL
57. Aria singer
60. Adjusts the FM
62. Island garland
63. It's used by a manicurist
66. Singer Geddy ___
67. More than a little damp
68. Carry the burden
69. Foot the column
70. Answers impudently
71. Kind of job

DOWN

1. Brits' raincoats
2. Earthy iron ore
3. The end
4. Truth follower?
5. Mole
6. Existed
7. Funnyman Johnson
8. Gasser
9. Unexpected sources of pleasure
10. Put away a sword
11. ___ legend
12. Pout
13. Actor Sean ___
18. Sort of estate
24. Escritoire
25. Bank deposit
27. Confesses
29. More senior
30. Riatas
31. Tropical nut tree
32. Pas
33. Time ___
34. Curved molding
35. Tied another knot
36. Low card
41. Proofreader's save
44. Trails
48. Rose family shrub
49. Expressions of disapproval
52. Emulates a Tiger
53. Burger fixin'
54. Right-hand page
55. Stew pot
56. Buy by Benny
58. Chocolate containers
59. Picnic problem
61. Distort
64. Turn right
65. Bitter vetch

❖ **Solution on page 276**

Ya Gotta Have It *Merle Baker*

ACROSS

1. Choose from this
5. Smell perceptions
10. DeMille specialty
14. Inferior
15. Rolling Stones bassist
16. Intangible quality
17. Longs for
20. Letter opener
21. Room in a house
22. Fed. loan agency
23. Please
29. ___ Stadium in Queens
30. Bibliography abbr.
31. King's Peak range
32. Comedian Margaret
33. Amer. mil. branch
34. Chum
35. Be consumed by jealousy
41. Literary monogram
42. ___ listening
43. USN address letters
44. Make knotted
47. Fly ball paths
48. From a distance
49. Adore
52. Mythical monster
53. Train unit
54. USN VIP
55. Disappoints
62. ___ *Misbehavin'*
63. Put up with
64. Greensboro's st.
65. Beach landers
66. Diminish
67. Hebrides isle

DOWN

1. AWOL chasers
2. Help wanted abbr.
3. Mediocre
4. Bearlike
5. Possess
6. Turn red?
7. Mantra syllables
8. Ardently enthusiastic
9. Villain's expression
10. Corn unit
11. Teases
12. Isaac Asimov classic
13. Northern neighbor
18. Extraction raw material
19. Insurance company employee
23. Freshwater fish
24. Safety standard org.
25. Ms. enclosures
26. Is in full swing
27. Some artists
28. Superficial luster
33. Clear
34. Out of style
36. Tyrant
37. Per unit
38. Betting venue
39. ___ the crack of dawn
40. Corrida combatant
44. Worldwide
45. Action star Chuck ___
46. Climb
47. It needs oxygen
48. Eve and Elizabeth
50. Like the early Dylan
51. German exclamation
56. Stick alternatives: Abbr.
57. Young parasite
58. E-mail ending
59. Cal. heading
60. Alpha or beta follower
61. Three, in Turin

❖ **Solution on page 276**

113

Inferiority Complex
Alan Olschwang

❖ Solution on page 276

ACROSS

1. Tease
5. Collector?
10. Heal
14. Director Gance
15. Gem
16. Two-toned treat
17. Mrs. Charles
18. Used article
20. Witnessed
21. Beer alternative
22. Bowling alley button
23. New Zealand's symbol
25. Pistol parts
27. Noncoms
31. Merged
32. Satan's realm
33. He wore gray
36. Expresses annoyance
37. Cunning
38. Acerbic
39. Highway curve
40. Ante follower
42. Parody
44. Warning from above
46. Mezzo-soprano Mentzer
49. Dark red
50. Socrates' star pupil
51. Helper for start-ups: Abbr.
52. Iranian currency unit
56. Like a failing business
59. Noriega feature
60. Wading bird
61. Great brilliance
62. Obtains
63. Low card
64. Free throws
65. Polishes the prose

DOWN

1. Lays off
2. Double reed
3. Inconsequential
4. Cloaks
5. Indicated irritation
6. Type of type
7. Johnnycake
8. Conclude
9. Sleep movement
10. Kind of art
11. Irregularly notched
12. Staircase support
13. No-nos
19. Swashbuckler Flynn
24. Beginning of some land?
25. Queue of quail?
26. Muhammad ___
27. Pear-shaped instrument
28. Burden
29. Funnymen
30. Greet in Galena
33. Irritate
34. Continental currency
35. See 21A
37. Rice wine
38. Passenger ship section
40. One who gives
41. A long, long time
42. Symington and Chase
43. Easiness initials
44. Johnny come ___
45. Positive
46. Sudden burst of energy
47. Relating to an arm bone
48. ___ Hawkins Day
51. WWII battle site
53. Chilled the chardonnay
54. Renegade
55. ___ we forget
57. Director Craven
58. Alas in Aachen

Suitability   Alan Olschwang

ACROSS

1. Masquerades
5. Singer Irene
9. Call
14. Marsh bird
15. Olfactory offense
16. Paddled
17. Prep
19. École's attendee
20. Biblical lion
21. Agile
22. Enlarge, in a way
23. Aquatic mammal
25. Much of the world
27. Causing pleasure
32. Holding instrument
35. Occur, briefly
36. Old French coin
37. Quarters
38. Bull's order
39. Irritates
41. Cal. abbr.
42. Leg
43. Most rational
44. Some rattlers
48. Chills and fever
49. Apt to snap
53. Eddy
56. Goddess of discord
57. Like sushi is served
58. Vietnamese city
59. A good place for socializing
61. A John
62. Sort of chest
63. Forest denizen
64. Forward
65. Pismires
66. Behaves humanly

DOWN

1. Indian state
2. Coconut oil source
3. Work out
4. Downcast
5. Leguminous plants
6. She reveres
7. Actor Calhoun
8. Place of refuge
9. Occurring before the conflict
10. System of treatment
11. Used plastic
12. Campbell of *Scream*
13. Utopia
18. Organic compounds
24. Attention getter
25. Get into the music
26. Literary initials
28. A digit
29. Coast sight
30. Some votes
31. Blowhard?
32. Goad
33. Places
34. Just a little bit
38. Commanded
39. Dissolute
40. Org.
42. Wildebeest
43. They write
45. Strand
46. Gawping
47. Precipitous
50. Closer to the target
51. Light show source
52. Still picture subjects
53. Where Mookie Wilson played
54. Runner's nemesis
55. Division word
56. North Carolina college
59. All the tea in China
60. Pindar work

❖ **Solution on page 276**

Seeing the Signs   Alan Olschwang

ACROSS

1. Affecting things past
6. Sedan sickness
9. Lava for a time
14. The heavens
15. Once he was Clay
16. UFO pilot
17. Keeper
19. Great brilliance
20. See 61A
21. Window topper
23. Vegas quote
24. Returned part of the payment
26. Away from the prow
28. A way the USA expanded
34. Philosopher Jean-Paul
37. Matadors' stimulation
38. More N than E
39. Silt deposit
40. Pub potion
41. Wink of an eye
43. Actress Claire
44. New Rochelle college
46. Gat
47. Gum doctor
50. *Wheel of Fortune* purchase
51. Most Bohemian
55. Springs of California
58. Chip dip
61. Atop
62. Baked brick
64. Military bigwig
66. Designer Beaton
67. Marie Saint
68. Chill
69. Rap
70. Start of a mark?
71. Toast toppers

DOWN

1. Happen anew
2. Storehouse
3. Pulsate
4. Performs again
5. Food morsel
6. Manage
7. Sir Guinness
8. Former Italian bread
9. Actress Whitman
10. *Little Men* author
11. Cover with gold
12. Honeyed spirits
13. Some are queens
18. Fred's first dance partner
22. Emulate a couch potato
25. Sort of bar
27. What 29D was, for a time
29. First name in pitching
30. Seine sight
31. The J in J.Lo
32. Nursery rhyme opener
33. Poetic contraction
34. Stumble
35. Reputable
36. Back of the line
40. A year in Acapulco
42. Sane
45. Keats works
46. King of Tyre
48. ___ pentameter
49. Sea between Australia and New Zealand
52. Invest
53. She takes shorthand
54. Legal wrongs
55. Prepare for the voyage
56. Middle Eastern gulf
57. Start of a motive
59. Scored an immediate point in tennis
60. Davis of golf
63. Member of a fraternal order
65. Pother

❖ **Solution on page 277**

Spinoff   *Merle Baker*

ACROSS

1. Elroy's dog
6. Nursery purchase
10. *The Untouchables* extra
14. Day with a sitcom
15. Operatic slave girl
16. Icy coating
17. From *All in the Family*
18. From 17A
20. Tore
21. Cable channel
22. Poughkeepsie college
23. Former *West Wing* actor
25. Part of HSN
26. From *The Andy Griffith Show*
31. In pieces
32. Granola bit
33. O'Brian role
36. ___ *Casey*
37. Columbo and others
41. Ghost's cry
42. K-6
44. "___ Blue?"
45. Heavenly hunter
47. From *M*A*S*H*
51. Degrees for attys.
52. Start of a counting-out phrase
53. Edith, to Archie
56. Women's ___
57. Golf hazard
61. From *Dynasty*
63. From *The Mary Tyler Moore Show*
64. Farm sound
65. TV part
66. Fitness centers
67. Subterfuge
68. Crystal gazer
69. "Don't ___!"

DOWN

1. *JAG* bigwigs
2. Katherine Helmond series
3. Like *Cops* episodes
4. Frank Gorshin role
5. Sugary suffix
6. Lacey's partner
7. Knee-slapper
8. Swearing-in phrase
9. Disparage
10. Ancient Athenian galley
11. Kathy Kinney role
12. Ed of *Daniel Boone*
13. Kristy McNichol show *Empty* ___
19. Highland hats
21. Local political div.
24. Scraps
25. *In the ___ of the Night*
26. The sweathogs' Kotter
27. German auto
28. French Impressionist
29. *Taxi* character
30. *The Love Boat* accommodation
34. ___ *222*
35. Fishing spot
38. Auto safety feature
39. Caesar and Nero: Abbr.
40. In a bit
43. Series with music by Henry Mancini
46. Some are jazzy
48. To boot
49. Hunt costar
50. Role for Buddy
53. Quiz show ___ *the Music*
54. TV doctor
55. Wine: Prefix
56. Waggoner of *The Carol Burnett Show*
58. *Third ___ from the Sun*
59. Arkin on *Northern Exposure*
60. Matador maneuver
62. Lovable aunt
63. Scandinavian rug

❖ **Solution on page 277**

All the World's a Stage   *Merle Baker*

ACROSS

1. Trump ex
6. Reed instrument
10. Pokes
14. Stinking
15. Pell-___
16. Part of QED
17. Irish dramatist (1880–1964)
19. Author Seton
20. Dog's treat, perhaps
21. Thai dough
22. Prom attendee
24. Wife of Zeus
25. Greek port
26. Nearest the horizon
29. Actor Delon
30. To ___ (everyone)
31. Henry V victory site
35. Short lead-in
37. Payment or profit start
38. Boring implement
39. The body politic
41. Nastase of tennis
42. Asian peninsula
43. Like much information
45. Italian theologian
48. *Rhoda* actor David
49. Stews with 52D
50. Wash. neighbor
51. Male cat
54. Fireplace shelves
55. Russian dramatist
    (1868–1936)
58. Billion follower
59. Secondhand
60. Construction pieces
61. Ollie's pal
62. Impudent response
63. Pester like a pup

DOWN

1. Should that be true
2. Go a different way
3. Rat attachment?
4. French diarist
5. Sun-dried bricks
6. Nebraska native
7. Brightest companion
8. ___ Miss
9. Blissful
10. French dramatist
    (1910–1987)
11. Golfer with an army
12. "Blue ___" (Roy Orbison
    song)
13. Vega and Polaris
18. Push or go follower
23. *All My Children* character
24. Norwegian dramatist
    (1828–1906)
25. "The elder" or "the
    younger"
26. Of the flock
27. Directional prefix
28. Unit of power
29. Greek square of old
31. Bancroft and Boleyn
32. Tropical fruit
33. Check
34. Ebony, e.g.
36. Prefix for sphere
40. British physiologist Darwin
43. Utah city
44. Noodle
45. Turkish leaders
46. Tossed ring
47. Shadow
48. Street layouts
50. Clumsy, stupid fellows
51. It might be baited
52. See 49A
53. Popular computer game
56. Gentle-lamb connection
57. Sash

❖ **Solution on page 277**

Weather or Not   *Alan Olschwang*

ACROSS

1. Mall event
5. Lava underground
10. Bugle melody
14. Fabricator
15. Waited for the green
16. Stew pot
17. Paquin of *The Piano*
18. Ontario city
20. Slinger's material?
21. There's some in Love's bag
22. Boors
23. More rational
26. Trouble
28. Lea low
29. It may be around a prison
33. Rings
34. Esters of an acid derived from milk
38. High peaks
39. Florence's love
41. Table seasoning
42. Fleeter of foot
44. Feminist Abzug
45. It goes from Texas to Iowa
48. Simian
51. Vietnamese holiday
52. Dustin Hoffman role
53. Santa Maria companion
55. Quite a bit
57. Reel companion
60. Ships at sea should avoid it
62. Finish the front lawn
63. Continental currency
64. Carl of the NFL
65. Seed
66. Comprehends
67. Couples
68. Two-tone treat

DOWN

1. Grand follower?
2. Hokkaido native
3. Sort of gardener
4. Important time
5. Cold-weather protector
6. Cling
7. Make 6D
8. Department store section
9. Foot the column
10. Corrida victim
11. Pictures' place
12. Socrates' prize pupil
13. Authority
19. Vote in
24. Ready
25. 2, 4, 6, and 8
27. On a single occasion
29. They're busy in Apr.
30. Shrill sound
31. Plants of a region
32. Atelier items
35. Formidable task
36. Nice lady
37. Judge's order
39. Yorkshire river
40. Concerning telepathic powers
43. Relating to a woman's marriage dowry
44. Clean up
46. Buzzed
47. Westerns
48. Church parts
49. Ire
50. Harden
54. New Mexico tourist spot
56. 1964 Oscar winner Kedrova
58. Fairy tale villain
59. Sample of a sort
61. Was at the forefront
62. Id companion

❖ **Solution on page 277**

119

Composers   *Michael Wiesenberg*

ACROSS

1. Miss
5. Accident memento
9. Old AMC
14. Heinz Holliger's instrument
15. Conduct
16. Run off
17. *Compositions* composer
20. *77 Sunset Strip* actor Byrnes
21. Where to find an iris
22. Guesses
23. Advanced in years
24. Lone fish?
25. Come down a cliff quickly
28. Wine that goes with raw fish
29. It approached $10 trillion in the U.S. in 2003
32. Indian, say
33. Starbuck's order
34. Seed cover
35. He collaborated with Romani on many operas
38. Brink
39. They row
40. *A Doll's House* playwright
41. ___ Plaines
42. Wear out
43. Frost lines
44. 1981 movie that won the Best Director Oscar
45. Rational
46. Lorraine's neighbor
49. Where to find red tags
50. Music of the '50s
53. *Fantasia on Greensleeves* composer
56. Snooty water
57. Cotton unit
58. CEOs, usually
59. Dustin in *Midnight Cowboy*
60. Dermatologist's concern
61. Confined

DOWN

1. Misplace
2. Sleeping
3. Automobile company that filed for bankruptcy in 1937
4. Frat party order
5. Turn in a chair
6. Crusader's adjective
7. Taj Mahal site
8. Automobile company named for its founder's initials
9. *Us* rival
10. 1966 hit song for Dionne Warwick
11. Invent
12. Dagger
13. Races
18. Home of University of Oregon
19. Part played by 20A
23. Swiftly
24. 900s or 9000s, e.g.
25. Went wild over
26. It's directed at the audience
27. Exhibits signs of not using a high enough octane gasoline
28. Singer of "Que Sera, Sera"
29. Something for the mill
30. San Francisco player, for short
31. Author of *Historia naturalis*
33. Russian rulers
34. *Who's Afraid of Virginia Woolf?* playwright
36. "Don't ask me"
37. Maker of O-gauge trains
42. Modern electronic music genre
43. Bed
44. Sitar compositions
45. Goes to sea
46. State
47. Kilauea output
48. Exec
49. Influence
50. Film pig
51. Muscat home
52. "Hey, you!"
54. *Las Vegas* home
55. Brat

❖ **Solution on page 277**

Composer Poser *Roy Leban*

ACROSS

1. Starbucks order
6. Lighter alternative
11. Some are classified
14. *Gil Blas* novelist Lesage
15. Accustom
16. Young'un
17. Rap is full of it
18. More irate
19. *Double Fantasy* vocalist
20. Part of a concerto?
22. Tight
23. Peter Fonda title role
24. Art appreciator
26. "Communism" has three
29. Anxiety
31. Brazen one
32. Gravy holder
34. ___ T
35. A billion years
36. Forward-looking invention?
42. "For sure!"
43. Jim Phelps's org.
44. Bed board
45. Broadway offering, perhaps
48. Big brother?
50. American purchase
51. Indy entry
53. Pennsylvania town near a lake
55. Baseball's Mel and Ed
56. Cost of a piano composition?
61. Louvre pyramid architect
62. Faint from excitement
63. Word heard in court
64. Dictator Amin
65. Art supporter?
66. Creates origami
67. Cycle starter
68. Small fellow of fiction
69. Armada

DOWN

1. Event for Bobby "Boris" Pickett
2. Earthenware pot
3. *The Godfather* actor James ___
4. Like Gandhi
5. Davis or Lansbury
6. Improperly acquired, slangily
7. Celebes ox
8. Tank feature
9. Green garnish
10. That girl
11. Does penance
12. Stereotypical meal for cops
13. Cheap cigar
21. Slow compositions
22. Railroad sidetracks
25. "You," biblically
26. Tide type
27. Kiwi's extinct relative
28. Cul-de-___
30. Sir, in India
33. Some spices
35. Elbow grease
37. AIWA rival
38. Steal, perhaps
39. Final: Abbr.
40. Type of deal
41. 12:00 at LAX, e.g.
45. "Spot" order
46. Like many movies
47. Shakespearean climax
48. Melodic composition
49. How to start a basketball game
52. Poe's middle name
54. Flamboyant Flynn of film
57. Part of a flower
58. Monty Python star
59. Relinquish
60. Formerly, formerly
62. Bundy matriarch

❖ **Solution on page 277**

At the Finish   Alan Olschwang

ACROSS

1. Fable
5. Steel mills' by-products
10. Judge's cover
14. Diva's solo
15. Mother-of-pearl
16. Engineer von Skoda
17. Discounter's promise, simply stated
18. Open courtyards
19. Window part
20. WIN
23. Act as the bank
24. Pindar work
25. Throws out with vehemence
29. Polo and his ilk
33. One system
34. Above
36. Actress Sara
37. PLACE
41. East of Berlin
42. Tatters
43. Basketball game
44. Wide-brimmed hat
47. More edgy
48. Fell
49. Without ice
51. SHOW
59. Cleveland's lake
60. Ballet dancer's practice aid
61. ___ Domini
62. Idi of Uganda
63. Mail
64. Article
65. Foray
66. Aims
67. Misplace

DOWN

1. It's good for chafing
2. Vicinity
3. Speech impediment
4. Bridge position
5. Trapper's instruments
6. Make tardy
7. Caustic
8. Beam
9. On the briny
10. Took ten
11. Neglect
12. Account
13. Nice lady
21. Extremist
22. Ms. Rehan
25. Highway curves
26. Tilt
27. Upper crust
28. Tom
29. Lob
30. Middle East bigwigs
31. Washing machine cycle
32. More enlightened
34. ___ Bator
35. Cribbage need
38. Lunch holder
39. Letter from Patrai
40. Heavyweight
45. Story conclusion
46. Uno, due, e tre
47. Circus workers
49. Fictional Rae
50. First name in swashbucklers
51. Equipment
52. La Douce
53. XII less IV
54. Card game
55. Type of pipe
56. Division word
57. Entities
58. Gold Rush city

❖ **Solution on page 277**

Cash in   *Norm Guggenbiller*

ACROSS

1. Scurry about
5. Russian summer house
10. Compact___
14. Gofer
15. Company in a 2002 scandal
16. Safety watchdog: Abbr.
17. Tabletop edge treatment
19. ___ Bator
20. Maidens
21. Up for grabs
23. Perfume compound
24. " ___ alive!"
25. *Arabian Nights* prince
26. Church section
28. Army div.
29. Popular putter
33. Embarrassed
34. Fall guy
38. Gala events
40. Brought up the rear
41. Lip curls
42. Hopkins Intl. luggage tag
43. Thomas Hardy title character
44. Take in
45. Picks
47. Henchmen
50. Racer Fabi
51. Worry
56. Studio sign
58. Theatrical company
59. Bandleader Puente
60. Concrete tool
62. ___ saccharum (sugar maple)
63. " ___ there yet?"
64. Basics
65. Coastal flyer
66. Fancy pool manuever
67. Twice daily, e.g.

DOWN

1. Moralistic tale
2. Turkish coins
3. That is, in Latin
4. Needle
5. Ball girls
6. Year, in Madrid
7. Fashioned
8. Israeli dances
9. "Me, myself, ___ "
10. Infantryman
11. Eastern religion
12. Guilt
13. Casual furniture, often
18. Bruce or Laura of film
22. Carries on
24. Composer Charles
27. "Give it ___ "
28. Key
29. Letter add-ons: Abbr.
30. Certain subatomic particle
31. Never, in Bonn
32. Newcomer
35. Iron starter
36. Mask or cap
37. USNA grad.
39. Computer command
40. Pedigree rival
42. Strong-arms
46. Poet Teasdale
47. Reached
48. Chilling
49. Playful swimmer
50. Fancy topper
52. Mobile home dweller?
53. Soup made with okra
54. Detailed instructions, briefly
55. Concise
57. In ___ (pressed)
58. Quaker pronoun
61. Current units: Abbr.

❖ **Solution on page 277**

Simon Says   *Dave Fisher*

ACROSS

1. Certain girders
6. Makes "it"
10. "7 O'Clock ___"
14. Souvenir
15. Winter bird feed, maybe
16. List ender
17. Supreme Being
18. Domain
19. Prego competitor
20. "___ all these years"
23. Dead, e.g.
24. Parapsychology subj.
25. Residue
28. Earlier
31. Fruit related to custard apples
36. Drive off
38. Brownie
39. Like a slob
40. "And whispered in the ___"
43. Says yes
44. Big ISP
45. First left-handed Masters winner
46. The Divine ___
47. Gillette brand
49. Croak
50. Rent to ___
52. Global standards grp.
54. "Are you going to ___"
63. Decorative work
64. Eye part
65. Last movement of a sonata
66. ___ of Man
67. Bait fish
68. Pays for a hand
69. First name for this puzzle
70. Winter transport
71. They have flat tops

DOWN

1. Gershwin and Levin
2. Wallop
3. "___ Need" (Temptations hit)
4. Tehran bills
5. Lug
6. Last one was shot in 1918
7. Halo, e.g.
8. Eccentric old man
9. Remains
10. Spongy toy
11. State in France
12. Salary
13. Aspersion
21. Stroke
22. Outrage
25. Famous Indian tea state
26. Japanese chess
27. Entry sign info, probably
29. Worldwide workers' grp.
30. Meat for pet food, say
32. ___ Good Men
33. Longed for
34. Common text code
35. Seeker's word
37. Snake eyes
39. Roughneck's locale
41. Discharge militarily: Abbr.
42. Tippler
47. Imaginary
48. Guru's community
51. Open country
53. *The Power ___* (Bryce Courtenay novel)
54. Berth
55. Maison in Mexico
56. Rights protection org.
57. Rod's partner
58. Storyteller's first word, often
59. Not new
60. Colony critters
61. Light bulb, figuratively
62. Phillie's famous Betsy

❖ **Solution on page 277**

E

Chapter 8

Closer Than It Themes

Stringing Up Lights   *Merle Baker*

ACROSS

1. Electricity pioneer
6. Like the English Channel, rarely
10. Muslim's journey
14. Quetzalcoatl worshiper
15. Carry on
16. Melville tale
17. Three lights
20. For example
21. Don't share
22. Takes on
23. Sundial figure
24. Big brass
27. Four more lights
34. Reluctant
35. Can't do without
36. Daisy ___
37. Lowdown
38. Toboggans
39. Greek cheese
40. Coll. hoops competition
41. "Something to Talk About" singer
42. *Dinner at ___*
43. Another four lights
46. Modern surgical tool
47. 42D has two
48. 100-eyed giant of myth
51. "Gotcha!"
52. Part of CBS
55. Yet another three lights
60. Uniform
61. Banjoist Scruggs
62. Plaintive piece
63. Delighted
64. Wharf
65. Mathematical base

DOWN

1. Keep ___ on (watch)
2. Old Testament book
3. Court order
4. Albanian coin
5. Winning straight
6. Big gulp
7. Jokester
8. "Yuck!"
9. NYC opera venue
10. Healing approach
11. Natl. counterpart
12. ___ de vivre
13. Exercises, in a way
18. Film genre
19. Tatar leaders
23. Nix
24. Hi-fi part
25. Did
26. Chums
27. Lark
28. Ancient Aegean area
29. A whole bunch
30. Connected, in a way
31. Last of a series
32. They're taken in court
33. Not o'er
38. Wanes in vigor
39. Père's junior
41. Humorous tribute
42. One who wipes out
44. Articulate
45. Classic soda pop
48. Draft selections
49. Split
50. FBI agents
51. ___ in the ointment
52. Went over the limit
53. Jellystone Park resident
54. River in which Achilles was dipped
56. Essential: Abbr.
57. Jr. Olympic Games sponsor
58. Monk's title
59. Kidnappers in 1974 news: Abbr.

❖ **Solution on page 278**

Male Call — Alan Olschwang

ACROSS

1. Powell or Wilson
6. Former Iranian ruler
10. Pond cover
14. Soft palate part
15. Sugar source
16. ___ la Douce
17. Open carriages
19. Scientists' milieus
20. Mode starter
21. It could lead to buyer's remorse
22. Merlot and meritage
23. Capone's nemesis
25. Dilapidated
27. Pequod's captain
29. Jots
30. North African palace
33. Proofreader's save
34. Lubricate
37. Chilled soup
38. Speller's contest
39. Escape capture
41. Type of tuna
42. Xenophanes' birthplace
44. Ohio city
45. Finish a room
47. Answer alternative
48. High jinks
51. Back talk
55. Turn away
56. Inflate
58. Agcy. once headed by a Bush
59. Fork part
60. Intimidating
62. Some are soldiers
63. Irritate
64. See 39A
65. Hebrew letter
66. Some votes
67. Apothecary measures

DOWN

1. From Havana
2. Minute plant structure
3. Director George ___
4. Kind
5. Captures
6. Type of beetle
7. Oda holder
8. Fine-grained volcanic rock
9. Subjects of this puzzle
10. Glassmaker's material
11. Mass-produces
12. Onion part
13. Billiards shot
18. First name in television
22. French painter Jean-Antoine
24. West Indies island
26. Work the land
28. He's from the wrong side of the tracks
30. Jefferson Davis's domain: Abbr.
31. Aachen expression
32. Deliveries to be
33. Start for a scape?
35. Words of commitment
36. Dykstra of baseball
38. Nautical warning device
40. Caustic substances
43. Fifth zodiac sign
44. Wood nymph
46. All over again
47. Goes fishing, in a way
48. Strait of the Far East
49. Sheeplike
50. *Dallas* matriarch
52. They turn litmus red
53. Scorch
54. Wise men
57. Michael or Richard
60. Supportive one
61. Menagerie

❖ **Solution on page 278**

On Your Feet! *Mark Milhet*

ACROSS

1. Risked a ticket
5. Short gig
10. Court foe of Andre
14. "Houston, ___ got a problem!"
15. Vietnamese capital
16. October birthstone
17. What the fat lady sings?
18. Madder than mad
19. Hypertext
20. Improve
23. Take a crack at
24. Past follower
25. Cumberland, for one
28. DEA agent
31. Small stone
36. Beginning at
38. Kasparov's corner man
40. "Andrea ___," subject of *The Perfect Storm*
41. Proved to be a suitable substitute
44. Hindu ascetic
45. Waiter's handout?
46. Hot fashion
47. Be short with
49. Offspring
51. Costa ___ Sol
52. Common title starter
54. *Norma* ___
56. Fetch fodder for Fido
65. Land measure
66. Amp feeders
67. Toast topper
68. Eschew
69. Still in the game
70. Chowder morsel
71. Diamond head?
72. Big rigs
73. Fabled also-ran

DOWN

1. Trade
2. Where the Amazon starts
3. Sinister
4. Gave a hand
5. Tanker's origins
6. Poi source
7. Words before instant or uproar
8. Observed
9. Occupies
10. The rest of Marco
11. *War and Peace*, e.g.
12. Combat vehicle
13. Fraternal fellows
21. Java holder
22. Top Wimbledon draws
25. Spears
26. Afghan or Thai
27. Piece for squeezeboxes
29. Part of a Clue board
30. Road markers
32. Physicist Niels ___
33. Like some shoulders
34. Feudal lord
35. Supporter of the arts?
37. Somersault
39. Game like bingo
42. Poetry Muse
43. Morning starters
48. Doubting one
50. Dispirit
53. Zola or Griffith
55. Miocene or Eocene
56. Blowout
57. Off-the-wall answer?
58. Snare, perhaps
59. Russo of *Big Trouble*
60. Milk choice
61. Jacob's third son
62. 1940s actress Raines
63. Bring up
64. To a degree

❖ **Solution on page 278**

Follow the Money   *Merle Baker*

ACROSS

1. Mishap
5. Enchilada flavoring
10. Farm newborn
14. Prefix with graph
15. Enticed
16. Affected, in a way
17. Desirable assignment
18. Clothing fiber
19. Purim's month
20. Dump in the army
23. Poetic preposition
24. Spud buds
25. Some pants
27. Release
30. Egyptian talisman
32. Act the usher
33. Like Paul's mission
36. GI's classification
37. Strike out
38. *Wheel of Fortune* buy
39. Smoking vis-à-vis health
42. Toot
44. Brazilian dance tunes
45. Hit the hay
46. Actor Steven ___
48. Trunk cover
49. Astaire film *Holiday* ___
50. World of commerce
56. Bunny hunter
58. Where you live is likely this
59. Piece of the Bahamas
60. Low card
61. Gluck work
62. *Hud* Oscar winner
63. Wizened
64. Informative
65. Like venison

DOWN

1. Drains
2. Humdinger
3. Ham ___ (overact)
4. City destroyed in A.D. 79
5. Became wearisome through excess
6. Range rovers
7. Doing nothing
8. Curve around
9. Never
10. Air safety agcy.
11. Catalog feature
12. Playstation forerunner
13. Ancient poetic accompaniment
21. Country singer Loretta
22. Acerb
26. ___ de Açúcar (Sugarloaf Mountain)
27. Ran through
28. Aloha State bird
29. Carpenter's tool
30. Bridges
31. Go for
33. Stretch
34. 1953 Pulitzer Prize winner for drama
35. Dorm denizen
37. Decorate brilliantly
40. Kind of doll
41. Muslim prayer leader
42. It's not welcome at the table
43. Hint
45. Ballpark promotion
46. Examines closely
47. Toughen
48. Bar servings
51. Hitchcock film
52. Had no doubt
53. Between continents
54. Exemplar of happiness
55. Hard to hold
57. Salon stuff

❖ **Solution on page 278**

Three in a Series   Michael Wiesenberg

ACROSS

1. Space
5. Tibetan monk
9. U.S., to Iran, once
14. ___ Spumante
15. Miners' goals
16. Sib's daughter
17. 6
20. Kosygin of the USSR
21. Do the hot tub thing
22. Shea player
23. Pier pronoun
24. Belief
26. *Star* ___
28. Agreed, with "with"
30. Bruited
34. Where to find System 7
37. Designer Cassini
39. Lamppost leaner
40. 13
43. Snoops
44. Red but not dead
45. Amazed
46. Persian ruler
48. Like Santa's helpers
50. Chills
52. "The racer's edge"
53. EMT skill
56. Selectric maker
59. Certain addresses
61. Fish hawk
63. 22 and 24
66. Taunts
67. Actress Skye
68. In the past
69. Agreements
70. Roe, for one
71. Equal

DOWN

1. Indian ruler
2. The start of Enrico Caruso's greatest hit
3. Else
4. Old Hillman model
5. French 20-franc gold piece issued after the Revolution
6. Jackie's second
7. ___ room
8. It's a tie
9. Bunkum
10. Assist
11. Two oxen
12. Maker of Wile E. Coyote's paraphernalia
13. Fit snugly
18. Ocean liner, briefly
19. Tale
25. Puts down cards, in rummy
27. Cruise's ex
28. White of the eye
29. Crusoe creator
31. Wade through, as mud
32. Architect Saarinen
33. Leaving
34. Brats
35. Her dad (Paul) cried when she got an Oscar
36. Debarked
38. A third of an Elvis tune
41. "If I could hazard an opinion"
42. Meat loaf, later
47. Run smoothly
49. ___ dixit
51. 1961 Heston role
53. Stretch
54. Parts of pounds
55. U-Haul rival
56. Pop of pop
57. Cheese served with wine
58. Crowds around
60. Gin fruit
62. Plash
64. "Take Good Care of My Baby" singer
65. Map analog of 2

❖ Solution on page 278

Seasick   *Dave Fisher*

ACROSS

1. Fundamental values
6. New Zealander
10. Apportion
14. Brit. general who captured Detroit (War of 1812)
15. Modern Persia
16. Current
17. Maritime migraine?
19. Wanton
20. Nothing to write home about
21. Part of A.D.
22. Valleys
23. Paternity determiner
24. Had arugula
25. Papier ___
29. Grand arranger gets canned?
35. His ___ (style choice)
37. Woman of order
38. Girasol
39. Waterfront feature
40. *Amerika* author
42. Green in Grenoble
43. Inst. where Clinton taught law
44. Sin
45. Bruce ___; Gyro Captain in *Mad Max 2*
47. Part of Poseidon's table setting?
50. A dervish has it
51. What___ (doodad)
52. Farm resident perhaps
54. Folksinger Billy
57. Christiana today
59. Odyssey
63. Turner who married seven times
64. Deliberately urge a dolphin?
66. Play opener
67. Image on a computer desktop
68. Wide open
69. Mind
70. Permits
71. Coral, e.g.

DOWN

1. Falls back
2. Cream or the Pointer Sisters, for example
3. Takes most
4. Quatro y quatro
5. Eclectic Jamaican music
6. Hold for gold?
7. You can chip with it
8. Baylor University locale
9. Red means losses
10. Ponder Pisces?
11. Pointless weapon
12. It can be up and down
13. Closes
18. Level for a martial artist
22. Pontiac's "Car of the Year" in 1965
23. ___ *Spiegel* (German daily)
24. Kournikova and Karenina
25. Do a closing-time chore
26. Popular Web font
27. Lobster claw
28. It helps deaf fishermen?
30. Supra's opposite
31. Pelagic diving bird
32. Overturn
33. Stupor, numbness: Prefix
34. Rearrange
36. Type of shoot
41. Pit opener
46. Butter ration
48. Metal tooth
49. They clutch arrows on a dollar
53. Negative conjunction
54. Dull
55. Dart
56. Entry fee
57. Not many times
58. Catch sight of
59. Some restaurant orders
60. Arabian note
61. WWW 007?
62. ___ up (maintain)
64. Roughneck's quest
65. Baby food

❖ **Solution on page 278**

Fowl Play   *Alan Olschwang*

❖ Solution on page 278

ACROSS

1. Rara ___
5. Catch sight of
9. Virus that infects bacteria
14. "___ Misbehavin'"
15. Beat it!
16. Wishes for
17. Expression of mock laughter
18. Preparation for a Thanksgiving meal?
20. List of candidates
22. Requisites
23. Keats work
24. Tab
26. Disney exec
28. Wedding party diversion
33. Gnaw
34. Unemotional
35. Religious denominations
39. Holiday forerunners
41. Symbol of slowness
43. Grimace
44. Family car
46. Bestow
48. Advanced deg.
49. Parader, perhaps
52. Stones' measure
55. Actress Ward
56. Before, once
57. A 16A for the accused
61. Ms. Shore
64. They're laid on muddy ground
67. Hibernia
68. Like the raging surf
69. Hart or stag
70. Vex
71. Dennis's brother
72. Sugar source
73. Pans' reversal?

DOWN

1. Exclamations of satisfaction
2. Lab container
3. Full of folks
4. Kind of electricity
5. East of Emden
6. Ostracize
7. Stoma
8. Oxen's burden
9. Course of study
10. Weather word
11. Chef's cover
12. Showy rock
13. Organic compound
19. Prairie near Minneapolis
21. Members of a fraternal order
25. Gives the green light
27. Appear
28. Average grades
29. He's from the right side of the tracks
30. A canonical hour
31. De Poitiers of France
32. They turn litmus red
36. Fellow traveler
37. Couch potato's diversion
38. Barbecue
40. Historical novel
42. Builder's buys
45. Remarkably
47. Lawn pest
50. Christiania today
51. Pair for the electrician
52. Closet liner
53. Caribbean attraction
54. Scout
58. Foot of a sort
59. Highlands hillside
60. Type of time
62. Diva's offering
63. Beatles hit
65. Glove material
66. Match part

Get a Move On   *Merle Baker*

ACROSS

1. Baker, at times
5. State of mind
9. Part of Fred's yell
14. Skirt type
15. Building piece
16. Mythological hunter
17. MOVE
20. Be at
21. Adobe dwelling
22. Island souvenir
23. Vietnam gulf
26. Joel's "___ to Extremes"
28. Pop-up paths
30. Singer Janis ___
31. Confer
33. "Stardust" composer Carmichael
36. French pointillist
37. MOVE
39. Despicable person
41. San Francisco Zoo attraction
42. Ma's instrument
43. Slippery critter
44. Damsel
48. *2001* villain
49. Like llamas
52. Hawkeye's rank: Abbr.
53. Tampa neighbor, briefly
56. Lineup
58. MOVE
61. Prefix meaning "sun"
62. Mirth
63. French kings
64. Delightful places
65. Cry of distress
66. Some bleaters

DOWN

1. African leaper
2. 2002 Peace Prize recipient
3. Kind of dancer
4. Ready to be eaten
5. Botch
6. UK award
7. Klutz
8. Casual visitor
9. Capitol feature
10. Saudi, for one
11. Kind of table
12. Lunchmeat
13. One or more
18. Canadian prov.
19. Operate
24. Close by
25. Paddled in the Olympics
27. Giant of note
29. River hazard
31. Earth sci.
32. Country
34. Greek liqueur
35. The Red Baron, for one
36. ___ Na Na
37. Disclosing
38. King of nursery rhyme
39. Acad.
40. Like some dogs
43. Physicist's study
45. Pitchman's phrase
46. Coined money
47. Focus on
49. Consumed
50. Sharon of Israel
51. Silent assent
54. Nabokov novel
55. Psyche parts
57. Dry
58. *Evita* character
59. "Livin' Thing" rock grp.
60. Repair, in a way

❖ Solution on page 278

Casablanca Dreaming   *Roy Leban*

ACROSS
1. "Ciao!"
6. 1948 Olympic locale
10. Bell system
14. See 61D
15. Web sites
16. Acoustic unit
17. He freed the Germans from the Romans
18. Like Ben Jonson, according to his epitaph
19. Addr. opening
20. Like some businesses
23. It never flew
24. Congressional investigations grp.
25. Gene sites
27. Dada's dad
30. Cool condos, perhaps
34. Kind of rug
37. You, to Yves
38. Opening in Vegas
39. Overly bold
40. Gin joint
44. Délibes opera
45. Day's doubled word
46. Phone for the hearing impaired
47. Some curves
48. Sorta
50. Gin drink
51. Golden rule word
53. Hall-of-Fame basketball coach Hank
55. Maple syrup, for example
57. Said to a head?
64. Like a button
66. Hoax, perhaps
67. Love, Italian style
68. ___ situation
69. One used by Ben Hogan
70. Quote man
71. Winner's margin
72. Sign in a diner
73. Sans pizzazz

DOWN
1. Common rhyme scheme
2. Crane
3. *My Friend* ___ (1949 movie)
4. Sealer
5. Shore shoe
6. Mod do
7. 1984 Olivier role
8. Exuberant
9. Take second, perhaps
10. Country first recognized at the Treaty of Paris, 1783
11. Know it all
12. Dividing word
13. Lawless character
21. Rack carrier
22. Martini's partner
26. Cyber security org.
27. Slows to ___
28. Parks and others
29. What a bridge player does
31. Hooch holder
32. *My Cousin Vinny* Oscar winner
33. Alert end?
35. Hit on a 45, perhaps
36. 1920s Hop: Var.
41. Famous last word
42. Roman holiday
43. Where the Shadow was
49. On deck
52. It may be golden
54. Mail, perhaps
55. Cat follower
56. One for the road
58. Something about someone
59. See
60. Pigs' digs
61. With 14A, ten-time World Series winner
62. Hurler Hershiser
63. Weak
65. Surrounded area in Go

❖ **Solution on page 278**

Ya Gotta Have Heart   *Roy Leban*

ACROSS

1. Type of drug
6. Harmon Killebrew was one
10. Long time on a PC
14. Oscar-winning movie of 1979
15. Loaded one
16. Lofty opening
17. Second highest rank in the USAF
18. Some whiskeys
19. Shakespeare's "honest" villian
20. Singer of "Ruler of My Heart," 1998
23. They just won't fly
24. Ma that baas
25. Port in Portugal
28. Mix, for one
29. Org. for 46A
30. ___ State (Idaho)
31. Shogun city
32. Siberian plain, for one
34. What he did to steal
35. Author of *My Heart Laid Bare*
40. Some exercises: Abbr.
41. 1996 Wes Craven film
42. January monogram
43. Faux follower
45. Capone's piece
46. Some members of 29A: Abbr.
49. Cowboy rival
51. To be in Spain
52. ___ le Pew
53. Actress, author of *My Heart Belongs to My Three Men*
56. "Gosh!"
58. Within opening
59. Film units
60. Rig
61. Steam
62. Stella on *The Joey Bishop Show*
63. Shape of 21D
64. Rip of *Coming Apart*
65. First woman in the House of Commons

DOWN

1. Medieval helmet
2. Last month
3. Woody plant tissue
4. Eats like a horse
5. "I" to the King
6. Quarterback's option
7. Marion Morrison's chosen name
8. Singer of "On Top of Old Smokey" in 1951
9. Willy Wonka company
10. Brides followers
11. Auto essential
12. A dyne over a centimeter
13. Farm sound
21. Renaissance instrument shaped like a 63A
22. What William Tell did
26. Jim Davis's dog
27. Bids at an auction
29. Greek goddess of vengeance
30. Clinton's college
32. IBM typewriter competitor
33. 2008 Olympic loc.
34. Tea party organizer, to his friends
35. Rockford and others
36. Peace prize city
37. Bay Stars city
38. Kids do it
39. Meal source
43. For each
44. Check
46. Ditch
47. Saturn topper
48. Motion follower
50. The pits
51. Ritual dinner
52. They're entered in court
54. Keen on
55. First name in humor
56. Psi power
57. Golly!

❖ **Solution on page 279**

Biblical Blooms   Michael Wiesenberg

ACROSS

1. What luck should be
5. Somewhat
9. Hold onto
14. Field
15. Like a poor excuse
16. Pelts
17. Biblical plant with small fragrant bell-shaped blossoms
20. God
21. Pay homage
22. Rainbow
23. Peruvian coins
25. Somewhat ill
27. Calloway of scat
30. That's a laugh
32. Coroner's initials
33. Mongolian tent
35. T-men and G-men
37. Smell
41. Plant associated with the magi story
44. Printer need
45. Wings
46. Baseball team
47. Personals
49. City west of Tulsa
51. Has too much of a bad thing
52. Heart-y
56. Sleep disturbance
58. ___ z
59. Atoll explosion
61. He's left the building
65. Aster associated with a fall holiday
68. Stomach disagreement
69. Doozy
70. Sol or real
71. The second is often called the first in Europe
72. Eye
73. On the other hand

DOWN

1. "I don't hear you"
2. Husk
3. Gateway competitor
4. *Get Yer ___ Out* (Rolling Stones album)
5. Fuzzy alien of '80s TV
6. Solomon's mother
7. Usenet or e-mail group posting disclaimer
8. MTV audience
9. Suit color
10. Abner or Orphan Annie lead-in
11. Dwight's '50s opponent
12. Oracles
13. College major, for short
18. "Don't look now, but . . ."
19. Bridge suit lack
24. "___ riot" (critic's review of a comic film)
26. Jack's *Five Easy Pieces* costar
27. It's a growth
28. Ford or Chevy
29. Muffin stuff
31. Fred Astaire's sister
34. Tire feature
36. Be a man
38. Subject of Pretenders' "My City Was Gone"
39. Fix
40. Home of ISU
42. Mundane
43. Son and ___
48. Stuff
50. Gave out
52. *The Stranger* author
53. Whirling
54. Visconti's ___ *and His Brothers*
55. It's a fiddle
57. Come in second
60. Self-satisfied
62. It's a fiddle
63. Wife of Osiris
64. Third word of a New Year's song
66. Not him
67. Johnny Cash's boy

❖ **Solution on page 279**

Almost Physical   *Alan Olschwang*

ACROSS

1. Bridge plays
6. Spoils the finish
10. Soup ingredient
14. Appropriate
15. Latin I lesson word
16. Supporting shaft
17. Radio component
18. Five after four
19. Prepare for the match
20. They can fix most anything
23. Hawaii holder?
24. Guileful
25. Where Hawks soar?
26. Diamond shape
28. They may let off steam
33. Like this entry
36. Possess in the Highlands
37. Olympian Devers
38. Advances
39. Leg
40. Melee
41. It holds things in place
42. Cid's leader?
43. A troubled state
44. They're held for future fighting
47. Takes advantage of
48. Shoe size
49. Sch. org.
52. Transfer taken
54. They're officious intermeddlers
58. Church part
60. Island excitement
61. Monotony
62. 1899–1902 war
63. Outlet
64. Followed a recipe direction
65. Sigmund's daughter
66. Advantage
67. Cubic meter

DOWN

1. Roman and Gordon
2. Typical
3. Kind of business?
4. Desi's pal
5. Nimbleness
6. Gulf of the Indian Ocean
7. Surrounded by
8. Sari wearer
9. Church topper
10. Dance step
11. Remove erroneous material
12. Overdramatic complaint
13. Florence's evening
21. Camel's hair fabrics
22. Aral or Aegean
27. Hole makers
28. Beaus
29. Scottish feudal baron
30. Sweet potato substitute
31. Average enhancers
32. Machine opening
33. TAE part
34. Coconut husk fiber
35. Danish explorer Knud
39. Station purchase
40. They grimace
42. Settle
43. Eye layer
45. Stimpy's cartoon buddy
46. Standing
49. Soho pennies
50. Closer to the mark
51. Stage direction, perhaps
52. Raisin rum cake
53. ___ request
55. Asserted a claim
56. Yin counterpart
57. Purl
59. Important time

❖ Solution on page 279

It Keeps Happening   *Michael Wiesenberg*

ACROSS

1. Billy of pop
5. Fishhook
9. Do
13. Like a comics crusader
15. It's a wind
16. Viking of note
17. "Ab Fab" role
18. Eroded
19. True cross
20. It keeps happening
23. Prepare for cooking, as game
24. Brief shirt
25. Revolutionary device?
28. City or Isle lead-in
31. Artist's studio
33. Age
34. Fuss
35. Sheepish one
36. It keeps happening
40. Everything
42. Exclamation that ends a card game
43. ___ Palmas
44. Drummer
47. Personals, e.g.
51. Iraqi port
52. Morsel for a horse
53. Wine storage
54. It keeps happening
59. Bonnie Prince Charlie's island
61. After dark in ads
62. Delete
63. Certain art
64. Poland's second-longest river
65. Hinder
66. Let it be
67. Less
68. Shockers

DOWN

1. We had one about 10,000 years ago
2. "Well, I swan!"
3. Something to soothe the masses
4. Cinematographer Riefenstahl
5. Ready for the prom
6. Home
7. Roman meeting places
8. ___ shui
9. Aloft
10. Border
11. Carnival site
12. Rubber-stamped, in headlines
14. VP before Al
21. On the loose
22. Stein filler
26. Cut
27. Before
29. Race
30. "We ___ the World"
31. Sum
32. Missed the boat
34. Twin of Abby
36. Dated
37. Broadcast
38. Beethoven preceder
39. NYC time
40. It might go out on police radios
41. Meadow
45. Most like a desert
46. Skedaddle
47. *The Wall* composer
48. Fly
49. She might be in distress
50. Navigates
52. Frequently
55. Son of Seth
56. Elton John musical
57. Sammy Hagar's favorite color
58. Banyan or baobab
59. "Mayday!"
60. Carson of the West

❖ **Solution on page 279**

Sin City *Dave Fisher*

ACROSS

1. Dick's dog
5. Delineate
10. Store
14. VIP transport
15. Large bird
16. Unconscious state
17. ___ time (never)
18. Thomas Stearns ___
19. Candid
20. Hawaiian abduction
23. Global sports org.
24. Anger
25. Mend
29. Head light
31. Container
34. Organic compound
35. Nice summer month
37. Callow
39. Alabama homicide
42. Rendezvous
43. Daniel's music maker
44. Spock's distinguishing features
45. Drench
46. Sorrels
48. Reproductive cell
50. Mayo to mayo
51. Slip
52. Indian seizure
61. Eager
62. Cherished
63. Olfactory sensation
64. Where the farmer is
65. Flat out
66. Sister and wife of Zeus
67. Put in a stake
68. Lets
69. Shish kebab option

DOWN

1. Chopped cabbage
2. Gyro
3. Present opener
4. Claimed
5. Islamic bible
6. Keepsake
7. Dry
8. Rocky was one
9. Require
10. Hunter's aid
11. Native of Arizona
12. Sign
13. Twinge
21. Davis Love letters
22. Tine
25. Musical notations
26. Chilly time in Chihuahua
27. Coral, e.g.
28. Handout
29. Polynesian rain dances
30. Rose oil
31. Curriculum ___
32. Head off
33. Laconic
36. Author Davidson (*The Best of Enemies*)
38. Attention getter
40. Expiate
41. Programmer's offerings
47. Arrest
49. Part of a circle
50. Confuse
51. Throw out
52. Nothing in Navarone
53. Tied
54. Sag
55. Bob
56. Famous dog watcher Pavlov
57. Former chancellor of Germany
58. Thought
59. Standard
60. Kind of bag

❖ **Solution on page 279**

Fishy Finish *Alan Olschwang*

ACROSS

1. They cruise on 28A
5. Runs easily
10. Russian despot
14. Came down
15. High home
16. Datum
17. Noria
19. Vietnam neighbor
20. Take care of
21. TV bovine
23. Opponent
24. The body of an organism
26. Diacritic marks
28. Buckeye State artery
32. Stephens of baseball
33. Cryptologic org. of the U.S.
34. Bar legally
38. Latin I lesson word
39. Afternoon respites
42. Make haste
43. Device for accelerating particles
45. Surfer's connection
46. E-mail subdirectory
47. Fountain treat
51. Upper ___
54. Goalie Tony ___
55. John or Jane plain
56. Goose
58. Center Patrick ___
62. ___ Bator
64. Banned import
66. Attention
67. Sermonize
68. Memo
69. Latin being
70. A Guggenheim
71. Rum drink

DOWN

1. Crows' calls
2. Winglike structures
3. Ceremony
4. Texan topper
5. Shooting marble
6. Practice, in a way
7. Pitcher Hershiser
8. Immobilizes
9. Ottoman Empire sultan
10. Poetic contraction
11. Foul-up
12. Walking
13. Vase material
18. The start of something bigger
22. Sommer and Aberle
25. Kind of bond, briefly
27. DDE's adversary
28. Shape of most famous office
29. Start of a sphere
30. Press
31. Kind of consonant
35. One of the Titans
36. Sty sound
37. Pistol ___
39. Actress Gia ___
40. Endure
41. Woe is me
44. Farewell
46. Now ___
48. Cpl., e.g.
49. Protect, in a way
50. Builder's directive
51. Elicit
52. Soft drinks
53. Pays heed
57. Auction milieu
59. Borodin's prince
60. Allied org.
61. A Norman
63. Born as
65. Saul's grandfather

❖ **Solution on page 279**

E

Chapter 9

The A-Theme

Getting Together   Alan Olschwang

ACROSS

1. David, for one
5. ___ up
10. Place for a jamb
14. Winglike structures
15. Wear away
16. Consequently
17. A place to invest
19. Dray
20. Porch piers
21. She signed up
23. She loved Hero
26. Southern Hemisphere constellation
27. Electronic device
33. Sit, differently
36. Subliminal
37. Let off some pressure
38. Mops
40. Sentence stretcher?
41. Municipal
42. Actress Sorvino
43. Ceremony
45. Pursue redress
46. They're well camouflaged
49. Batter's desire
50. Gala
54. Able to serve
59. A ship to remember
60. Silver screen star
61. Where fleecing in practiced
64. Interoffice communication
65. Equine
66. Danish actor von Trier
67. Pub purchase
68. A kind of protest
69. Beat it!

DOWN

1. Secret scheme
2. Going solo
3. Ray
4. Tough teacher
5. Type of turtle
6. Behave humanly
7. ___ up
8. Utopia
9. Vitiate
10. Bridge player, at times
11. Dental exam
12. Fairy tale villain
13. Mechanical routine
18. Chest adornments
22. Toledo gold
24. Clean air advocate: Abbr.
25. Save
28. Lives in a loft
29. Invests
30. Puts on paint
31. Jacob's bro
32. President Coty
33. Distinctive doctrines
34. Ridicule
35. Rani's cover
39. Degree level
41. Of last month
43. German theologian Albrecht ___
44. Alas in Aachen
47. Related
48. Symbols of slowness
51. A Shore
52. Ice breaker, briefly
53. Plaster of Paris preparation
54. An arm or a leg
55. Cannes conception
56. Join the party
57. *Time Machine* victim
58. Sort of straits
62. Trident-shaped letter
63. *Dawson's Creek* girl

❖ Solution on page 279

Places, Please   *Viv Collins*

ACROSS

1. *Finding* ___
5. Once more
10. Comedian Jay
14. Historic stretches
15. Knight's weapon
16. Algonquian language
17. Taj Mahal site
18. *L.A. Law* attorney
19. Lose your footing
20. Moline's neighbor
22. Word with breve
23. Hammett hound
24. Automotive transmission
26. Van Gogh's loss
29. Cat without a tail
31. First st.
32. Rode the wind
34. Fate date
36. Cavalry weapon
40. Big brass item
41. Kin of viol
43. PBS science program
44. Pulverize
46. Geometric art style
47. Activist
48. Make lace
50. The Nutmeg St.
52. Melodic syllable
53. Driving force
57. Sgts, e.g.
59. Poet Sandburg
60. Outskirts
65. Code type
66. Companion to *The Odyssey*
67. Theatrical lover
68. Legal claim
69. Mother-of-pearl
70. Small, confining room
71. Banker's option
72. Slate and charcoal, perhaps
73. Boat part

DOWN

1. Close by
2. Therefore
3. Actor Singer or McClure
4. City on Honshu, in Japan
5. Galbraith of *Psychos*
6. Like a Christmas tree?
7. ___ *Christie*
8. Cake topping
9. Required
10. Spanky in *The Little Rascals*
11. Famous name in toothbrushes
12. Word on a nametag
13. Take five
21. School of thought
25. DDE adversary
26. Newts
27. Astringent
28. McEntire's comedy series
30. Three-masted vessel
33. T. S. Eliot title with *The*
35. Minor or lesser
37. Heavy shoe
38. Perpetually
39. ___ avis
42. Gives in
45. Derby, for one
49. River sport
51. Neither
53. Poker player's response
54. Miss Osmond
55. Smooth one's feathers
56. Power or system
58. Unlike a tug-of-war rope
61. Edgar ___ Burroughs
62. " . . . sting like ___": Ali
63. Locale of a Christie book
64. Wooded valley

❖ **Solution on page 279**

Words of Understanding   *Norm Guggenbiller*

ACROSS

1. Once around
4. "Final Four," e.g.
9. Beelike
14. Comic Philips
15. Pat's other name, perhaps
16. Healthy, reddish complexion
17. *All Things Considered* network
18. Palmer, to his pals
19. Cuts back
20. Find time for the task
23. Railroad bridge
24. Good friend, to Henri
27. Submarine
28. *Star Trek* counselor
31. What the suspicious smell
32. Young___ (kids, informally)
35. Supporter
37. Iron starter
38. March, in a way
43. Altar answer
44. Zhivago's love
45. Blue
46. Off limits, to a child
48. Cheerful tune
50. Border on
54. "Sure, why not?"
56. Pooh's creator
59. Try the impossible
62. Jazz dance
64. Actress Lenya
65. Cambridge sch.
66. Board
67. L.A. Laker MVP
68. Legal suffix
69. Coeur' d ___, Idaho
70. Spitballer Gaylord
71. Comprehend, and a hint to this puzzle's theme

DOWN

1. Span
2. Current unit
3. Baggage handler
4. Set out
5. He played *Gentleman Jim*
6. Slow, graceful dance
7. "The doctor___"
8. Removed
9. ___Detoo of *Star Wars*
10. Pet food name
11. Musher marathon
12. Nav. officer
13. Yankee logos
21. "I didn't tell ___"
22. Govt. notes
25. Filly, formerly
26. Road to the Forum
29. 1986 Indy winner Bobby ___
30. Three-fourths of a margarine stick
33. Cambodia's Lon
34. Lawn low spots
36. Vote for
38. Done, in Tours
39. Baseball's "Blue Moon"
40. Like one of Barry's homers
41. Cycle starter
42. Oil well firefighter Red ___
47. Scullers
49. Shred
51. Finds a fall guy
52. Not too swift
53. Guinea pig
55. Cabinet choice
57. ___ *Is Born*
58. Nev. peak
60. Sit (down)
61. First-rate
62. Relaxing place
63. 1960–61 Soviet chess champ Mikhail ___

❖ **Solution on page 279**

Right Wings *Lane and Anna Gutz*

ACROSS

1. "Same here!"
6. Pen grub
10. Relinquish
14. Square
15. Increase the staff
16. Crease creator
17. Part of an act
18. "I goofed!"
19. It's between two banks in Cairo
20. 1966 TV series with Bruce Lee
23. Musical gift
24. Some of it is Minor
25. Showy trinket
28. David Seltzer film, with *The*
31. Needing a diet
35. Beard that never gets shaved
36. Some scream at the sight of this
37. Klink clink
38. Cio Cio San, a.k.a.
41. Appropriates
42. Letter starter
43. From abroad: Abbr.
44. Type of paper
45. Type of nuts
46. Module
47. Story starter
49. Roomy vehicle
51. Schoolboys gone wild movie?
58. Banca deposit, once
59. Mayfair's neighbor
60. Charlie Tuna's concern
61. Running route, perhaps
62. It's dated with rings
63. Actor's dream
64. Awesome archer
65. E-mail button
66. They unwind at the theater

DOWN

1. Maid's list item
2. Ruler's mark
3. Old pronoun
4. Incorporated color
5. Horse tail?
6. Horse tail?
7. Fierce predator
8. Annie, e.g.
9. Baja bling bling
10. Mercury's origin
11. Noted canal, port, or lake
12. MENSA reject
13. Compass dir.
21. Wears by wind
22. Policeman's woe
25. Kit and caboodle
26. Flooded
27. Not warranted
29. Group of *Sopranos*
30. Don't get caught!
32. Spritelike
33. Actor Albert ___
34. Suez site
36. Loom
37. Don't feed
39. Car care company
40. Peg of the PGA
45. Once
46. Remove Reeboks
48. Price tag amounts
50. Burner beginner
51. Not taped
52. Word before B
53. Not now
54. Killed weeds
55. Cruise destination
56. Etc. in Latin
57. Acting sites
58. Builder's buy

❖ **Solution on page 280**

Higher Education   *Norm Guggenbiller*

ACROSS

1. Run through
5. Search (with "into")
10. Collars
14. Writer ___ Stanley Gardner
15. Unfamiliar
16. Baseball family name
17. Moms go by it, at times
20. Condition
21. Drill type
22. Croquet site
25. Sushi selection
26. Close interrogation
33. A dance, when repeated
34. Wine opener
35. Pickle or broccoli unit
36. Dynamic start
38. Rights org.
41. Get fresh with
42. Giant
44. It's often checked
46. Harden
47. Record-setting accomplishment
51. Chemin de ___ (casino game)
52. DEA agent
53. Parade decoration
58. Tonto's horse
62. Alter vacation plans, e.g.
65. German import
66. Hells Canyon locale
67. Interest in numbers
68. Goods for sale: Abbr.
69. Hose material
70. Sharp criticism

DOWN

1. Leaves in stitches?
2. Harness-race pace
3. ___ mater
4. Bug
5. Prosecutors, briefly
6. New Haven student
7. *Mod Squad* character
8. Turned down, formally
9. Used to
10. Part of NRA: Abbr.
11. "That's ___!"
12. Scary sounds
13. Gets some color
18. Cool
19. Shifts into neutral
23. At what time
24. 1492 sailor
26. "___ crowd"
27. Western writer Bret
28. Nocturnal insect
29. Tracking system, for short
30. Phrase the question differently
31. Lessens
32. Prefix for while
33. Roman statesman
37. Clod
39. *Fargo* director Joel
40. Sunscreen ingredient
43. Like some yogurts
45. Trunk
48. Stay behind
49. Fashionable
50. Dawns on (with "to")
53. Type of artist
54. Sound often associated with failure
55. X-ray units
56. Sight from Cleveland Browns Stadium
57. Convincing
59. Grad student's exam
60. Its members are often courted
61. Abound
63. "___ is it?"
64. Fool

❖ **Solution on page 280**

Where in the World?   Michael Wiesenberg

ACROSS

1. Window piece
5. Window piece
10. Devils
14. Rival rival
15. Colorado resort
16. Lowdown
17. Mideast Gulf
18. Where to find Nouakchott
20. You might have to write this off
22. Over
23. Geller the bender
24. Glossy alternative
25. Where to find Freetown
32. Where to find all these places
33. Restaurant patron
34. El Dorado, familiarly
37. Supplies for 33A
38. Gave pills to
39. Common e-mail mistake
40. See it in a Chevrolet
41. California senator
42. Wipe out
43. Where to find Cebu
45. Sandbar
49. "This Is No My ___ Lassie" (Robert Burns poem)
50. Bank jobs
53. Of old
57. Where to find Skopje
59. ___ ex machina
60. Jacob's twin
61. Render weaponless
62. "My Way" penner
63. Remains
64. You need 140 to get into it
65. Textile worker

DOWN

1. Swedish jet maker
2. *Same Time, Next Year* actor
3. Hied
4. Where to find Santa Rosa de Copan
5. Where to find Banjul
6. Aspiring atty.'s exam
7. Subject of a Satyajit Ray trilogy
8. Repeated word in hit song from remake of *The Man Who Knew Too Much*
9. Pique
10. Bucky Beaver's toothpaste
11. Water lilies painting
12. Aim
13. Hammett creation
19. Circus star
21. Missteps
25. Star of 1940's *The Thief of Bagdad*
26. "___ a far, far better thing . . . "
27. End of a Napoleonic palindrome
28. Paul V's papal predecessor
29. It stands for a painter
30. Cheri of *SNL*
31. Actor Beatty
34. Primary color in prints
35. Church recess
36. Deer ones
38. Homer's word
39. Where to find Port-of-Spain
41. Almost an A
42. Homer's *Iliad*, e.g.
44. Where to find Colon
45. More reserved
46. Put up
47. Gymnast Korbut and actress Tschechowa
48. One score after deuce
51. Sinecure
52. Of sound mind
53. Broadcasts
54. Start of a counting rhyme
55. Microwave
56. Ivan or Peter
58. Forefront

❖ **Solution on page 280**

Ail from Ale — Lane Gutz

ACROSS

1. Wide, to Caesar
6. Bombeck and others
11. Pipe type: Abbr.
14. "I ___ decent wage"
15. Gets warmer, perhaps
16. Water under the pont
17. Long-distance relationship?
19. ATM company
20. Anti–Rush Limbaugh
21. Wheaties competition
23. Buried genetic code?
25. Lake in Paris
27. Restrain
28. They fit to be tied
29. Clint Eastwood in a bucket seat?
31. Alaska Time: Abbr.
32. Feed follower
33. Uncle Fester's cousin
34. Theaters in Italy
37. Cape Evans location
41. Wedding words
42. +: Abbr.
43. Campus in Nashville
44. Get one's fodder out of jail?
48. Herring or Jack
50. Tear up
51. Female with pincers
52. On ___: tethered
53. "Earth ___"
55. Pottery for pekoe
57. Was, at birth
58. Yachting enthusiast?
62. ___ Kapital
63. Steak stabbers
64. Verdict readers
65. East, in Essen
66. Essen, in Essen
67. Rival of Sealy and Simmons

DOWN

1. *The Cyberiad* author Stanislaw ___
2. BMW tower, maybe
3. Betting option
4. Take cargo from the boat
5. NHL team in Buffalo
6. Feminine suffix
7. Warning of danger
8. Cocktail with curaçao
9. Valiant kid
10. U.S. Army rank
11. Score divided by four
12. Leave for good
13. Hair ___
18. Like Mother Hubbard
22. Paper section
23. Blind part
24. "___ the pain!"
26. TV commercial awards
29. Gaucherie with "faux"
30. BMW paths, maybe
32. Theatrical assassin?
35. This: ~
36. BMW paths, maybe
37. Oar's job
38. *Casablanca* villain
39. Those, in Mexico
40. Short writer?
42. Finished, as a basement
44. Antony portrayer in *Julius Caesar*
45. Trojan War hero
46. Gobble up
47. It's light sensitive
48. Gets rested
49. NASCAR racer Andy ___
52. Venomous African viper
54. G.I. transporters, once
56. Helper: Abbr.
59. Cay kin
60. Table scrap
61. CIA kin

❖ **Solution on page 280**

Auto Motive — Alan Olschwang

ACROSS

1. Lucy's love
5. Ballroom dance
10. Pine
14. Final
15. Small singing groups
16. Hard labor
17. Farmer's delight
19. Piece of meat
20. Pother
21. Tightwad
22. Social sufferers
23. He was no. 40
25. Shipped
26. A fast-moving fighting force
32. Backer
35. Obliterate
36. Jr. of jr.
37. Plenty, e.g.
38. Bacon buys
39. Seaweed
40. Actor Wallach
41. Leaf
42. Sources of irritation
43. Muscle management
46. Odyssey
47. You can count on it
51. Homer's epic
53. Hive denizen
56. Hill denizen
57. Legislature of Japan
58. Railway's main line
60. Relaxation
61. Flinch
62. Katmandu's place
63. Ballet, literature, etc.
64. Voted yes
65. Ship's principal structural feature

DOWN

1. Forbid
2. Ooze forth
3. Pacific Ocean island group
4. Diminutive devil
5. Kind of bean
6. Circle parts
7. Quag
8. Clod
9. Cleo's downfall
10. Goddess of Wisdom
11. More dashing
12. Posterior
13. Antlered ones
18. Interoffice communication alternative
22. Actress Campbell
24. Cove of New York
25. "Say it to the hand," for instance
27. Georgia greeting
28. "Drops of Jupiter" band
29. 15th-century English explorer John
30. Irritate
31. Shrill sounds
32. Attention getter
33. ___ contendere
34. Most plucky
38. Team member?
39. Soda flavorer
41. Dancer Astaire
42. Serious
44. Sermonizes
45. Classified
48. Effect partner
49. Ready for removal
50. Violate a commandment
51. Conception
52. Half of a Jim Carrey movie
53. Plumber's pursuit
54. Littlest of the litter
55. Nursery rhyme opener
58. Tango team
59. Acorn, eventually

❖ Solution on page 280

Bright Ideas   *Lane Gutz*

ACROSS

1. *Untitled Robe* artist Jim
5. *Zigzag* actor Ivan
10. Tanner's woe
14. Orser's character in *Rebel Yell*
15. Nice last word
16. Picante producer
17. Arthur Schawlow invention
19. Scraps
20. Wives (slang)
21. Church-style anthem
22. Defeat unexpectedly
25. Craven Walker invention
27. Sweetheart, e.g.
30. Minoxidil alternative
31. Balaam's beast
32. Spline
33. Will Smith role
35. Bemire
37. Garrett Morgan invention
41. Musical symbol
42. Ingest
43. Start to cut
45. Slip
47. Prevarication
49. Church tome
51. Georges Claude invention
54. Be demanding
55. Brief ending
56. Favorable conditions
59. View from a pew
60. Conrad Hubert invention
64. Burpee product
65. Beneficiary
66. Film addition
67. Current rotation
68. Rock monolith in Australia
69. Like some meat

DOWN

1. Not too bright
2. Zeus's Mount?
3. Votes against
4. Like the invention of the light bulb?
5. Iced tea garnish
6. Nanotechnology inventor Cohen
7. Mexican agave
8. Park sight
9. We, possessively
10. Fabric shop purchase
11. Disciplines with belts
12. There are four in an IP address
13. Adventures: Var.
18. Pro ___ : in proportion
21. Biblical region
22. DHL competitor
23. Hide
24. Ill-fated
26. Drops by
28. *The Sopranos* character
29. Inventor Whitney
34. Finish the cake
36. Start of the end of a letter
38. Uses an ax
39. Sticky stuff
40. Dregs
44. Sardonic
45. Box up
46. Used a scythe
48. Utilize
50. Fratricide victim
52. Not rich
53. Aeronautical invention
57. Help desk caller
58. Women
60. Drug tester: Abbr.
61. Head start?
62. The man
63. Bring to court

❖ **Solution on page 280**

Off with Their Heads!   *Douglas Fink*

ACROSS

1. Lit up
5. Panaches
10. Surly person
14. Tight fitter
15. Team representative
16. Late KGB chief
17. Captured
18. Natural gas component
19. Not quite right
20. Fiber source
21. Lawyer, briefly
22. Military main room
24. Limit
26. Edge-of-tears look
27. Prepare coffee
29. Least clean
33. Northwest capital
36. Hung open
38. Suzette's school
39. City near Provo
40. With the most muck
43. It doesn't hurt to have this
44. Braid
46. Noble horse
47. Comprehends
49. Gate people
51. One way to play it
53. Overseas reporter, for short
54. Move like a snake
58. Get brushes ready for painting
62. Vintner's very dry
63. Time-turning singer
64. Extremely important
65. Packed
67. Deadly sin count
68. An imperfect ten
69. Tell
70. Last name of Candace's dad's "partner"
71. Like some coalitions
72. Customary practices
73. They're "nice" in some TV ads

DOWN

1. With a nasty look
2. Ad pitch
3. Wiccan collectives
4. Bowled over
5. Pave
6. Wishy-___
7. Sparkly fleck
8. Swedish coin
9. Early video game
10. Topical
11. Goldfinger's apropos first name
12. Like cool weather
13. Reunion group
21. Of a certain heart chamber
23. Moon base?
25. Stay on fire
28. He played Mingo on *Daniel Boone*
29. Like a miser
30. Low ones on the pecking order
31. L.I. resort town
32. British guns
33. Uncle Miltie
34. Gather, bit by bit
35. Mail in a bill
37. Andy's boy
41. Ones who can read
42. Bosporus or Bering
45. Went for a walk
48. Homer's lad
50. Entrapment device, slangily
52. Fools
55. Not bristly
56. Bill designers
57. They're more than fads
58. Handholds
59. Flower part
60. Startle
61. Bomb dropper
62. Kingdom of King Minos
66. Plunder
67. Wound remnant

❖ **Solution on page 280**

It's in the Hole   Michael Wiesenberg

ACROSS

1. Staff people
5. Eager
9. Lhasa ___
13. Dostoevsky subject
15. Early SMERSH head
16. Sling mud
17. ___ Amsterdam (1600s Dutch colony that became NYC)
18. Fasten, as skates
19. Indiana team
20. Sacred burial ground, e.g.
23. Past
24. Not so near
25. Nail polish remover
27. Threatened
30. Gaming place
32. Pepsi, for one
33. Not tacit
35. It's two mints in one
38. Songwriter Axton
39. Like a diamond
41. Summer drinks
42. Altogether
44. City near Phoenix
45. Penny
46. It rubs things out
48. Go back over
50. "What thou ___, write in a book": Revelation
51. Performed
52. Half a pint
53. Aykroyd-Murphy hit of 1983
60. Girasol, for one
62. Addict
63. Beethoven's "Für ___"
64. First name in horror of the '30s and '40s
65. 27th U.S. president
66. Indy 500 prize
67. Shores up
68. *American Beauty* star
69. Part of DOJ

DOWN

1. Completion of 32D
2. Apathy or boredom
3. 100 sen, in Cambodia
4. What James Brown has
5. Humanist psychologist
6. Honored, as with one's presence
7. "He's expecting you; go right ___"
8. Get somewhere
9. Cleopatra's nemesis
10. Click "buy" in an Internet form
11. Rush of power
12. About
14. Doppelganger villain Harvey Dent in DC Comics
21. ___ cash (card-counter's supply)
22. Acid in vinegar
26. Like some plays
27. Unification Church leader
28. Residence of French president
29. Essence
30. Supply food
31. Renaissance festival drinks
32. Ho ___, together with 1D
34. Popular saying at recess
36. High bridge combination
37. The late Concorde
40. Bobby ___ of "Splish Splash" fame
43. Aerial support
47. Cakewalks
49. Gardener's tool
50. How Big Bird is, when asked
51. Nasty
52. Actor Lee J. ___
54. Tout de suite!
55. Mar
56. Situated
57. Parasitic insects
58. Best two-pair poker hand
59. Labor Day mo.
61. Vegas opener

❖ **Solution on page 280**

Cow's Word Puzzle *Dave Fisher*

ACROSS

1. Dems opposite
5. Tie
9. Indian tea state
14. Relating to the ear
15. Scintilla
16. Bessie's favorite wild ruminant?
17. Bessie's favorite tune?
19. Peels
20. Glove material
21. Food critic's concern
23. Appropriate
25. Possessed
26. Most retiring
29. She can't be married
34. Russian news agency
35. Word with phone or block
37. Raccoon relative
38. ___ roll
39. What Bessie will do at a bovine bash?
41. Stanley Cup org.
42. House bug
44. Put together
45. Pulitzer Prize novelist James ___
46. Lake state
48. Fix origami, maybe
50. Que.'s neighbor
51. Sow mate
52. Absence of pain
57. Hitachi rival
61. Flat
62. Where Bessie finds bliss?
64. Bessie's favorite Bond?
65. Long
66. It might be beveled
67. Kournikova and Freud
68. Survivor's first word?
69. Red and Black

DOWN

1. Stir up
2. Europe's tallest volcano
3. Brad ___
4. Plans secretly
5. Faint
6. Perch
7. Not beneath
8. Arab equivalent of an arroyo
9. Surroundings
10. Euphemism for a scumbag
11. Tender
12. Quizzes
13. Eyesore
18. Maiden name users, often
22. Tai's follower
24. Score
26. Project for Triton
27. Saigon's adversary, once
28. Violinist Stern
29. American painter John F. ___
30. Trudge
31. Argentine dance
32. Lucy's landlady
33. Irked
36. *Kate and Allie* role
39. Building material
40. Goose egg
43. Third World menace
45. Cottage style
47. Corp. swallowed by Verizon
49. Assuage
51. Cleanse
52. Soprano Gluck
53. Light gas?
54. Bard's river
55. ___ dish
56. Move slowly
58. Connecting point
59. Hindu philosophy
60. Washington bills
63. Get timber

❖ **Solution on page 280**

From the Director's Chair   *Matthew Skoczen*

ACROSS

1. Eyeglasses, for short
6. "You Shook Me All Night Long" band
10. Hindu honorifics
14. Moral man?
15. Out of port
16. Frat wear, maybe
17. Oscar's 1954 Best Picture winner, directed by 38A
20. Sluggo's funnies friend
21. Early arrival?
22. Wrestling, for one
23. *Birth of a Nation* group
26. Actor Ralph
27. Close to church
29. Pass a bill
32. Sharp
33. Drop back in on
35. Jack of rhyme
37. Some HS kids
38. Two-time Academy Award–winning director
41. AWOL chasers
44. Small finch
45. Appointed, in a way
49. Aphrodite's son
51. Coffee brand, with no caffeine
53. Up for it
54. Point of argument
56. Lip-___
58. Network for *All Things Considered*
59. Retinue
62. Salsa grabber?
64. 1957 film starring Andy Griffith, directed by 38A
68. Carson's successor
69. Rival of Adidas
70. Looking better
71. Word in a memo
72. Essence, in a way
73. Stuff in a file?

DOWN

1. ___ Paulo
2. Elia or Saki, e.g.
3. Mogul's mansions
4. Harry who boosted Columbia Pictures
5. Dust sighting?
6. Road travelers' grp.
7. TX time
8. Sea or space beginning
9. Author Caleb or Singer Vicki
10. Classic '70s fad
11. Some college friends
12. Match, e.g.
13. Shiny fabrics
18. *ER*'s Noah ___
19. Not much
22. Carol, to Bobby
24. 1950s Cochise player
25. Lap covers?
28. From birth
30. Curmudgeonly
31. Looney Tunes character, for short
34. They loop the Loop
36. Change under the sun?
39. Book ending?
40. Annoy
41. *Roseanne*'s Laurie
42. Double-checker, say
43. One HBO family member?
46. Ed Norton's way in and out
47. Authorize
48. Article of Freud
50. ABC's TGIF component
52. Henry VIII had one, twice
55. Bee chaser?
57. Looter's lair?
60. Singer Vannelli
61. City west of Tulsa
63. A quick study?
65. Ring ending, for short
66. Pronoun for a ship
67. Like some martinis

❖ **Solution on page 281**

Moneymaker *Alan Olschwang*

❖ Solution on page 281

ACROSS

1. Average
5. Sacred bird of ancient Egypt
9. ___ Mesa
14. Napoleon's exile site
15. Hawaiian state bird
16. Come to pass
17. Northerner who supported the CSA
19. Outscores
20. Necessitate
21. Madison Avenue offerings
23. Choir part
24. Blue nose
26. It's in the middle of an alley
28. Working folk
33. Sty sound
34. Ice cream servings
35. Expressions of satisfaction
38. One of the UC schools
40. Prince Valiant's son
41. White heron
43. English Cathedral city
44. Heated
47. Provoke
48. Assai and its ilk
50. Chewy candy
53. Norse god of wisdom
54. Island accompaniment
55. Cravat
58. Secret
62. Coarse files
64. Hard slap
66. Or else, in music
67. Runner's distance
68. Univ. course
69. Gangling
70. Finished a steal
71. Without

DOWN

1. Ancient Iranian
2. North Carolina college
3. Neighbor
4. Kyushu city
5. Washing machines need them
6. Actress Arthur
7. Machu Picchu native
8. Germ
9. Male swan
10. Indian and Arctic
11. Head part
12. All, in music
13. Fiery felony
18. Posterior
22. Pas
25. Baking soda, briefly
27. Scottish Gaelic
28. Foreshadow
29. Iran's currency unit
30. Covet
31. Rae of fiction
32. All other than the conscious self
35. Seed cover
36. Tiller
37. Fr. holy women
39. Mop
42. They get the aid
45. Drive the getaway car
46. Surmised
48. Canine
49. A panther's color
50. Decider of fact
51. Fiat
52. One of the James brothers
56. Distinctive doctrines
57. Expressionist painter Nolde
59. Killer whale
60. Fish eater
61. Puts on
63. Utter
65. The Greatest

Power Source   *Alan Olschwang*

ACROSS

1. Fete
5. Raisin rum cakes
10. Lola, for one
14. *The Plains of Passage* writer
15. Expect
16. Chills and fever
17. It keeps food hot
19. Sea in Antarctica
20. Medical specialty
21. Sort of loss
23. Former draft org.
24. Clampett patriarch
25. Swiss stream
26. It's part of politics
31. Type of tiger
34. Singing group, "The Four ___"
35. Durocher of baseball
36. What a judge does, for starters
37. Sorority members
39. Spill the beans
40. Behave humanly
41. Bring home the bacon
42. Extreme diets
43. They always come out on top
47. Not quite so many
48. King's leader?
49. Defensive hockey great
52. Frustrate
55. Black South African homeland
57. Anna went there
58. Unit called dalton
60. Gumbo ingredient
61. Pitcher Ryan
62. Fencer's foil
63. Spots
64. ___ vita
65. Funny folks

DOWN

1. Pants
2. Freeway fillers
3. West Yorkshire city
4. Jai ___
5. Pancake material
6. Emmys and Obies
7. Sort of boomer
8. Trouble
9. Ship workers
10. Heterogeneous
11. Eager
12. It's encouragement to the team
13. Dennis the Menace, for one
18. One of the Ursas
22. Important times
25. 30D opposite
26. Milady
27. Queen of Italy
28. Evils
29. Without ice
30. Oodles
31. Expression of relief
32. Dynamic leader
33. Young salmon
37. Hack haven?
38. Galena and mispickel
39. ___ Mitzvah
41. Fulda feeder
42. Former French bread?
44. South American ruminants
45. Airport surface
46. Marilu in *Taxi*
49. Zoo attraction
50. Verb after a power failure
51. Gets up
52. Chicken, generally?
53. Be a trailblazer
54. Hard finish?
55. Commuter's cost
56. Fish-eating duck
59. In addition

❖ **Solution on page 281**

Rights of Passage *Alan Olschwang*

ACROSS

1. Lead the nomad's life
5. Essential oil from flowers
10. Ripened
14. Former Hawks home
15. Nemo's creator
16. Ore source
17. Intermediate stopping point
19. Butcher's offering
20. Muse of poetry
21. Right now
23. Cassowary cousins
26. Traveling
27. Obstruction
31. Dundee daughters
35. Behave humanly
36. WWII battle locale
37. Alpine cottage
38. Lyricist Hart
40. Lover
42. Beret filler
43. Spain or Portugal's place
45. Bring home the bread
47. Pique
48. Louise and Turner
49. Desire, for one
51. Nastase of the nets
53. Northern Hemisphere constellation
54. Chilean novelist Isabel ___
57. Food item
61. Final
62. Explorer
65. Mr. Strauss
66. Say
67. Radial
68. Fiber source
69. Lachrymose
70. Put on cargo

DOWN

1. English dramatist Nicholas ___
2. *Funny Girl* guy
3. Writer Seton
4. Drizzled
5. A Gardner
6. Vietnamese holiday
7. Stumble
8. Parka
9. Get a new "Life"
10. Stray of a sort
11. Enter
12. Red pencil
13. Lair
18. Archaeologist's finds
22. Obi
24. Extremist
25. Flight school final
27. Pay the piper?
28. Small African antelope
29. Composer Harold ___
30. Astronomer's attraction
32. Kind of acid
33. Colorful tropical fish
34. Pilot
37. Pavin of golf
39. It has raisins, nuts, etc.
41. Nobleman
44. Wight or Skye
46. Italian architect Pier Luigi
49. Quell
50. Blemishes
52. Viewpoint
54. Skater's jump
55. Magma exposed
56. Singer James
58. It starts a road to a lode
59. Sleuth Wolfe
60. Funnyman Carey
61. Seasonal worker
63. Johnson pet
64. Stir follower?

❖ **Solution on page 281**

Chapter 10

The Themey Side

A Spicy Puzzle   Roy Leban

ACROSS

1. Aides: Abbr.
6. Star with a computer language named after it
11. The U.S., after the 18th Amendment was passed
14. Cootchy-cootchy girl
15. *M* star
16. Indian prime minister in the '90s
17. Atlas, for one
18. Not being straight
19. A grad may be working on it
20. Spicy saying?
22. Arizona elevation
23. 1998 Final Four team
24. *Fantasia* frame
25. The America's ___
26. *West Side Story* tune
28. *Daredevil* crime boss
32. What you might test the water with
33. Woody's son
34. She raised Cain
35. King in a Steve Martin song
38. Spicy traveler?
40. Scotch alternative
41. ASCAP competitor
42. Hand cleaner brand
43. Memory measurement
45. Christopher Robin's father
47. Least hard
51. Miler Sebastian ___
52. Dead or tight follower
53. 2001 follower
54. Verb, for one
56. Spicy plant?
59. 1040 month
60. Liquid dynamite
61. *The ___ Sanction* (1975 film)
62. Slicer's goal
63. Jetson kid
64. Baseballer Hal ___
65. Not to be trusted
66. Secluded valleys
67. Depot postings, informally

DOWN

1. Pantomime
2. Words on a mailing label
3. Shiny fabric
4. Trains and more
5. Part of many a business name
6. Ready
7. Dedicated
8. Cheerless
9. *Deephaven* author Sarah ___ Jewett
10. Part of a relay
11. Spicy drink?
12. Cheer words
13. Luke's mentor
21. Level
22. Beer holder
25. Big bills
27. Search engine
28. Malayan isthmus
29. Poorly constructed
30. Poison follower
31. It can be gained at the altar
33. Nile biter
35. *TV Guide* abbr.
36. *Pulp Fiction* star Thurman
37. Spicy actor?
39. He's anonymous
44. Magician's prop
46. It's not neutral
47. Diplomatic agents
48. Asylum seeker
49. Singer O'Connor
50. Concentrations of a solution
52. Company infamous for shredding
54. Newborns need lots of them
55. Sputnik's birthstone
56. Kind of pickle
57. Raison d'___
58. Radiation units
60. Charge for a 46D

❖ Solution on page 281

160

A Poker in the Study   *Michael Wiesenberg*

ACROSS

1. Like Schwarzenegger
6. Andy's radio partner
10. Beatles' "___ a Woman"
14. WWII scourge of the shipping lanes
15. Tirade
16. Late-night talk show
17. Bushwhacker
19. Loosen
20. Bluesy James
21. It might be auld
22. Brainwave, for short
24. Trying to take over big companies, say
30. "Mais ___"
31. Clad
32. Get an ___ (ace)
35. Where you might see C:\>
38. Spanish ayes
39. Covert
43. Opposite of floor
44. Depart
45. Part of CBS
46. Rebels
49. "___ Dien" (motto of Prince of Wales)
51. Hidden reserve
56. Religious path whose name means "way"
57. Call, in poker
58. Upset
60. Home of Zion
63. Inscrutable
66. Front
67. Angered
68. Many a whiskey
69. Was in debt
70. Light
71. "If it was up to me . . ."

DOWN

1. Erato, for one
2. What you might take with poor stock investment advice
3. *Reuben, Reuben* star Tom
4. Tried something
5. NY wagering
6. Specialized vocabulary
7. Zsa Zsa and Eva's sister
8. U2 hit of 1992
9. Mason's secretary
10. Torpid
11. Rooster's mate
12. Finish
13. ___ Canals of the Great Lakes
18. Aid
23. Werner Erhard's system
25. Cronyn of *Cocoon*
26. Buckwheat groats
27. Sign of spring
28. Like a bachelor's pad
29. Uses stets and deles
32. Capital of Ghana
33. Acid used in soap
34. White ___
36. Action star Lundgren
37. Suffix with Capri
40. Emulated Holmes
41. More wicked
42. Gospel singer Winans
47. You might find jets here
48. Eden
50. Proclaim
52. Glacial ridge
53. Run-down
54. Bad habits
55. Actress Verdugo
59. Swirl
60. It might be a dish
61. Remove a car
62. "Chances ___"
64. Center of many a threat
65. Hoover's org.

❖ **Solution on page 281**

Frightful   *Alan Olschwang*

ACROSS

1. Freeway exit
5. Removes impurities
10. Baby's first word, maybe
14. Diva's piece
15. Zagreb denizen
16. Power source: Abbr.
17. *Dead Man Walking* star
18. Lugosi feature
20. Hack
21. Sort of valve
22. Turn right
23. Irish luck
25. Large African antelopes
27. Flintstone tot
30. Gemstone
32. Platoon leader's command
33. Tennessee team
34. Copies
38. Crib components
39. Tick-tack-toe loser
40. Rubbish
41. Placed the cellular call
42. WWII weapon
43. Roast host
44. Pigment material
46. Classes in Hindu society
47. Street crosser
50. Confederate
51. Not well lit
52. Weather phenomenon
55. Mop
59. Some NFL players sport them for effect
61. Fish story
62. The Swedish Nightingale
63. Soap substitute
64. Final
65. Icelandic literary work
66. Ice cream holders
67. Vidal's Breckinridge

DOWN

1. Glued to the tube
2. Vicinity
3. Jezebel
4. It's always hit in haste
5. Breach
6. Actor Jeremy ___
7. Iowa's ___ Dodge
8. *Gone with the Wind* home
9. They feed fires
10. Dict. entry
11. Finish a tire job
12. Marked for removal
13. They're always on top
19. Depend
24. Rearranged seat?
26. It's for home safety
27. Grouper, e.g.
28. Party of a ready trio
29. Bewail
30. Pugilist
31. North Carolina college
33. Exercise suffrage
35. Ancient Brit
36. Its blade is fluted and blunt
37. Gets it
40. Blue/green color
42. Seal wood
45. Brought to mind
46. Earns a save
47. Befuddle
48. Bright green
49. Correct
50. Tarsi's milieu
53. Pitcher Hideo
54. Picture on your monitor
56. Pale
57. Banned substance
58. Synagogue platform
60. Nabokov novel

❖ **Solution on page 281**

Getting Down   *Mark Milhet*

ACROSS

1. Tile shade
5. Video game pioneer
10. Slays, in slang
14. Speech part
15. Von Steuben's title
16. Club in a bag
17. You can get down here
19. Centers of activity
20. Arnaz-Ball company
21. Complete collections
23. Kiddie pie
24. Twitches
26. Pass on
28. Agt. Scully's employer
31. "Boy!" or "girl!" preceder
33. Sudden longing
34. Web page item
36. Hence
38. Pigeon's perch
41. You can get down here
44. "Fiddlesticks!"
45. Jury member, in theory
46. Home to billions
47. Scraped, with "out"
49. Yemen's capital
51. Shade maker
52. Thought the world of
55. Naldi of the "Ziegfeld Follies"
57. Brazilian hot spot
58. Polish partner
60. Estevez of *Repo Man*
64. Egg cell
66. You can get down here
68. Intro to physics?
69. Royal
70. *The Time Machine* race
71. Stadium near Shea
72. Devices to catch the unsuspecting
73. Sahara sight

DOWN

1. OK city
2. Baskin-Robbins order
3. Features of habit?
4. Like many a Nolan Ryan fastball
5. Taken, as by an alien, perhaps
6. Athenian T
7. Second Amendment concern
8. Did a cowpoke's duty
9. Marching to the rhythm
10. Vinegar's partner
11. You can get down here
12. Get a clear picture
13. Like a snicker, perhaps
18. Essayist's alias
22. Neck wrap
25. Purse feature
27. ___ *Gay* (famous B-29)
28. Dud
29. Storage containers
30. You can get down here
32. Moorehead of *Bewitched*
35. Soldier material?
37. Kind of liner
39. Potting need
40. Ore carrier
42. Water pitchers
43. 1997 U.S. Open winner
48. Expel from a country
50. Dough dispensers: Abbr.
52. Potpourri emanation
53. Sleazy bars
54. Restaurant patron
56. Was under the weather
59. Gaius's garment
61. Doozy
62. Clickable symbol
63. Dust Bowl migrant
65. West of Hollywood
67. Catch some Zs

❖ **Solution on page 281**

Going the Distance   Alan Olschwang

ACROSS

1. Goya's duchess
5. Iowa community group
10. Invader of Rome
14. Existed
15. Biblical weeds
16. Too
17. Measuring devices
19. The last one in line brings it up
20. More agile
21. Unyielding
23. Pen
24. Try truffles
26. It can move when locked
27. Making very slow progress
33. New England component: Abbr.
36. Spasm
37. Rancor
38. Faced the day
40. Look after some little ones
42. Gift recipient
43. Razes
45. Blynken's buddy
47. Headland
48. Trudging along
51. James's creator
52. Ripen
53. Type of dog
56. Language units
61. Run out
63. Golfer's target
64. Important events
66. Sacred bird of ancient Egypt
67. Decree
68. Plumber's pursuit
69. Pirate's take
70. Philippine president Fidel Valdez
71. Platters hit "___ You"

DOWN

1. Gulf
2. Bounded
3. "Maybellene" singer
4. Vocalist Williams
5. Lure
6. ___ tai
7. Circle parts
8. Free swimmers of the sea
9. Mollify
10. Attire
11. Bread spread
12. Russian despot
13. Plenty, e.g.
18. Witnessed
22. Mark the former stray
25. Not that
27. Map in a map
28. Cake topper
29. South China inhabitant
30. Hamburg unit
31. Old-time actor Roscoe
32. Coloring agents
33. Leg part
34. Two-tone treat
35. De ___: from the beginning
39. Borden bovine
41. Forum wear
44. Stir
46. Abridged versions
49. City near Syracuse
50. Teller's announcement
53. Closet item
54. Spacial
55. Annoying
56. Singer Collins
57. King of the road
58. Potpourri
59. Kind of egg
60. Slender
62. Water sport
65. Author Umberto ___

❖ **Solution on page 281**

Halloween Happenings   *Dave Fisher*

ACROSS

1. Float
5. Bills
9. Turkish title
14. New money
15. Cross letters
16. ___ Martin
17. Did a Halloween thing
20. Holy man
21. Repeat
22. Tom, Dick, or Harry: Abbr.
26. Two or more periods
27. Cummerbund
31. What some turtles might do
33. Jazz great Herbie ___
37. Aggressive foreign policy
41. One weighed against Wade
42. Did a Halloween thing
44. Put-on
45. Jack-o'-lanterns, for example
46. Wastage
48. Smart
49. Quarry
50. Shelley's shtick
53. Type of egg
55. Terra-cotta instrument
59. Japan's oldest city
64. Did a Halloween thing
68. Tiny bit of land
69. Lamented
70. Smack
71. Instructions to eraser-happy proofreaders
72. *Beetle Bailey* dog
73. Desires

DOWN

1. Gets hitched
2. Halo
3. Barney's buddy
4. Reggae star Peter
5. Bow, e.g.
6. So-so connector
7. It may have been burned in the '60s
8. Spanish ayes
9. Phone alternative
10. Buddhist retreat
11. Greek walkway
12. Parasite supporter
13. Stake
18. Adder's target
19. Got down
23. Playwright's device
24. Take rudely
25. Actor Rory ___, star of many Westerns
27. Grass used for fiber
28. Exxon alternative
29. Dandy apparel?
30. With-it
32. South Dakota's capital
34. Passion
35. Peter of Herman's Hermits
36. Informative
38. Mississippi tributary
39. Gets a bug
40. Where Will Hunting washed floors
43. Tuck's partner
47. Frozen dessert
51. Gives up something
52. Last word in films
54. A spinner's delight
55. Geisha's girdles
56. Amount
57. ___-bodied
58. Jimi's hairstyle
60. Agile
61. Not windward
62. Eager
63. Demands
65. Not safe
66. Inactive: Abbr.
67. Stir

❖ **Solution on page 282**

Why, Why, Why!   *Michael Wiesenberg*

ACROSS

1. Ann and Nancy Wilson
6. ___ dire
10. 640 acres: Abbr.
14. Mr. Yale
15. ___ facto
16. *Clan of the Cave Bear* author
17. ___ malorum est cupiditas ("Greed is the root of evil," from Chaucer's "Pardoner's Tale")
18. Ardor
19. Southern address?
20. Wows
22. He's an Eastern player
24. *Deep Space Nine* constable
25. Hip young man
26. Home office necessity
31. Seattle neighborhood, familiarly
32. Wheel holders
33. Offhandedly?
35. Command ctrs.
38. New York's Jacob ___ Park
39. Pry open
40. '50s TV's Yiddish family sitcom actress
41. Gin inventor's first name
42. 1960 movie *The World of ___ Wong*
43. Brag
44. Unsettle
45. Prepares for secure transmission
47. *St. Elmo's Fire* actress
50. "Le ___ est mort, vive . . . "
51. Movie magic
54. First name in Mideast politics
58. Ugandan bad guy of yore
59. "Oops!"
61. Wild dog
62. Birthplace of Beethoven
63. Time in office
64. Gene Vincent's "Be Bop ___ "
65. Hook's second
66. Gabs
67. Plant tissue

DOWN

1. Sister of Zeus
2. Old Western character actor Jack ___
3. 2000 Tony winner
4. Subterranean plant stems
5. Formal wear
6. Namely: Abbr.
7. Revealed
8. John Watson's words
9. Cuddly
10. Verbally vote against
11. Shaky or tremulous
12. Fracas
13. More sick
21. Auld ___ (Ireland)
23. Partner in war
26. It might be humble
27. Leaf angle
28. Old 42
29. She's queen: Abbr.
30. Ike's spouse
34. Wolverine et al.
35. Pile
36. OP followers
37. NCOs
39. What people often try to get out of
40. Just like a kid
42. Former Iranian president Bani-___
43. Forester's tool
44. Dixon of prediction
46. Bawl
47. Sailors
48. What a first-time TV contestant might blurt out
49. Wired or Salon
52. Moon of Saturn
53. "The Noble Duke of ___"
55. James Brown's genre
56. *Cosmo* topper?
57. 500 sheets
60. Pinafore preceder

❖ **Solution on page 282**

A Little House Cleaning *Mark Milhet*

ACROSS

1. Off-key, in a way
5. Arouse
9. Nincompoop
13. Ade flavor
14. Construction markers
16. Lessen the load
17. Touched down
18. "Ho" preceder
19. Wheel holder
20. Press not required
23. Its tip may be felt
24. Plan
25. Weather phenomenon
27. "Clue" weapon
29. Mounts
32. Bachelor's home
35. Practices punching
38. Sing the praises of
39. Border on
41. Flat-bottomed boats
43. Ocean motion
44. Mexicali moola
46. Cures
48. Ann's larger neighbor
49. Fifth-century scourge
51. Simone of jazz
53. Points the finger
56. Brunch beverage
60. African antelope
62. Replaced by transistors
64. Top-of-the-line
66. Satisfy, as thirst
67. The eye has it
68. Word before tail or ride
69. Goalie's stat
70. To be, in Latin
71. Terrier type
72. Microphone word
73. Ahead of ewes?

DOWN

1. Imperfections
2. Pale purple
3. Some Pennsylvania Dutch
4. Restraint for Rover
5. Peppermint liqueur
6. Pigeon follower
7. Thunderstruck
8. Make merry
9. It's served in spots
10. Become the bard
11. Man, but not woman
12. Magazine with dating tips
15. Actors Penn and Connery
21. Pop singer Tori ___
22. Baptism, e.g.
26. On deck
28. "To ___ his own"
30. Dummy
31. Reindeer trailer
32. One of three bears
33. Aid's partner
34. Pet under the sofa?
36. Wade's legal opponent
37. Last song one might sing?
40. Slave away
42. Most thin
45. Czech or Croat
47. State of agitation
50. Squirrel away
52. Charm
54. Dazzling display
55. Debonair
57. More than chunky
58. Have a feeling
59. Obstinate ones
60. Adjusts, as a spark plug
61. Cranny counterpart
63. Strings for a luau
65. Contact's place

❖ **Solution on page 282**

More Changelings   Michael Wiesenberg

ACROSS

1. Flat-topped
5. Curtain
10. *Arms and the Man* playwright
14. "___ neighbor and weigh"
15. Affirmations
16. Sole
17. Downside of making a beach comedy?
20. Bad name to give a boy
21. Woodland deity
22. Tip of a shoelace
23. Ticklish Muppet
24. Spanish Mrs.
25. Margarita maker's lament?
31. Makes a picture
32. Neutron's place
33. Free (of)
35. ___ Land
36. Mess up
38. Clown
39. Moon, say
40. Mob boss
41. Perhaps most famous Trojan of all
42. Pinniped cyclists?
46. Memorized
47. First hippie Broadway hit
48. On the wagon
51. Slaves
53. It's a wrap
56. Heirs to a chocolate fortune?
59. Verdi's slave girl
60. Lithe
61. Like Kerouac
62. Cap'n's mate
63. Ready
64. Northern capital

DOWN

1. It might be critical
2. Jacob's brother
3. Math wave
4. Part of many company names
5. Go-getter
6. Gymnast Mary Lou ___
7. Pale
8. Equal
9. It's often to the left of F1
10. Catchphrase
11. Ginsberg epic
12. Sister to Charles
13. Batman portrayer
18. They might be British
19. Anaheim Stadium player
23. Austen novel
24. Skedaddle!
25. They don't tell the truth
26. "A monkey's uncle" preceder
27. Dave of Traffic
28. Paystub abbr.
29. Amusing
30. Dress figures
31. Andy Capp's missus
34. Mob boss
36. Spar
37. VC's concern
38. Whiskey chaser
40. Actress Bow
41. Bank job
43. Burroughs creation
44. Spins
45. Golden circles in old paintings
48. Attempt
49. Drew Carey's state
50. Kips
51. Prelate's address: Abbr.
52. Theatrical award
53. They have queens but not kings
54. Certain exam
55. Regarding
57. Far out
58. Sopranos' home

❖ Solution on page 282

First Person   *Matthew Skoczen*

ACROSS

1. Darkroom supply
6. Like some lingerie
10. Ponch on *CHiPs*
14. Vast expanse
15. About
16. Reviewer Shalit or Siskel
17. Rock used for flagstones
18. Nice hot times
19. Anthem opener
20. Meek one's lack
22. It has a point
23. Where to find gnus and emus
24. Gotten honestly
26. Outdoor hiding spots
30. Islam follower
32. Mosque feature
33. Available
35. *Carmen,* for instance
39. Deity to 30A
41. JFK posting
42. Bit used in cooking
43. Part of Columbus's ship with the shortest name
44. Antismoking politician
46. Latin being
47. Weighed down
49. In order
51. Sarong spot
54. Bat wood
55. Flatten
56. Bestseller in 1848
63. ___ top
64. Candles can't burn at both of them
65. Apropos for Halloween
66. For short, for short
67. Slanty print, for short
68. Avoided the restaurant
69. Nyets in Nantucket
70. Reebok rival
71. Reached one's full potential

DOWN

1. Salary determiner, often
2. It's annoying
3. Duck in the water
4. No, to Noah
5. Type of guard
6. Deceive
7. Opposite of fold
8. Actress/singer Summer
9. Smithers and others
10. One with 9D
11. Amber, for one
12. Just plain silly
13. Data-entered
21. Eh
25. Years in the Yucatan
26. It might have a loran
27. Type of tangelo
28. Pitch
29. Celebs
30. Attack
31. Word processor key
34. Lap pup
36. Once, once
37. Come up
38. Like fine wine
40. It might be packed
45. Hey, buddy
48. Enter all at once
50. Last song in *Ferris Bueller's Day Off*
51. Rocket series
52. Tropical island, but not 51A
53. Fun use of time
54. Airplane seating choice
57. One opposed
58. Minn. or Mont. neighbor
59. It comes from goats
60. Malevolent one
61. Sundial numeral
62. 1996 Tony winner

❖ **Solution on page 282**

Where Does the Time Go?   Dave Fisher

ACROSS

1. His and her
6. ___ Romeo
10. Pillage
14. Best
15. Garlands
16. Island dance
17. The start of many tales
19. Heartthrob
20. Lace ends
21. Part of a book
22. Subject of Arthur Golden's bestseller
25. Type of scan
27. Yours in Tours
28. Map abbreviations
29. Franklin's oft-quoted quote
33. Like good wine
35. ___-la-la
36. Ribbed fabrics
40. Plasma
42. Ball
44. Coddle
45. Bungalow, maybe
47. Draft holder
49. Ford in *Star Wars*
50. Occasionally
53. Adipose
54. Awkward one
57. It's company
58. Blondie's agent?
60. Nest material
62. Computer fix, often
65. Headlight?
66. Nine saver
70. Made do (with "out")
71. Darn
72. Yogurtlike drink
73. Great American Ball Park players
74. Vanden ___ (Jag model)
75. Narrow openings

DOWN

1. Overly
2. Fourth-century European invader
3. Catchall abbreviation
4. Some are bright
5. Bad spell
6. Succulent plant
7. Quitting time?
8. Disaster
9. "___ Goes By" (Herman Hupfeld classic)
10. Bark or junk
11. Verify
12. Dolly, e.g.
13. Collards
18. Braid
21. Broods
22. Understand
23. Garden tool
24. Grenoble's river
26. Woody's Z-4195, for one
30. Sign of a sellout
31. Make no progress
32. Chihuahua's chatter
34. Simpson's suds
37. Natural facecloth
38. Blooming shrub
39. A deadly sin
41. Bazaars
43. Stake
46. Take a ___
48. '80s toy that rivaled Transformers
51. Mouthful
52. Safe features
54. My significant ___
55. Wide-eyed
56. Registered
59. Big ___ (Jughead's pursuer)
61. They may demand sacrifice
63. Europe's highest volcano
64. Proposals
66. Roadie's responsibility
67. "___ Fell" (Beatles song)
68. Lousy egg?
69. Some race officials

❖ **Solution on page 282**

The Family *Merle Baker*

ACROSS

1. Catch forty winks
8. Place to serve mint juleps
15. Asmara's land
16. They might be tickled
17. Merry old soul in London
19. Hankers
20. Sheer fabric
21. Pirate, briefly
22. Symbolic logic pioneer
23. Garbage hauler
27. Aus. neighbor
28. Gaea
30. Galileo's university town
31. Having a bluish-gray tint
32. For the time being
34. Tries (with "at")
36. *Goldfinger* actor Gert
37. Like some frozen water
38. One not likely to be nominated
41. Good or goose follower
44. Wall St. abbr.
45. Hardly calm
46. Essential part
47. Disciplinary
48. Placement
49. Radioactive decay result
54. Pat on the back
55. Hamlet's quest
56. "Appears that way"
57. Evening events

DOWN

1. Render harmless
2. Ancient seer
3. Appalachian dulcimer, e.g.
4. Upper regions of space
5. Mine finds
6. Not "agin"
7. Right-hand man
8. Brawny
9. Not as upright
10. Stood up
11. Columnist Buchwald
12. Matchstick game
13. Narc's org.
14. Lugger out west
18. Ruckus
22. Portend
23. Light lunch
24. Rugged rock
25. Conductor Klemperer
26. Tot's question
28. Alma ___
29. Ruhr Valley city
30. Address, for some
32. British baby buggy
33. Gallivant
34. Pool hall denizens
35. "___ Named Sue"
36. High school agr. club
37. Labor leader Chavez
39. "Understood"
40. Find on the dial
41. Geological epoch
42. Nirvana's genre
43. Notable exploits
46. Rising star
47. High degrees
48. Son of Jacob
49. Baseball twin-killings: Abbr.
50. Draft pick
51. Mideast fed.
52. Mouthful, maybe
53. Summer zodiac sign

❖ **Solution on page 282**

Fly-byes   *Douglas Fink*

ACROSS

1. Stationery item
5. Closet wood
10. Woody Allen's *Scenes from a ___*
14. Terrible one?
15. Acclimatize
16. It's topical
17. It last flew in 1914
20. Before that goes before
21. Least complicated
22. Grant on TV
25. Be of use
27. It last flew on October 24, 2003
32. Keg need
33. Rod's mate
34. One way to travel
36. Goes by
38. Barber's spot
41. ___ contendere
42. Run away
43. Rhoda's mom
44. It went bankrupt in 2001
49. Extra in *The Matrix*
50. Top
51. Tribe in Connecticut
55. One in the know
56. It last flew March 23, 2001
62. Apiece
63. " . . . billions and billions" guy
64. Recent currency
65. Friend of Clifford the Big Red Dog
66. The doctor ___
67. *Saving Private Ryan* setting

DOWN

1. Piercing spot, for some
2. Eggs
3. A reason to pull over
4. Without a contract
5. French film
6. Half of a noted pair
7. ___ date
8. Outstanding debt
9. Stamp for ending an 8D
10. Star gazers
11. Skipper's command
12. Elton's johns
13. Time to do without
18. Proofreading catches
19. Dot on a map
22. Time for a scholar
23. Hello or goodbye
24. Katmandu tongue
25. ___ *High*
26. Abbr. on a knob
28. Formerly named
29. Madras mister
30. Like the ocean
31. Squiggles in print
35. Minimal
37. Sci-fi or pea container
38. Thin aperture
39. Rocket ender, in the serials
40. It's catching
42. Type of club
45. Living ___
46. Winner at Wimbledon and the French Open
47. They have the gift of gab
48. Pressed
51. Unit in telephony
52. October object
53. It is in Spanish
54. It has a comeback
55. Milk measure
57. In the past
58. Cross shape
59. Kid's pie material
60. Roth ___
61. Dale's partner

❖ **Solution on page 282**

Signs of a Storm   Michael Wiesenberg

ACROSS

1. Understated
7. Loss of resources, of a sort
11. Poured
14. Of Kiev
15. Captain of the Pequod
16. Miracle-___
17. Greek of principles
18. Italian port on the Adriatic
19. NRC predecessor
20. State gambling game
21. Element 39
23. That gal yonder
24. B&O et al.
26. "Git along little ___"
28. Wings
30. Word on a greasy spoon's marquee
33. Clears
34. Kept in check by will power
38. Match
39. Boat cover
40. Corner
42. Baseball player Tim or actress Ella
45. Whiplash preventers
50. Lena ___ of *Chocolat*
52. Cross letters
53. Worshipers locale?
54. Bigwig
56. Wrench
58. Green-lights
59. It's topographical
62. Queen's "___ the Champions"
65. Broadcast
66. El ___
67. Make lovable
69. "___ I hear you right?"
70. Guinness of film
71. Start of a carol
72. Cloning need
73. Short cut
74. Holds back

DOWN

1. Petition
2. Ho do instrument
3. Reef material distinguished by ridges and furrows
4. Pinball punishment
5. Cafe au ___
6. Where Saul consulted a witch
7. Played nanny
8. It might keep your hair dry
9. Dodge of old
10. Cuckoo or roadrunner
11. Weather equipment
12. Hermit
13. Holliday, for one
22. It carries a charge
23. Owns
25. Cross over
27. Boston time
29. Little salamander
31. A ride on the Reading
32. Dried up
35. A cheer
36. Part of the famous palindrome attributed to Napoleon
37. ___ Plaines
41. Rough landing?
42. "Don't ___ my parade"
43. Joy
44. Cold place of exile
46. Bestselling pediatrician author
47. Ecological treasure of Brazil
48. Go by Amtrak
49. SAT takers
51. And not
55. Cranium
57. Macintosh, e.g.
60. Where to find Timbuktu
61. "Wait ___!"
63. Author of *The Neverending Story*
64. Summer drinks
65. Sum
68. It's a legal matter

❖ **Solution on page 282**

Hot Movies — *Merle Baker*

ACROSS

1. Statute
4. Nip in the bud
10. Zhivago's love
14. Neither partner
15. Shirley's *Terms of Endearment* role
16. From scratch
17. Philosopher Lao-___
18. Hot movie of 1960 / Elvis Presley Western
20. Gazes at
22. Grating
23. Mine find
24. Fervor
26. Hot movie of 1974 / Gene Wilder comedy
33. Capital of Nigeria
34. Pond scum
35. Tolkien creatures
37. French article
38. Aggregation
39. With 44D, share with
40. Corn servings
42. Overhang
43. Pageant prop
45. Hot movie of 1966 / WWII pseudo-documentary with Kirk Douglas as Gen. Patton
48. Bulky bovids
49. Former Chairman
50. Easy ___
53. Pretentious person
58. Hot movie of 1983 / Cheech and Chong comedy
61. Corrida cry
62. Kid
63. Blindingly intense
64. La preceder
65. Unemployed
66. Got older, perhaps
67. Kind of cat

DOWN

1. Add to the pot
2. By the fire, maybe
3. Authentic
4. Expeditions
5. *The Price Is Right* host Bill
6. Tough test
7. Some cats
8. Dernier ___
9. Solo on screen
10. The Bunkers' old car
11. Industrious insects
12. Bring in
13. Out of kilter
19. Kind of school
21. TV clown
24. Capital of Croatia
25. Wax-coated cheese
26. Dejected
27. Hawaiian island
28. Golden following
29. Knight of the Round Table
30. Ukrainians, e.g.
31. Zhou ___
32. Austere
36. Kind of party
38. Dried-up
41. Sour
43. Like some fleas
44. See 39A
46. Eddie's *Beverly Hills Cop* role
47. Diamond authority
50. Nora's pooch
51. River of Hades
52. Highway
53. Silents star Negri
54. Acceptable
55. Tease
56. Lotion additive
57. Pup's cry
59. Wane, as spirits
60. Diamond auth.

❖ **Solution on page 283**

E

Chapter 11

How Do I Love Theme?

In Line   Alan Olschwang

ACROSS

1. Killer whale
5. Swedish rock group
9. Spill the beans
13. Peruse
14. Sort of soda
15. High quality
16. Baum dog
17. "Faerie Queen" character
18. Black in Bordeaux
19. Start of first series
22. Temple of Zeus site
24. Extra funds for retirees: Abbr.
25. Aaron's brother
26. Coach Parseghian
27. Sort of serve
29. Lobby group with big guns?
31. Start of second series
33. Puts up with
38. Cantor and Lupino
39. More of second series
41. Salsa server
42. They misplayed
44. End of second series
46. Nightmare street
47. British rule over India during the 19th century
48. Keanu in *The Matrix*
49. Miss Dinsmore of kid books
53. Mimic
55. Actress in *The Maltese Falcon*
57. End of first series
60. He's got all the answers
61. Sort of space
62. Entrée go-with
65. Mr. Morales
66. *Advise and Consent* author
67. Big lib. books
68. Riga native
69. Clan division
70. Ready

DOWN

1. Food for Fido
2. Classic car
3. Boat with floats
4. Baked brick
5. Stem
6. Grouses
7. Meet unpleasantly
8. Indian nursemaid
9. Dueler's instrument
10. Checks out
11. Old-womanish
12. Road shoulders
14. El of Spain
20. Storm front?
21. Mosque prayer leader
22. It only gets better from here
23. Age, in a way
28. Region of Germany
30. Missouri university city
32. More E than S
33. Former draft org.
34. What a bill might become
35. More than a little shoddy
36. Pitcher Nomo
37. Tiger's track
40. Loudspeaker part
43. Will of the Waltons
45. Bitterroot peak
47. Backslide
49. *The Glassy Sea* writer
50. Skunk
51. The ultimate dieter
52. Spoilsport's statement
54. Advance
56. IT guru
58. Spreads the green
59. Crooked
63. ETO general
64. Reader's letters

❖ **Solution on page 283**

It's Patriotic   *Alan Olschwang*

ACROSS

1. Theater seat
5. Hornet
9. Henry Cabot ___
14. What Hamlet smelled
15. Actress Chlumsky
16. Projecting bay window
17. Event for Bobby "Boris" Pickett
18. Lead actress
19. Desert greenery
20. A safer investment
23. Tax rebate use, sometimes
24. Uno, due, e tre
25. Ananias, e.g.
28. *Cheers* cry
30. Meeting manager?
32. Notorious marquis
35. Massenet work
38. Scion
39. It's often clerical
43. They loop the Loop
44. Martin and Pickford
45. Hostelries
46. Driver's inconvenience
48. Purim's month
51. Organic compound
52. Expressions of surprise
55. *Tenant Farmer* painter
58. Times to remember
62. Bristles
64. A Diamond
65. Korean president
66. Severe
67. Jody Foster film
68. Highly regarded
69. Change the shoe color
70. War god
71. Sort of sister

DOWN

1. Mary's charge
2. Tests by panels
3. Patronize the pump
4. A computer-related technology
5. Nut holder
6. Nonconformist
7. Goes over the edge
8. Break down a sentence
9. Start of a motive?
10. Prophet
11. Poet Emily
12. Obtain
13. Mr. Whitney
21. Corporate bigwig
22. Crown
26. Decorate
27. Corporal and colonel
29. Heathcliff's heath
31. Long-snouted fish
32. Gal from Goteborg
33. City near Muenster
34. Exaggerated
36. Layer
37. Lioness in a film
40. Cassowary cousin
41. Noel
42. Spin out
47. Fire starter
49. Resides
50. Scottish river
53. Middle Eastern shrub
54. Bum chaser?
56. California/Nevada lake
57. Serengeti scavenger
59. British valley
60. Floor piece
61. Play a child's game
62. Georgia, formerly
63. Somme summer

❖ **Solution on page 283**

Concealing Little   *Merle Baker*

ACROSS

1. Actor Conrad ___
5. Toothbrush brand
10. Features of 9D
14. Arm bone
15. ___-nez
16. Treat with cream
17. Justification for territorial expansion
20. Treats with irreverence
21. Motorola rival
22. Way to enlightenment
23. Quantities having only magnitude
27. Stylish
31. German coal-producing region
32. Bleat
33. Made a mistake
34. Emulated Scheherazade
36. Minnesota Twins all-time winningest pitcher
37. Short glasses
38. Dash gauge
39. Definitely not well
41. Magazines and newspapers
42. Falsehood
43. Mideast carrier
44. Cure
45. Elizabeth ___ Browning
47. Cushion
48. Communication for the deaf: Abbr.
49. Go up
54. There may be a message here
58. River in Switzerland
59. Indian lute
60. Bound
61. One feeling remorse
62. Jazzman Artie and journalist Bernard
63. Not straight

DOWN

1. Night sound?
2. Banned apple spray
3. ___ uncertain terms
4. Credulous one
5. One who starts the betting
6. Out of bed
7. Hill builders
8. Watch numbers: Abbr.
9. Recyclable items
10. Kind of eclipse
11. Shipping magnate, familiarly
12. Pa Cartwright
13. Asian condiment
18. Rattled
19. Frightful
23. Impertinent
24. Chafe
25. Far from fresh
26. Square-dancing figure
27. City in northern Illinois
28. Lawrence's land
29. Supplicant
30. Parrots, perhaps
31. Binder or bound beginning
34. Water balloon sound
35. "Up and ___!"
37. Like some pretzels
40. Nixon aide
41. Get the gold
44. Speeders
46. Less experienced
47. "I don't believe that!"
49. Singer James
50. *Zorba the Greek* actress Kedrova
51. Once more
52. Pull apart
53. Catch sight of
54. Ingot
55. ___ de Cologne
56. Three, in Turin
57. Medical research agcy.

❖ **Solution on page 283**

Seeing Double   *Michael Wiesenberg*

ACROSS

1. Italian sports cars
6. Theda ___ of the silents
10. Rover sender
14. Pounds
15. Loan
16. Sigh
17. "Ordinary World" group
19. Deli offerings
20. Ripening agent
21. Nest egg
22. Gone by
24. Nabokov antihero
30. Talking head offering
31. Riser?
32. Tease
33. Unhappy
35. Owing
36. Actress Lupino
37. Poured out
41. Chamberlain, once
44. Williams of folk
45. End of GI's reply
47. Spenser's Faerie Queen
48. "Evil Woman" group, for short
49. Happen
51. Displays
54. Sinatra hit from 1980
57. "___ were king of the forest"
58. ___-fi
59. Mother Earth, once
61. First president of South Korea
64. German spa city
67. Mr. Boffo's first name
68. Perot's stand out
69. Paths through the brain
70. "Impaler" upon whom Dracula was modeled
71. ___ Inn
72. Vice ___

DOWN

1. "___ pocket full . . . "
2. Guffaws
3. Start
4. Chicken Little, say
5. xxx-xx-xxxx
6. As seen by the myopic
7. Made bubbly
8. Genetic material
9. Excessively
10. Potentate
11. Everything
12. Made a lap
13. Pack animal
18. It might be cast
23. London time, for short
25. ___ Brith
26. Schlep
27. ___ the Red
28. Sally into space
29. Lift type
34. Limned
37. Eve's home
38. Masculine
39. Frigate front
40. Slangy detective
42. Frilly
43. Abolish officially
46. Peters out
49. Reaction to sucker punch
50. Adjournment
52. Vic or Joe
53. Users of 29D
55. Give way
56. Prevail
60. Vase handle
61. Race, as an engine
62. "I'm sorry, Dave, I can't do that" speaker
63. Age
65. Tower coordinator
66. Hip-hopper Bel ___ Devoe

❖ **Solution on page 283**

Out of Sorts   Grace Becker

ACROSS

1. Another name for Jupiter
5. Big gig
9. Proton holders
14. Did impressions of
15. Singer Redding
16. Golf great ___ Nelson
17. Nautical hazard
18. Units of electrical resistance
19. "The Final Frontier"
20. Use it to request merchandise by mail, for instance
23. Sommer of the screen
24. ___ kwon do
25. Extra wide shoe size
26. *Pygmalion* playwright
28. Links limos
30. At sea without an anchor
34. Tools for making holes in graduated sizes
37. Hammer user
38. No more than a smidgen
39. Give
41. Beginner
42. Toyota rival
45. Unresolved detail
48. ___ Milano of *Who's the Boss?*
49. ___ Rice, author of *We the People*
50. "___ off the old block" (spittin' image)
52. Part of R and D: Abbr.
53. It's subjective
56. Item for Jack and Jill
59. Send the same message in this kind of communication
62. Racetrack in *My Fair Lady*
64. Peau de ___ (Wedding dress material)
65. Cole Porter musical comedy *Kiss Me___*
66. Ski resort
67. Questionable contraction?
68. Ken or Lena
69. Robert Urich in *Vegas*
70. Woods's accessories
71. Early prop in *It's a Wonderful Life*

DOWN

1. Blouse ruffle
2. *Aida* or *Carmen*
3. Chili color in Mexican restaurants
4. Maugham's *The Razor's ___*
5. Chocolate-covered peanuts
6. Basketball players
7. Succotash ingredient
8. Special interest grps.
9. Sit-up targets
10. Place to find keys
11. Like some exams
12. Make fun of
13. Large knife found in crossword puzzles
21. Kind of estate
22. Ricardo Montalban role
27. Bridge professionals org.
28. High-school funny man
29. Like week-old bread
31. Nastase of tennis
32. Frond-bearing forest growth
33. Trampled
34. Actress Merrill
35. Muddy up
36. "The ___ Bitsy Spider"
40. Prospector's dream come true
43. Wood for bats
44. Babe in the woods
46. Some are Western
47. Golfer Ballesteros
51. Suggest
53. In the least
54. Fix laces again
55. Market analyst concern
56. Historian's subject
57. Nick and Nora's dog
58. Graphic symbol
60. Former Kennedy matriarch
61. Some ring victories
63. It's in the bag

❖ **Solution on page 283**

Just in Case   *Verna Suit*

ACROSS

1. Motorcycle add-on
8. Screen denizen
15. Question of courage
16. Be on a spree
17. Brownish pigments
18. Isolde's lover
19. Slogan
21. Shaggy rug
23. Trompe l'___
24. Calabrian coins
27. Red dye ingredient
29. Clean
32. Paid guy
33. Door opener
35. Painter Chagall
37. Interjections
38. Atty. test
40. Birthright seller
42. Computer support dept.
45. Trip calcs.
47. Great shock
51. It's smoked, sometimes
52. Formosa Strait island
54. Caruso or Gedda
55. Bulgars and Poles
58. HS student
60. Popular '60s cars
61. Lawn-fouling fowl?
65. Procedure start
67. Russia neighbor
70. Crew car
71. Worked on wedgies?
72. Chronologically, e.g.
73. Curls

DOWN

1. '60s rads
2. Intro course number
3. Like some soldiers
4. Mystery author Buchanan
5. Ethnic food that's less spicy than its neighbors
6. ___ against time
7. Send order again
8. Pituitary hormone
9. John Dickson ___
10. Ordeal
11. Winemaker Carlo
12. Muse of music
13. FICA agency
14. Yen fraction
20. Choice morsel
21. Yankee foe
22. Second person
25. Dep. opp.
26. Quick cry for help
28. Bad
30. ___ Dawn Chong
31. While opening
34. Pro ___
36. Dray power
39. Pompon place
41. Trucial States, today
42. DDE competition
43. MD neighbor
44. Sugar pill
46. Swinger Sammy
48. Lays bare
49. Hay storage
50. ___ *Poetica*
53. Dieter's lunch
56. Fog
57. Lass's headgear
59. Flush game
62. French Caribbean cove
63. Bambi and Rudolph
64. Portuguese saints
65. Bio. or chem.
66. Author Amy
68. Born in Bruges
69. Begley and Begley

❖ **Solution on page 283**

LPs   *Merle Baker*

❖ Solution on page 283

ACROSS

1. LP spinners
4. Going up
10. Bambi's aunt, and others
14. Dull routine
15. Bakery treat
16. Abadan's land
17. Bustle
18. Clinton's budget director
20. Succeed
22. Tizzy
23. Shrink's org.
24. Half an LP
25. Founder of the science of microbiology
30. Wallop
31. Rural structures
32. Sample
35. Lady Jane ___
36. Aspect
37. Gambling game
38. Critter for carrying
39. Pigeonhole
40. Element number 5
41. Two-time Nobel Prize–winning chemist
43. Takes it easy
46. Med. scan type
47. Cheers
48. "Eureka!"
53. Nixon Supreme Court appointee
55. Pursue
56. Lodges
57. Muse of astronomy
58. Former Texas governor Richards
59. Check alternative
60. Empty ___
61. Come out with

DOWN

1. Party pooper
2. Olympic sport since 1964
3. Come to a standstill
4. Turn for the worse
5. Much of Greenland
6. Blackthorn fruit
7. Fleming and McKellen
8. Winter air quality
9. An incline
10. He's not a glutton
11. Combining form meaning "correct"
12. No longer on the table
13. Kind of drum
19. Spider nest
21. Nonclerical group
24. *Silkwood* actress
25. Dinah Shore Classic grp.
26. Sculling gear
27. Manipulates
28. Manual calculator
29. Goldman ___
32. Delhi wrap
33. Essential mineral
34. Early video game
36. Excessively subtle
37. Manuscript sheet
39. Turns thumbs down on
40. Second-story man
41. Nearly on time
42. 2001 Best Foreign Film nominee
43. Attic find, maybe
44. "Maria ___" (hit of 1941)
45. Croquet sites
48. "As ___ saying . . . "
49. Express openly
50. Yuletide story start
51. Hebrides isle
52. *Amadeus* award
54. Mined find

It's Easy! *Douglas Fink*

ACROSS

1. Rebound
6. Clean up a deck
10. Village idiot
14. Public venue
15. *Adventures in Babysitting* icon
16. 7D
17.
20. Laugh track content
21. Hot under the collar
22. Cabin sleeping accommodations, perhaps
23. King David's predecessor
24. She's just out
25. It's subtle
28. Off yonder
30. "We ___ Family"
33. European opener
34. Future MENSA members, perhaps
36.
39. Behaving like a mob
40. A weather's antonym
41. Center of control
42. It's what's not for dinner
43. Multitudes
45. Giant legend
46. Brouhaha
47. *Dynasty* actress
50. Supplies from the IRS
52. Dawn, for one
55.
58. Skater Lipinski
59. Cracked
60. *Buffy* spinoff
61. Farm verb
62. Unamusement
63. Bronco buster

DOWN

1. Check alternative
2. Region
3. Gets ready to drag
4. Three Dog Night hit
5. *Flashdance* song title word
6. Try to be way off base
7. 16A
8. Top quality
9. It's uplifting
10. Be a pain?
11. Chow call
12. Part of MIT
13. Melanie, in *Working Girl*
18. Faithful
19. Man of the cloth
23. Hardy-har-har sound
24. Early word or art style
25. Liquid for blow-ups
26. Out of the know
27. Bodega bye-bye
28. Coats in the wild
29. Brown role for Grier
30. Garlicky sauce
31. Check it out again
32. Serpentine paths
34. Call from an alley
35. Nana's hubby
37. Piggie
38. Sturdy minor shelter
43. Mater leader
44. Sly one
45. Readily available
46. Jacques of song
47. *Fear Factor* snack, perhaps
48. Test tube
49. Linc's locks
50. Samoa neighbor
51. Office shape
52. Part of a Baha Men title
53. 1001 ___!
54. 1952 Olympic site
56. Like the *Queer Eye* five
57. The other genetic acronym

❖ **Solution on page 283**

It's Not Over *Mark Milhet*

ACROSS

1. Read quickly
5. Cabbage sides
10. Big chunk
14. Ocean motion
15. Ornamental loop
16. Good sign?
17. Proton's place
18. Wise leader
19. Say for sure
20. Where subs are found
23. Got fed up?
24. Came down with
25. Equality
29. Uptight
31. Scribble down
34. Lickety-split
35. Fall birthstone
36. Bar or car opening
37. Ailing
40. Black and White
41. Black cat, maybe
42. Indicators
43. Pencil holder, at times
44. Lad's love
45. Obstacle
46. "Why, certainly!"
47. Tennessee jock
48. Extremely vile
57. Similar
58. Like a haunted house
59. Jim Ryun's distance
60. Fast time?
61. Cinema's stock
62. Qom home
63. Invention beginning
64. Winter hazard
65. Tear to pieces

DOWN

1. Hamlet did it through an arras
2. Tailed flier
3. Teen hero
4. Note
5. Like dalmatians
6. Supple
7. Tylenol target
8. Reasons to complain
9. Proceed with difficulty
10. Ore corridor
11. Magma on the go
12. An acting Baldwin
13. Party pooper
21. Cooler contents
22. Dale's mate
25. VCR button
26. Sleeping problem
27. Clerk of the 4077th
28. Chills
29. Choices for fencers
30. Tony Orlando's backup
31. Crusade of a sort
32. *Access Hollywood* co-anchor Nancy
33. Short-spoken
35. Resistance units
36. Tend to the sauce
38. Bun warmers
39. Grown-up
44. Flock's place
45. Like Abe
46. Gossipmonger
47. Sheer fabric
48. "___ Hai"
49. ___ out (just managed)
50. Right fielder, to the scorekeeper
51. Cad
52. Canadian tribe
53. Arab potentate
54. Wet spongy earth
55. Leave nothing to chance
56. Take care of

❖ Solution on page 284

Three Squares   *Merle Baker*

ACROSS

1. Understand
6. Recipe directive
10. Fountain choice
14. It might be broken on the stand
15. Hose shade
16. City north of Provo
17. Miller character
18. Geometric calculation
19. *Harlequin's Carnival* painter
20. Denny's offering
23. Runner down under
25. Pub potables
26. Driveway application
27. Hocus-pocus
29. Fifties fender feature
30. Some AARP members
31. Former Yugoslav strongman
32. Highest point
35. '60s sit-in locations
40. Elm, e.g.
41. City of France
43. Spanish article
46. Co. name abbr.
47. Not a ___ in the house
49. Spice tree native to Indonesia
51. *The Grapes of Wrath* wayfarer
53. Call of the hounds
54. What nobody wants to be called
57. "Put a lid ___"
58. Elec., e.g.
59. Karatelike exercise program
62. 18A measure
63. Cause of cramming
64. Benefit
65. Action
66. Grounded streakers
67. Outcropping

DOWN

1. Guy's date
2. "Evil Woman" grp.
3. The ends of the earth, figuratively
4. Construction piece
5. Sorry trait for a musician
6. Untrustworthy one
7. Some racetracks
8. "What's the big ___?"
9. Put in another post
10. Cause for a pause
11. Projecting windows
12. Loewe's partner
13. Affairs
21. ___ Khan
22. Doctrine
23. Young newt
24. Word with call or order
28. Seemingly forever
29. Final ___
32. Current choice
33. "The Gold Bug" writer
34. Hard to grasp
36. ___ Justice
37. Malls, to teens
38. Reuben wrapper
39. Tofu source
42. Napoleon aide
43. Disburden
44. Subtle difference
45. Garb
47. Racket
48. Kind of car
50. Doled out
51. Dryden or Keats
52. Highland wear
55. Hwy. numbers
56. Roof edge
60. ___ brother
61. Roar of approval

❖ **Solution on page 284**

Play Option   Merle Baker

ACROSS

1. Yep opposite
5. Slumber
10. Muted trumpet effect
14. Inter ___
15. Pooh creator
16. Mimic
17. Feature of some courses
20. Hindu incarnation
21. Process flour
22. Hot time abroad
23. Minstrel's instrument
25. Negative conjunction
26. Jailbird
27. Do lab work
32. John's *Pulp Fiction* costar
33. Zero
34. Silent
35. Observe unobserved
38. Menlo Park monogram
40. Olympics reward
44. DDE opponent
46. Dock worker's org.
48. Pup's lament
49. Cavort
55. *Double Fantasy* singer
56. Needle
57. Plane that doesn't need a
    runway
58. Cesar Chavez org.
59. Pot starter
61. Baltimore baseballer
65. Try to find in the dark
68. Out of port
69. Atlas, for one
70. Slaughter on the diamond
71. Lawless role
72. Dummy Mortimer
73. Stadium cover

DOWN

1. California wine valley
2. Norwegian saint
3. Tower town
4. Calif. barrio city
5. Spruce up
6. Full deck in old Rome
7. Pipe elbows
8. Power source
9. Carry out
10. Roll of bills
11. Each
12. Continued
13. Silvery
18. Mythical goat-man
19. Sun room
24. Way out
27. Neighbor of Ukr.
28. Diamond arbiter
29. Anti vote
30. Without toppings
31. Marseille Mrs.
36. Symbol of strength
37. Brain-related
39. Height: Abbr.
41. Turn red?
42. Feel feverish
43. CD forerunners
45. Small pianos
47. Shock with wonder
49. Drysdale teammate
50. Imbue (with)
51. Ranchers
52. Acquire
53. Rhino feature
54. Omitted in speaking
60. *Harper's Bazaar* illustrator
62. "It's ___ consequence"
63. Harris Tweed machine
64. Celtic language
66. Call in the meadow
67. Sculler's need

❖ Solution on page 284

Let's Settle This   *Merle Baker*

ACROSS
1. Babies
6. ___ California
10. Heats in the microwave
14. Bovine attraction at the 1939 World's Fair
15. Jai ___
16. In the event that's true
17. He has his eye on the target
18. Starting up
20. Stereotypical hard labor
22. Brazilian resort
23. Actress Thompson
24. Residue of a sort
27. Wraps
31. Siren
33. Make known
34. Street of nightmares
36. Set loose
37. Snip producer
42. "Lovergirl" singer Marie
43. Used a settee
44. Scot's negative
45. Put on a pedestal
48. Bum out
51. Cherry or fuschia
52. Freak out
54. *Norma* ___
55. Like presents, often
60. Bend an ear
63. Henry's tutee
64. Enlarged
65. Greek mountain
66. Prepared potatoes, perhaps
67. Understands
68. Lights out
69. Word with charmer or eyes

DOWN
1. MM, for one
2. Potpourri
3. Armed Forces branch: Abbr.
4. Hall of Fame knuckleballer Phil ___
5. Pet, perhaps
6. Swelter
7. Wanted poster word
8. Wolf's cousin
9. Japanese martial art
10. Oomph
11. Neighbor of Pak.
12. Greek letter
13. Heir, often
19. Going nowhere fast
21. Cowboy display
24. Like edelweiss
25. Fancied to be
26. Depends (on)
27. Christian festival
28. Christian creed
29. Confidant
30. Camera type
32. Med. specialty
35. Submissions to eds.
38. Cone or -Cat head
39. Israeli natives
40. Uncouth fellow
41. In ___ (unborn)
46. Sycophant
47. Extremely
49. Concrete layers
50. Catch, as a fish
53. Uneven
55. Nave seats
56. Number crunchers
57. Costa ___
58. Book before Dan.
59. Miami-___ County
60. Omelet need
61. Have being
62. Nov. honoree

❖ Solution on page 284

Say It Again, Sam   *Merle Baker*

ACROSS

1. Hospital units
5. Shelled out
9. Bandleader Kay ___
14. Muffin topper
15. French cleric
16. ___ barrel
17. One of the Simpsons
18. Plaintiff
19. Takes a snooze
20. It doesn't stop a lot
23. ___ *Bravo*
24. Abigail Adams, ___ Smith
25. Qom resident
29. Prefix meaning straight
31. Secret bar
33. HS subject
35. Does wrong
36. U.S. soldiers
37. British conservative
40. Perplexed
42. Sound quality
43. Humphrey's *High Sierra* costar
44. Gator's kin
45. Mad Hatter's party
47. Woofer element
50. August 15, 1945
54. Get delivery
55. "___ to Joy"
57. Biblical priest
58. Degree-conferring institution
61. Taco topper
64. Tough test
65. Pop star
66. "If I Had a Hammer" singer Lopez
67. Stratagem
68. Social misfit
69. Tempting one
70. Call for
71. Driving supports

DOWN

1. Ravel composition
2. Alchemist's quest
3. Saddam Hussein, formerly
4. Fly like an eagle
5. Outworn
6. Mistreats
7. "Yeah, right!"
8. Rear
9. Alaska bears
10. DeCarlo of *The Munsters*
11. "___ who?"
12. Afore
13. ___ Tafari
21. Organic compound
22. Noah's landfall
26. Shakespearean villain
27. A ___ apple
28. IPO's venue
30. " . . . and that ain't ___!"
32. *Goodfellas* actor
34. Grateful Dead leader
37. VCR alternative
38. Skunk's defense
39. Sudden attack
41. Home of Roger Rabbit
42. ___ Mahal
44. Positive
46. First name in daredeviltry
48. Corporate transportation producer
49. Setting
51. Political analyst Myers
52. Former Blair House resident
53. Bond payments
56. Gave (out)
59. Pennsylvania port
60. Pocket collection
61. Ave. crossers
62. Coach Parseghian
63. On

❖ **Solution on page 284**

The Listener   *Michael Wiesenberg*

ACROSS

1. That's not my cross ___
5. Popeye's female foe
11. Coal carrier
14. Military group
15. Fly
16. Close by
17. Question deeply
19. Oy follower
20. Pinafore preceder
21. Rocky unit: Abbr.
22. "Forever Will ___" (Virgin Steele song)
24. Top news story
28. Paddock dwellers
31. Kind of patch
32. Hangs heavily, like a stormy sky
33. Listening device
37. Boo-boo
38. 37A, e.g.
40. ___ Brith
41. Tub need
43. Getting warm
44. High nest
45. W.C. in Lompoc
46. Party leader
50. Kali worshiper
51. House part
52. CIA preceder
55. Like a ewer
56. Put up a good defense
61. And so on
62. J.R.'s mom et al.
63. Part of a metaphysics title by Robert B. Pirsig
64. ___-wop
65. Processes ore
66. Deep Purple hit written by Joe South

DOWN

1. ZZ Top's first top 20 single
2. Slot feature, often
3. Disposable lighters
4. Your home
5. Secret ___ (anonymous gift-givers)
6. Occurrence
7. Sue Grafton's ___ *for Alibi*
8. Sardonic laugh
9. With ___ in my eye
10. "Let's start this rumble"
11. Anarchy
12. NBA's Shaq
13. Oh my!
18. Signs
23. Frodo, for one
24. What a tennis player may try to improve
25. Like some magnets
26. Get paid again
27. Nocturnal insect with abdominal pincers
28. Steve McQueen's first major movie, with *The*
29. Davenport locale
30. Fit
34. Indigo
35. "___ my Annabel Lee" (Poe)
36. Where one lives
38. Marsh bird
39. Refuge
42. Tempts
43. Physicist Bohr
45. Like Capp's Fosdick
46. Clipped
47. Attach, as a tarp
48. Sears, Roebuck ___
49. Poet Stephen Vincent
52. Luau locale
53. Political attacks
54. Clockmaker Thomas
57. Advanced deg. for an atty.
58. Baseball Hall of Famer Combs
59. Drill for this
60. Ultimate

❖ **Solution on page 284**

Running on Empty *Mark Milhet*

ACROSS

1. Buds' function
6. Inspired poet of Hinduism
11. Highest degree
14. Basic beliefs
15. Destaff
16. Tick off
17. Can't come up with the answer
19. Pool tool
20. Take-out order?
21. Wise up
22. Molt
23. Scold
25. Forbidden
27. Depp movie of 1999
32. Geisha's prop
35. It follows that
36. Simple type of answer
37. "Work without ___"
39. Goes bad
42. Punch
43. He may make you do it
45. Land for the looney
47. Born, in bridal bios
48. Whisper from your honey
52. Bill attachment
53. Ticker-tape event
57. Butler's last word
59. Low man at the opera
62. Yemeni seaport
63. Whitney or Wallach
64. No longer valid
66. Tons of time
67. Divvy up
68. Twilled fabric
69. Barber or Buttons
70. Name on a check
71. Pattern

DOWN

1. Victoria's Secret purchase
2. Up ___ (cornered)
3. "We ___ Overcome"
4. Beach needs
5. Snaky curve
6. *Hee Haw* type
7. *To Live and Die ___*
8. Kind of pants?
9. Title role for Mia
10. Squid squirt
11. The president in *Mars Attacks!*
12. Quiz option
13. Pay mind to
18. Shortens in the sleeves, perhaps
22. Cobbler's inventory
24. Pub quaff
26. Lad following a bus?
28. Trip for a narcissist?
29. Young pheasant
30. Not a second time
31. Turned off the alarm
32. They're in
33. From square one
34. "Forget it!"
38. Marketing ploy
40. "Yay team!"
41. Type of sandal
44. Inc., over there
46. Santa ___ winds
49. Interstellar cloud
50. Way of taking medicine
51. More severe, as consequences
54. Love lots
55. Condescend
56. Wrapped up
57. "Home on the Range" critter
58. Natural emollient
60. Plumlike fruit
61. Fill to excess
64. Catch some Z's
65. "Spring forward" letters

❖ **Solution on page 284**

Chapter 12

Who Told Theme That Thou Was Naked?

Small Starts   *Matthew Skoczen*

ACROSS

1. They show hits: Abbr.
5. Popular music genre
8. Silly syllables?
13. "Enter!"
14. Judi Dench's 2001 title role
16. Rice ___
17. Construction beam
18. Big swig
19. George, to Abuelo
20. Organization founded in 1831
23. " ___ Secret" (Kylie Minogue song)
24. Rhine feeder
25. Quick crosser
28. Mayberry's main man
33. Comedy partner of 52A
36. Land of St. Pat
37. Blunder
38. Neil Armstrong, John Glenn, et al.
41. Demonic diminutive
43. They come up from a deck
44. First name in spoon-bending
45. Then mate
46. Chef's cutlery
51. Org. that took Hearst
52. Comedy partner of 33A
53. Michael Caine title role
57. Australian territory
62. Lead to *Beach* or *Waterfront*?
64. Dodge type
65. Famous last words
66. Hawk's hook
67. Add-ons
68. "Copper!" in a way, say
69. Approval
70. "The Raven" poet's monogram
71. Wild plum

DOWN

1. Literary genre
2. Character in 1D, maybe
3. Epps and Sharif
4. Court sister
5. *Mystery!* host since 1989
6. Make ___ for it
7. Take in a war?
8. Muslim pilgrim
9. End of a buck?
10. Mooches
11. Director Lee
12. You, on the Danube
15. Opera prop
21. Charged item
22. When doubled, an amulet
26. Short notetaker?
27. Cast
29. Cacaphony
30. 1941 and 1984, e.g.
31. Hoover's grp.
32. After: Abbr.
33. Turkeys, in a way
34. Ryder rival
35. With reserve
39. Non-Rx
40. Cigar ending
41. West end?
42. Leon Uris novel, *QB* ___
44. Tiny Tim played it
47. North Pole sighting, perhaps
48. Arledge of ABC sports
49. Mi followers
50. Corby and Burstyn
54. Movie attraction?
55. Emcee's task
56. Draw out
58. Cries of discovery
59. Las Vegas competitor
60. Nut used to flavor Coke
61. Clouseau, briefly
62. Extra quarters: Abbr.
63. Sports org.

❖ **Solution on page 284**

Fuzzy Logic   *Grace Becker*

ACROSS

1. Hawaiian sushi item
5. Woodland babies
10. He yelled "Show me the money!"
14. Actress Raines
15. Notions
16. Rich Little is one
17. Open to men and women
18. Play by an epee wielder
19. Words of understanding
20. Both sugary and tangy
22. Maria's *West Side Story* friend
23. Mort ___ from Montreal
24. Attempted to persuade
26. Disk readers
29. Word with free
30. Actress Arden
33. Actress Ryan of *Beverly Hillbillies*
34. Soft drink competitor of Pepsi
35. Jewish month
36. PC alternatives
37. Board game enclosures
38. Associate of Mr. Applegate
39. Woodwind instrument
40. Horse's gait
41. Turns on the tears
42. Nine-digit ID
43. Ser. staters
44. Baseball great ___ Mack
45. Throw water on
47. College in New Rochelle
48. Burt Ward role
50. Small piano of epic size
55. With *The*, a 1976 horror film
56. Toyota model
57. Quarterback's trouble spot, usually
58. Cher movie
59. Golf shoe feature
60. Line-___ veto
61. Tolkien tree giants
62. Hold responsible
63. Pianist Peter___

DOWN

1. Parts of mins.
2. Invention of John Deere
3. Sheltered side at sea
4. Sounded reasonable
5. Liquor measures
6. TV's *Let's Make* ___
7. Kind of river dam
8. Island resort off Cape Cod
9. It has a funny nose
10. Captain Queeg's command
11. Bottom side up
12. Sugar source
13. L × W
21. Container's weight
22. FBI guy
25. Deer with three-pointed antlers
26. Prom night rentals
27. Graceful horses
28. Not quite tops
29. Flies alone
31. Frankie of the Four Seasons
32. Clean the chalkboard
34. Pitcher's specialty
35. *The In-Laws* star, 1979
37. Courses of travel: Abbrs.
41. Sound of a large bell
43. Compete in a meet
44. Road Runner's adversary
46. Porcine sounds
47. Skyscraper support
48. Setting for Rossellini's *Open City*
49. Yemen's neighbor
51. Out yachting
52. Poker pot builder
53. Poet's "at no time"
54. Audition platter short
56. Environmental hazard, for short

❖ Solution on page 284

Web of Intrigue   *Douglas Fink*

ACROSS

1. Cinema souvenirs
6. Doc bloc
9. *Jurassic Park* ore
14. Harmonic
15. It's not so pretty
16. Amscray!
17. Susan's Emmy role, finally
18. Start of school
19. Suitable for piercing
20. Part 1 of quote
23. Harry Potter's strength
24. Pro follower
28. Car option
29. Dick's Trueheart
33. Lacking ethics
35. Spanish stuff with rice
37. Part 2 of quote
38. Part 3 of quote
39. Nonetheless
41. She lies over the ocean
42. Musical symbol
43. Sculpture part
47. Lacking
48. One of the Fates
50. Part 4 of quote
57. Soul-ful TV role
58. Lend a hand
59. Tale-telling Mother
60. It's nothing to get excited about
61. Fore-man's need
62. Delivery-related
63. Confirm a sum
64. Blow it
65. Junkyard dog's action

DOWN

1. Stay in a funk
2. Spelling on TV
3. Troop group
4. Composer for Ahnold to be?
5. They're tossed
6. Current unit
7. Caballero's rattle
8. They're the tops
9. Mixture
10. Persian's peep
11. Hoggett's hog
12. Penultimate fairy tale word
13. *That '70s Show* role
21. Call in the army
22. Get ready
24. Tortoise or hare
25. Make ___ (act)
26. They have many pages
27. ___ you ashamed?
29. Swallows at sea
30. Catherine, in *The Mask of Zorro*
31. Executed
32. Fills the bill
34. Pack animal
36. In the past
40. Kevin's Oscar role
41. Doofus
44. Fancy
45. Less dreary
46. Puzzle shape suggesting the quote's source
48. Plant pest
49. Stop and yield
50. Symbol for Indiana Jones
51. Sicilian spouter
52. Type of missile
53. Consider it a ___
54. It's nothing much
55. Rigid ruler
56. Billy Idol title word
57. That girl

❖ **Solution on page 285**

Going Native *Lane Gutz*

ACROSS

1. Michael Douglas movie
5. Mad, to Juan
9. Plague, to Albert Camus
14. Wears out
16. Way to speak
17. Creeks
18. Break in the skin
19. Letters on an ambulance
20. Dramatic genre
22. Fixed by agreement
23. Tommie or James
24. Forest denizens
29. Adjusts a clock
33. Ali at birth
34. Cordillera Central's range
36. NOW goal
37. Fill the hold
38. Assiniboine allies
39. Roberts method of communication?
40. Santa ___
41. Melchizedek's land
42. Places to find pips
43. F-14 follower
45. L.A. DJ
48. Een, ein, un, y uno
50. Gives birth to
51. Productive person
56. Reason for poor driving perhaps?
59. Use a soapbox
60. Grand jeeps?
62. Bristles
63. Fire starters
64. Some farm workers
65. Show disrespect
66. Magistrate in Genoa

DOWN

1. "___ Together" (John Lennon)
2. Chromosome carrier
3. Dirty accumulation
4. Vessel on Ararat
5. Bandage
6. Resources of 34A
7. Average grades
8. Alternate passage
9. Caddoan speakers
10. Skips the ceremony
11. Type of train, according to Don Cornelius?
12. Subway choice
13. Belgian bicyclist Merckx
15. Sot
21. Gore's anagram
22. Hordeolum
24. Standing ovation
25. Plain, to Enrique
26. Palendromic title
27. 1930 Triple Crown winner Sande
28. Grinch's look
30. Like déjà vu
31. Extremely small amount
32. Quota for some
35. Bruce's ex
38. Supplement a soirée
39. In conflict, with "at"
41. Eastern Sioux
44. Belushi or Aykroyd in *The Blues Brothers*
46. Three or more pitches in unison
47. Composer Szymanowski
49. Siphons
51. British blackjack
52. Breyer's flavor
53. Morris of Boyz II Men
54. Plant of the mint family
55. Change for a twenty
56. Union general Jesse Lee
57. Safecracker
58. De bene ___
61. Sundance, for one

❖ **Solution on page 285**

Things Are Looking Up *Verna Suit*

ACROSS

1. Take on
7. Act doglike at dinner
10. Raised platform
14. Like pond surfaces
15. Poet's palindrome
16. *Educating* ___
17. Homemakers' get-together
20. Mont Blanc
21. ___ de cologne
22. Daiquiri ingredient
23. Short wrongdoer
26. Blacksburg, VA, school
28. Walk the floor
31. Experienced performers
33. It was nothing
35. Graphic opening
36. Loosen
38. "___ bin ein Berliner"
39. Crush, like grapes
42. Like many "collectibles"
44. Weave companion
45. Canine cry
47. It finds a way out
48. Pertaining to royal court
50. Two-family dwellings
53. Musician John ___
54. Cone type
55. Housing payment
56. Coal scuttle
58. Underdog's voicer
60. Patty H.'s kidnappers
62. Cadence count
68. Samoan seaport
69. Buckeyes school
70. Deliver comeuppance
71. Russian ruler
72. Disorderly hair
73. Actor Wesley ___

DOWN

1. Thin Man's pooch
2. Create *The Thinker*
3. Family gathering place
4. Ref cousin
5. Medoc Mrs.
6. Brontë governess
7. Sainte Anne de ___
8. Drop the ball
9. Walton patriarch
10. Soap operas
11. Lung filler
12. Addams cousin
13. Express with words
18. Goodbye gesture
19. Shari Lewis, e.g.
24. Study or den
25. Dog baby food
27. ___ Dinesen
29. Soul medicine
30. Every
32. Lodz resident
34. Kid's question
37. Perch beneath a pane
39. Incomplete schedule inits.
40. Disorderly defeat
41. Ancient times
43. Former duchy ___-Coburg
46. Make livelier, as a speech
49. Beatty-Hoffman movie
51. Unfortunate
52. Gospel healer, briefly
57. Sad fate
59. Generation
61. Zeus and Hera's son
62. " . . . too sexy for my ___ "
63. P.O. alternative
64. ___ Zadora
65. General who ate chicken
66. Velvet finish
67. *X-Files* overseer

❖ Solution on page 285

A Two-Step Program
Merle Baker

ACROSS

1. Adjusts
5. Reddi-___
8. All of us
13. It's worn out
15. John and Paul
16. Start of good advice
18. Mirthful countenance
19. Susan of *L.A. Law*
20. Answer back
21. Swiss peak
22. Scrap
23. Heston's org.
24. Kind of cat
26. Advice, part 2
30. Old Faithful emanation
31. With 22D, Sinatra hit
32. Role for Ingrid
33. Breathed new life into
37. German industrial area
40. Clean bus fuel: Abbr.
41. Come close
45. Advice, part 3
49. Tokyo, formerly
50. Popular vehicle, for short
51. Perpendicular to vert.
52. Mineo or Maglie
53. Swimmer Mark ___
55. City of Iran
56. Disorderly accumulation
57. End of the advice
60. Vinegary prefix
61. Movie buff
62. What a slacker might get
63. Catch sight of
64. Part of ROM

DOWN

1. Vivid red
2. Planetary orbit shape
3. Word with hall or house
4. RR depot
5. Informed about
6. Black
7. West Coast power supplier: Abbr.
8. Seem
9. *The Naked Maja* artist
10. Momentous
11. News agency
12. Old map initials
14. Electric or dynamic beginning
17. "Misty" composer Garner
18. Chatters
22. See 31A
23. Canadian prov.
25. Handheld device
27. Remain
28. Latin dance
29. Farther off the mark
34. Maladroit
35. Concerning
36. At any time
37. Ed.'s request
38. Et cetera
39. Family addition
42. Site of an important stone discovery
43. Struck together
44. Snaky swimmers
46. Surpass in cleverness
47. Vexatious, as a situation
48. French man
54. Greek letter
55. Clever remark
56. Ponder
57. Bran source
58. Place for prospective lts.
59. Canoe necessity

❖ **Solution on page 285**

Splitsville   *Norm Guggenbiller*

ACROSS

1. Lowlife
4. Sully
9. Former Browns QB Bernie ___
14. Whiz
15. Bewildered
16. ___ nous (confidential)
17. Mid-12th-century date
18. Cleansing powder
19. "Darn it!"
20. Rorschach inkblot, for one
23. Stuck, figuratively
24. Michener epic
25. Eye problem
26. Like some excuses
29. Portent
30. Paper size: Abbr.
33. Center
35. Work unit
36. Cool when the heat is on
39. State div.
41. "Are not!" reply
42. Soda
43. Seniors' gp.
45. Decor finisher
47. Humane org.
51. Downhill course
53. Loser
56. George Bush, once
59. Jung's inner self
60. Bête ___ (bane)
61. Chemical suffix
62. Cap feature
63. Santa ___, Calif.
64. Patty Hearst's captors, for short
65. Unable to sit still
66. "You've got mail" receiver
67. Nighttime, to a poet

DOWN

1. University grounds
2. Say "yes" to an offer
3. ___ Beach, Calif.
4. Small drum
5. Make amends
6. Neighbor of Jordan
7. Oscar-winner Patricia ___
8. Curbside call
9. Nairobi's nation
10. Type of punch
11. Flowed, as a river
12. More pretentious
13. Lying on the couch
21. Engraved pillar
22. Beat ___ (get away with)
27. "Bless you" preceder
28. Stooge name
31. Dam-building org.
32. Send back to a lower court
34. Tokyo, once
36. Songwriter
37. WWII troop carrier: Abbr.
38. ___ salts
39. Tapioca source
40. Conned
44. Special TV offers
46. Ethnic
48. Accolades
49. Lit light
50. Of a South American range
52. Consisting of a single element
54. Peter ___ of *Casablanca*
55. Daub
57. Peoples of Peru
58. ___ contendere (plea)

❖ **Solution on page 285**

Sticks and Stones   *Alan Olschwang*

❖ Solution on page 285

ACROSS

1. Steam bath
6. Makes a move
10. Nicholas or Alexander
14. Say
15. Mets' milieu
16. Sub
17. Auto alternative
19. Eye part
20. Sword section
21. Inventor Nikola ___
22. Cincinnati nine
23. Glacial period
25. Billfold filler
27. It's moss free
33. Put on
36. Goulash
37. Beret fillers
38. Willingly
40. City on the Mississippi
43. Power
44. Tablelands
46. Diva's solo
48. Witness
49. Hard-to-find animals
53. Ump's call
54. Chortle
58. In addition
61. Nimbi
64. Sound quality
65. Stadium selection
66. Sharpening device
68. Type of duck?
69. Alleviate
70. Lukewarm
71. Writer Bagnold
72. Dispatched Biblical style
73. Some votes

DOWN

1. Bar buy
2. Storage place
3. Functional
4. Delicious drink
5. Place of refuge
6. Tennis great
7. Letters from Patrai
8. Like an oily politician
9. Thai currency unit
10. Craved, in a way
11. See 12D
12. Desiccated
13. End of a Mamet play title
18. Stanley Kowalski's love
24. Sentimental drivel
26. East of Berlin
28. Abner's size
29. Jots
30. He had his ups and downs
31. Hawaiian state bird
32. Italian noble family
33. Supplicant's request
34. Middle management
35. Lucy's love
39. ___ in (took into account)
41. Galena or mispickel
42. Put in a cubbyhole
45. Go cross-country
47. Had a bite
50. Politicians' concerns
51. Kind of network
52. Small sofa
55. Hard court entertainment
56. Astronomer Jump Cannon
57. Lawn spoilers
58. Fit
59. Incline
60. Big rig
62. Face the day
63. Once again
67. Slop spot

The A List *Verna Suit*

ACROSS
1. Soaring
6. Subject to debate
10. Sex researcher Shere ___
14. Breathing anomaly
15. It's a real pain
16. Popular author
17. A-list photographer
19. Non-jock
20. Country Patsy
21. Magnifiers
23. Lung filler
25. A-list tennis player
28. Hybridized
30. British ref.
31. Clark's classic role
32. Daubs
35. British honorific
37. A-list Russian poet
42. Water ice
43. Arctic resident
45. Sprang
49. Collar
51. Lingerie item
52. A-list psychiatrist
56. Permit to
57. Journalist William ___
58. Like hawthorn leaves
60. Bridge part
61. A-list architect
66. "From where ___ . . ."
67. Crime fiction genre
68. Distance runner
69. Musket additions
70. Model Parker
71. Roof type

DOWN
1. Highway help org.
2. Hosp. staffer
3. In a movie
4. Have emotions
5. Actress Shire
6. Got along
7. Andes tuber
8. Resistance unit
9. One weber per square meter
10. ___ *and Her Sisters*
11. Existing in Latin
12. Where a rolling stone comes
13. Breaks up (with someone)
18. Late Landers
22. White herons
23. Pecs neighbors
24. "___ la Douce"
26. Lucy was one
27. Waxed cheese
29. Pacer Patch
33. Whitewater rider
34. ___ Mineo
36. West or Murray
38. Hawaii's ___ Coast
39. Briefly approves
40. Ballet dancer Edward ___
41. Pierre's girlfriend
44. Choose
45. Highland girl
46. Go by
47. Big do
48. Lithographs
50. Blurred
53. James and Jimmy
54. Misspell
55. Moves like a buffalo
59. Go boating
62. Rawls or Reed
63. Relative of i.e.
64. Hanoi holiday
65. Cinnabar, e.g.

❖ **Solution on page 285**

Initially the Same   *Douglas Fink*

ACROSS

1. Prevailing mood
6. Copy
10. Expansive
14. Where the girls are
15. Not excluded
16. Crow's-nest cry
17. Insider Broker
19. In the neighborhood
20. A bicycle built for two
21. Sch. org.
22. Pew's place
23. Dentist's discovery
25. Satan's realm
26. Support
30. Neither partner
31. Fight
32. Puts lotion on
34. Smite
39. Gloria Gaynor's verb
41. One way to write
42. Relying on observation
44. Like old bread
45. Society page word
46. Trail behind
48. Periods of time
49. Cinema receipts
52. For a special cause
54. Louise of *Gilligan's Island*
55. Get one's goat
56. Piggie protector
61. Red one?
62. Detective, Forensically
64. Put the kibosh on
65. Cognizant of
66. Tropical fruit
67. Its original occupants were kicked out
68. Brood
69. Lulus

DOWN

1. Voucher
2. Rock that rolls
3. Abadan's land
4. Darn
5. Put PR with GIs
6. Casino cube
7. Fix for fishing
8. Gumby's horse
9. "Orinoco Flow" singer
10. Vowel Whirler
11. In the future
12. Dry white wine
13. They'll roll you under "Max headroom" signs
18. A sign of things to come?
24. Trig. calc.
25. Boss and Lulu, on '80s TV
26. Diamond point
27. Grad
28. Ltd. in the U.S.
29. Kinematic Balance
31. Deplore
33. Horse fathers
35. Muslim's Almighty
36. A way up before going down
37. Actress Raines
38. Bakery goods
40. Go for the gold
43. Slightly hard
47. Asian desert
49. Martin who sang "King Tut"
50. In need of a nap
51. Get together
52. Do not exist
53. Jerry's TV pal
55. Words at weddings
57. The face ___ angel
58. Melody
59. MIT grad
60. Some are inflated
63. This instant

❖ **Solution on page 285**

Creature Features   *Grace Becker*

ACROSS
1. Entrance feature
5. Marina sights
10. Producer's nightmare
14. Turgenev's birthplace
15. On the ball
16. Get up
17. Carrie Fisher role
18. Gunpowder ingredient
19. "With the greatest of ___"
20. Weismuller film
23. Scottish uncle
24. Hot tub locale
25. "Air Music" composer
30. Traps
35. Movie starring Will Smith
36. Movie star, for one
38. Strip of shoe leather
39. Paul Hogan movie
43. Jaffe or Barrett
44. Revoke, as a legacy
45. "____ Stand By My Woman Man"
46. Kind of lace
49. Excellent
51. ____ Angeles
53. Alias letters
54. Oscar winner for Katharine Hepburn
63. Mischievous one
64. Top of a form to be filled out
65. Health food
66. Atmosphere
67. Garden tool
68. Tolkien creatures
69. NFL players
70. Big name in tractors
71. Meth.

DOWN
1. Jar
2. Kind of code
3. Golda___
4. Team jacket
5. Mild-___ (Clark Kent's style)
6. Came down to earth
7. Green of the movies
8. Green giants
9. Sandal parts
10. Liberate
11. ___ Neeson, actor
12. Peak in Greece
13. Hammer end
21. Citgo competitor
22. Rave's opposite
25. Mother-of-pearl
26. Youngest of the Jetsons
27. Moon of Saturn
28. ___ Kazan, director
29. Pinochle combos
31. Bristlelike appendage on plants
32. Corrected a mistake
33. Fragrant resin
34. Place
37. Warning signal
40. Baseball's Ripken
41. The Blue Hen state
42. Miyoshi ___, Oscar winner in *Sayonara*
47. "___'s Coming" (Three Dog Night)
48. Drove (around)
50. Edict site in France
52. Subtly nasty
54. Word with fly or mouse
55. Happy___
56. Continental currency
57. Meadows
58. Little Sheba creator
59. At no time, to bards
60. Theatrical award
61. Shorebound newts
62. Corrode from disuse

❖ **Solution on page 285**

Enterprising Personalities   *Douglas Fink*

ACROSS

1. Melancholy
5. Finger throw option
9. Prayer places
14. Former attorney general
15. Flat end of a certain tool
16. Be
17. Dedicated
18. Mah-jongg piece
19. Bay for the Buccaneers
20. Cause for a delay
22. Happiness
24. Chow follower
25. Perfectly logical baby doctor
28. Over or ever
31. Zilch
32. "Nevermore" quoter
33. Commanding actor
40. Border lake
42. It needs volume control
43. Perfectly logical
44. Navigational yeoman
49. Grissom who wasn't gloomy
50. It's between roses, for Shakespeare
51. Like some occasions, or when they might be
53. Engineering coach
59. Yiddish spot for a yarmulke
60. Banner ad, perhaps
61. Like a yenta
65. It's not to be taken literally
67. Lettuce option
69. Tiny amount
70. Biblical gift
71. At any time?
72. Shift
73. Printer's device
74. Flu fighters
75. Knitted

DOWN

1. About 15 grains
2. An avenger of Dinah
3. O/S that's a fan of Korn?
4. Curriculum unit
5. Select
6. Stoop
7. Perry's aide
8. Curl the lip
9. Lay it on the line
10. They're for display
11. Copy
12. Molded jelly
13. ___ to high heaven
21. Bonus
23. Best of show
26. Kobe robe closer
27. ___ City (popular computer game)
28. Impersonator
29. Dumb gal on *Match Game*
30. It goes to the heart
34. Darling of diamonds
35. Green parrot
36. CM / II
37. Prego rival
38. It's a burden
39. Worm destination
41. First printings, for instance
45. CO clock setting
46. Coral reefs
47. Escape
48. Kublai Khan dynasty
52. Banded rock that sounds good?
53. Cut on the cost
54. Closet filler
55. Be a blogger, perhaps
56. Toylanders
57. Spinach eater's go-with
58. *Wings* actor
62. Arose
63. Be in a snit
64. Emulate a cavern
66. More, por favor
68. Car front protector

❖ **Solution on page 286**

B-Minus *Adrian Powell*

ACROSS

1. Panhandles
5. Wax-covered cheese
9. On the trail of
14. Brainwave
15. Unless, in law
16. Fret
17. Insect in a hurry (one's best shirt)?
20. Eight-based
21. Adam's oldest
22. Driving aids
23. Sound system
25. Moray and electric
27. Bug elder (prized jewelry)?
33. Candidate's cash cow
36. Hokkaido native
37. Cleanser commercial word
38. Turkish leader
40. Haughty response
43. It'll do, once
44. Stagecoach controls
46. Settled the bill
48. Former country music channel
49. Peruse then orate (simple meal)?
53. Serengeti hair-raiser
54. North Pole vehicle?
58. Choral range
61. Quarter acre
64. ___ firma
65. Social services con job (poor earnings group)?
68. Leonine group
69. Bathroom scent
70. Goddess of youth
71. Intuition
72. Underworld river
73. Lyric poems

DOWN

1. Types of ballpoint pen
2. Extracted chemical
3. Beau ___
4. Tuareg region
5. Draw to a close
6. Spinal shock absorber
7. Tibet's locale
8. Environment
9. Cobbler's tool
10. Hiker's complaint
11. Steadfast
12. Language of the glens
13. Bakery choices
18. Spanish princess
19. Leg joint
24. Elevator man
26. Step up from med.
28. Rustic lodging
29. Inca calculator
30. Isn't doing badly
31. Hot to trot cry
32. Cut
33. Salmon spawn
34. *Go Hang a Salami! I'm a Lasagna Hog!* author
35. Pet seen on TV?
39. Futuristic robots
41. Jack Sprat's enemy
42. Is the right size
45. ___ Paulo
47. Mississippi feature
50. Drug cop
51. Gives in to gravity
52. Bounce back again, and again . . .
55. Ticked off
56. Loon cousin
57. Abhors
58. *Sound of Music* locale
59. Folktale
60. Castor, to Pollux
62. Miss out
63. Disavow
66. Born as
67. Harrison of *My Fair Lady*

❖ **Solution on page 286**

Animal Behavior *Adrian Powell*

ACROSS

1. Yoko ___
4. Dead heat
8. Monastic jurisdiction
14. Make smaller
16. Good point!
17. Very distressing events
18. Long-vowel mark
19. Friends from Italy
20. Security Council bigwig
22. Twists
23. Gloomy
24. Say repeatedly
26. Wrap
28. Profound
32. The best of times
35. GMT minus five
36. Use the Remington
37. One kind of angle
38. Keats specialty
39. Role for Valentino (1921)
40. Iranian leader, once
41. Tussle
42. Penetrate
43. Sharpen
44. Most vinegary
46. One who ascribes
48. Bring in the sheaves
52. Artist's plaster
55. Biodegrade
56. French woman
57. Lives
59. Bankrolls
61. 17th-century dance
62. Episode
63. Cold, ruthless
64. Mountain pond
65. Possesses feature

DOWN

1. Group of eight
2. Bellini opera
3. Recording studio sign
4. *G.I. Jane* star Moore
5. Gene material, briefly
6. Perceptive
7. Evaded an obligation
8. Bill outlet
9. Blow one's own horn
10. Went against the grain
11. 4,840 square yards
12. Chuck wagon grub
13. Distinctive desires
15. Avoided a direct answer
21. Got out of bed
24. Wall climber
25. Suitable
27. Not in Scotland
29. Peeping Tom, maybe
30. Lengthy movie
31. Short Chinese canine
32. Gridiron mark
33. Sonic bounce
34. Beijing dough
38. Bouquet to a Brit
39. Lisa, to Bart
41. North African reptile
42. For each
45. Eye receptor surface
47. Two-star stopover, maybe
49. Event host
50. Grace periods
51. Irritating insects
52. Garnet and peridot
53. Theater sign
54. Triangle ratio
56. Gladly
58. Hog heaven
60. Cash register co.

❖ **Solution on page 286**

Either Way   Alan Olschwang

ACROSS

1. Land buy
5. Tend tom
10. Family friend
14. Son of Noah
15. Goad
16. Gumbo ingredient
17. Ms. Turner
18. Wakes up
20. Augury
21. Bambi's aunt
22. ___ off
23. Goody bag kin
27. Hardy heroine
28. Breakfast companion
29. Chinese philosophy
32. Icy
35. Stuffed
37. A Ladd
38. Hotel's offering
40. Sort of estate
41. Hyping
43. Care for
44. Downcast
45. Khan of Pakistan
46. Middle time?
48. Rioter getting a better break-in device
53. Harden
56. Classic auto
57. Fair
58. Places to arrive at and sharpen
61. First to round the Cape of Good Hope
62. West Valley's state
63. Elève's place
64. Like some hands
65. Apothecary measure
66. Nimbi
67. Headland

DOWN

1. Fur trader John Jacob
2. Set of bells
3. Get a new *Life*
4. Giving off
5. Great apes and men
6. Changes the law
7. Asparagus unit
8. ___ Aviv
9. Ernie ___ of the PGA
10. Grinding tooth
11. Island accompaniment
12. Baobab
13. Bugle song
19. Germs
24. Embarrassed
25. Neighbor
26. Existed
29. Stadium section
30. Literary collections
31. Leer
32. Apertures
33. Scat queen
34. Panegyrize
35. 1988 Tom Hanks flick
36. Bet on
38. Farm outbuilding
39. College credit
42. Brits' jails
43. Born as
46. Small interstice
47. Searches blindly
48. River of forgetfulness
49. Part of the old ballgame
50. Binary compound
51. Gemstones from Down Under
52. Finishes fourth
53. Cry before throwing a ball high
54. Baum dog
55. Important times
59. One of the magnificent seven?
60. Fort Worth inst.

❖ **Solution on page 286**

Leapers   *Douglas Fink*

ACROSS

1. Cake mate
4. Secret supply
9. Following
14. Rotary disk
15. Gardening products name
16. Bordeaux brother
17. SWS reversed
18. Ryan of the mound
19. Put on cargo
20. *American Idol* judge, born 2/29/56
23. ___ one's time
24. Seek guidance
25. Trees in Hershey Park?
29. Hopper
31. It's nothing much
32. Groaner
33. Meal before a race
36. Sage
38. Diva ditty
39. *General Hospital* actor, born 2/29/72
42. Bleacher feature
43. Good Xmastime name?
44. Melodic
45. Ballet pointer
46. BBQ holder
47. Each
48. Like some hotel pools
50. Miss Piggy's question
52. Bridge position
56. *Crime Story* actor, born 2/29/44
59. A Hawaiian of Japanese parents, for one
62. Enlighten
63. Collection
64. Home of the All-American Soap Box Derby
65. Fred's dancing sister
66. "Fever" singer
67. Living entity
68. Viking sendoffs
69. Slip up

DOWN

1. Bitter
2. Porch for poi?
3. Correct
4. Walkman maker
5. Horse of holding
6. Book of maps
7. Crude domicile
8. Felix Unger's sound
9. In the black
10. French bread, once
11. WJM news anchor
12. Prior to
13. *That '70s Show* patriarch
21. Micawber, for one
22. Do dish work
26. What to wear when doing dish work
27. Board for beyond
28. Flub a fishing line
30. Actor McKellan
31. Like some medicine
33. Page of song
34. It's very negative
35. Mrs. Peel's partner
36. Proceed
37. Take advantage of
38. Fan
40. Do grounds work?
41. Downed
46. Aviation company
47. Balderdash!
49. Music hall
50. Future ensign
51. Willow
53. Aviation seat option
54. Rude reaction
55. Starchy vittle
57. Tide type
58. Votes in favor
59. Capture
60. *South Park* baby brother
61. Hindu honorific

❖ **Solution on page 286**

Chapter 13

I Loved Theme Once; I'll Love No More

Bad TV *Merle Baker*

❖ **Solution on page 286**

Family Tree *Adrian Powell*

ACROSS

1. Palatable
6. Chicken piece
10. Soft splash
14. Senseless
15. ___ fixe
16. Ready for picking
17. Metric heavyweight
18. Actor Connery
19. Forewarning
20. Leader of the trees?
23. Kind of admiral
24. Change in Madrid
25. Bringer of legal action
27. Nothing at all
28. Crow sound
31. Comedic couple in the forest? (with 37A, 42A)
34. Divide in two
36. Bests Snidely Whiplash
37. See 31A
39. Stonecrop plant
40. Oust from the database
42. See 31A
44. It's subjective
45. Genetic compound
47. Problem for old autos
48. Like a snake
50. Mischievous children
54. Pledge from a healing tree?
57. Greek sandwich
58. Cereal container
59. Flora and fauna
60. Cecil B. DeMille production
61. Wicked
62. Floridian key
63. Netting
64. Turn down flat
65. Ogle

DOWN

1. Ravi Shankar's instrument
2. Iguana relative
3. Endangered animal
4. Shoe insert
5. Wapiti, for one
6. Ornamental vine
7. Thoughts
8. Make shipshape
9. Inherited type of code
10. Grad rituals
11. Peruvian center
12. Ready for business
13. Animal enclosure
21. Went like a bullet
22. Becomes sickly yellow looking
26. Release the seat belt
28. Mafia chief
29. Ardent
30. Small cyst
31. South African with roots in Holland
32. Pleasant pitch
33. Terminate
35. Writer for *Playboy*?
36. *21 CFR Part II* authors
38. Toward the back
41. Dressed like a judge
43. Wind spike
46. Wall niche
48. Geological age
49. Field marshal Rommel
51. Dough, colloquially
52. Mater's mate
53. Do like Stojko
54. Promote unashamedly
55. Marsh bloom
56. Sacred bird to the pharaohs
57. Sapphire, for example

❖ **Solution on page 286**

Similar Endings *Douglas Fink*

ACROSS

1. Make a selection
4. Kevin Smith film
9. Cheese alternative
14. Cattle call
15. Its sign-off is "Out"!
16. Lovebird
17. Swiss summit
18. Hit film musical
20. Aristide's former domain
22. Injury
23. Enigmas
25. They're not original
29. A famous Marx, unrelated to Groucho
31. Italian port and WWII battle site
32. Said yes to
36. Abby's twin
37. *Queer Eye* teasing request
42. Fall behind
43. Slender cigar that sounds like a comedy duo
44. They make you happy
49. Put under
50. Like a wasteland
52. Like some tomatoes
56. *Friends* role
58. *Awakenings* drug
59. It goes downhill fast
63. Opie's portrayer
64. *Taxi* boss
65. Word signifying purity
66. One-time threat to the bald eagle
67. DEA target
68. Wild guesses
69. I told you so!

DOWN

1. Mutual of ___
2. Like the ends of the earth
3. It's to be discussed
4. Like an alpha male
5. Her band was plastic
6. Early France with a chutzpah sound?
7. Certain runner
8. Comes up
9. Official document of old
10. Mass wedding participant
11. Lending letters
12. Trip part
13. Long leader
19. Thatch
21. Apprehended
24. Fancy-shmancy
26. Fad
27. Make void
28. First name in skating
30. Astral cat
32. Didn't do so well
33. Wetlands region
34. Palindromic stories
35. Not an orig.
38. Slot filler
39. It's hard to bear
40. Tiny bakery items
41. Like an ill eye
45. Baseball's Agee
46. One who leaves to unite
47. Rajah's wife
48. Little pig building material
51. Panache
53. Cruciverbalist's love
54. A nice thing to say
55. *Gremlins* director
57. Certain something
59. Past one's prime
60. John, to Ringo
61. Uh-huh
62. It's a gift

❖ **Solution on page 286**

X Appeal *Douglas Fink*

ACROSS

1. Sub
5. Hello or goodbye
10. TV Superman portrayer
14. Norwegian patron saint
15. Bathroom fixture
16. Story starter
17. Harold Lloyd prequel?
19. Flaky material?
20. Gives responsibility for
21. Adapt
23. *Desire Under the ___*
24. It's known for its zoo and cheer
25. Secret organizations
28. More than threatens
31. Came up
32. Royal Asian woman
33. Put away
34. Alluring
35. The root of all evil
36. But
37. ___ port in a storm
38. Type of check
39. Sandal part
40. Elder's attribute
42. Lab sample items
43. Dub over, perhaps
44. Close
45. Officially recognize
47. Payback mission
51. Stickers
52. "I need to give the dinosaur back his card game"
54. Rim
55. Royal one, or a measure
56. Prepare for takeoff
57. They hold you over the blades
58. Database unit
59. Votes

DOWN

1. Egg contents
2. Spunk
3. Whitewater craft
4. Egg order
5. Vast chasms
6. Dryer collections
7. Nice things to say
8. A not-so-nice thing to say
9. Court professional
10. Trig ratio
11. What Jerry Stiller did a-courtin'?
12. Revered one
13. Former Mr. Speaker
18. Sheer fabric
22. Harassed
24. Prepared fish
25. Hombre homes
26. Spectacle site
27. *Seinfeld* star needs to hit the gym?
28. Astute
29. Military marine
30. Procedures
32. 66, for one
35. It's the humidity
36. Sharp dagger or heel
38. Read into a fax
39. Lamp accessory
41. Comes up
42. Need
44. Passover event
45. Go along with
46. Art form, often
47. It's shocking
48. Varmint's yap
49. Proofreader's printout
50. ___ of Evil
53. Person of habit

❖ **Solution on page 286**

Allentown   *Douglas Fink*

ACROSS

1. Come off of
5. Florentine cathedral
10. Dose, often
14. Give up
15. Early anesthetic
16. Hodgepodge
17. Woody Allen film of 2002
20. Be outstanding
21. CEO or CFO
22. Ode pro
23. Singer Cruz
25. Providence sch.
26. Woody Allen film of 1995
33. Arctic dweller
34. Game with an it
35. Turk's title
36. Nine-digit ID
37. 911 service
40. Coffee break hour
42. Actress Tyler or Ullmann
43. Tot's wordless requests
45. Alias initials
47. Show remorse
49. Woody Allen film of 2000
53. As of ___
54. Fencing maneuver
55. Mountain lakes
58. Baby food or comment
59. J. Low gp.
62. Woody Allen film of 1999
67. Part of NEA
68. White sale item
69. Part of QED
70. Bakery loaves
71. Shoes or apartments
72. Back of a car?

DOWN

1. It talks back
2. Cat call
3. Being lax
4. Business card abbr.
5. Like a sleepy-eyed one
6. Paradise
7. "So that's it!"
8. Vacation club?
9. It's in pretty rough form
10. Olla ___
11. They stand on knees
12. Schmutz on a shirt
13. It stands for something
18. Actress Mimieux
19. First name in orchid-growing detectives
23. Frat X
24. Clever
25. Sudden whim
26. *The ___ of Avalon*
27. Putting it all together
28. Din preceder
29. Doffed item
30. Blockhouse?
31. Use your mind
32. Icicle sites
38. He plays Joey on *Friends*
39. Hit the slopes
41. Slim
44. Cunning
46. Box by the mosh pit
48. Plaything
50. ___ we forget . . .
51. Li'l national symbol
52. Warbles
55. Romanov ruler
56. Not according to plan
57. Natural network
59. Popular vote getter of 2000
60. Ugly duckling, later
61. Highest-grossing film that featured Woody Allen
63. TV E.T.
64. Zip
65. CSI evidence
66. Society gal

❖ **Solution on page 287**

Characters in a Series   *Douglas Fink*

ACROSS

1. State of dread
6. *Dracula* role
10. Dances like Cyndi Lauper?
14. Dance where a foot pivots
15. Image
16. Author Ludwig
17. Spousal relative
18. It's a gas
19. Later!
20. *Designing Women* actress
22. In a bit
23. Makeshift bed
24. Making the sidewalk safe, perhaps
26. Mini-hahas
31. Grant or Marvin of film
32. Title word in a song by Tevye
33. Famous cookie man
35. Test
39. Exhausted
41. Mountaineer's challenge
42. Ward
43. Point a finger at
44. High time
46. Finger-throw call
47. Camp asst.
49. Coffee shop supply
51. Minor flaws
55. IRS expert
56. Beatle place of song
57. Leader types, stereotypically
63. French Sudan, today
64. Barbershop item
65. Winter getaway city
66. Scraped by
67. They may have you over a barrel
68. Dickens's Drood
69. Angel food?
70. Ship wood
71. Used car price reducers

DOWN

1. Like a desert
2. Above quantity?
3. Chutzpah
4. Shoo
5. Glove-slap sound
6. Colonist posse member
7. Bakery employee
8. Secretive places
9. Toughen
10. Software release determiner
11. Muscat man
12. Climber's tool
13. Jargon
21. Gaucho's weapon
25. Fields
26. Sideways walker
27. Dune or butte
28. Abdul-Jabbar's alma mater
29. *Boston Public* actor
30. Times in the limelight
34. Take a random sample
36. Word-processing key
37. Swear
38. Desires
40. He's known for moonwalking
45. Palm drink
48. Tempest spot?
50. Hit
51. Got really sore
52. 1970 World's Fair site
53. Out-of-the-way place
54. Downhill skier's domain
58. Appeal
59. Gal Friday
60. Croquet place
61. Send off
62. They're not nice

❖ **Solution on page 287**

Street Performers *Douglas Fink*

ACROSS

1. Wallop
6. Wiggler on the roof
10. One-third of a WWII movie
14. Winter drink
15. Bowie beau
16. This is only a test
17. Neighborhoods
18. Big rig
19. First name in pants
20. Places for pigeons?
22. Angry, accused dry cleaner's complaint?
23. Doc bloc
24. Buffy and others
26. Sidewalk throw
31. 911 responder
32. *Peter and the Wolf* duck
33. *Airplane!* star
35. Grunge shirt design
39. Spinning sound
40. Made public
42. Machu Picchu resident
43. Make foot noise
45. Art ___
46. R.A.'s neighbor
47. Grampa's namesake
49. They help tide you over
51. Disney's Dwarves and others
55. Elected ones
56. Like those in a nave
57. Red preacherman?
63. Blog author, for one
64. Pie in the sky?
65. A nephew of Donald Duck
66. Early physics?
67. Sicilian spiller
68. Desert sustenance
69. Meat loaf portion
70. Lentil dish
71. Carpet choices

DOWN

1. Someone who crossed a line
2. Unsatiated one's plea
3. Court pro
4. Painting layer
5. Starchy sides
6. Panel for Perot
7. "Rag Mop" brothers
8. Donny and Marie
9. Treat like Napoleon
10. Thin 69A, like a triangle?
11. Type of daisy
12. Verbose fan
13. Wrong
21. Mutual of ___
25. Band aid
26. Takes away
27. Life sentence?
28. Mr. Dither's bane
29. Green grouch?
30. Lorry wheels
34. Parlor piece
36. Shortly
37. Like some tea
38. *My Two* ___
41. Up to
44. Chart type
48. Calculated, old-style
50. Biblical book
51. *The ___ of Beverly Hills*
52. Stand for art
53. Ste. art
54. Two- or three-toed animal
58. Bette title role
59. Couples cruise director?
60. Large fish
61. Bathtub woe
62. Parliament pro votes

❖ **Solution on page 287**

Alphabet Run *Adrian Powell*

ACROSS

1. Throat problem
5. Team cheer
11. Blacktop material
14. Lhasa holy man
15. Evil reputation
16. Street in Montreal
17. Like a comfortable old armchair
19. Packers' lineman
20. All out of clothespins
21. Blows one's top
23. Escargot
24. Sedimentary layers
26. Illusionist's forte
31. Bar balance
34. No longer fresh
35. *Sesame Street* muppet
36. Surrounded by
38. Mea ___
40. Takes home
41. Artist's headgear
43. Pork cuts
45. Bashes
46. Actor's backups
49. Turkey piece
50. Clock sound
54. Cornflakes, for example
56. Common bed resident
58. Wood sorrel
59. Cufflinks kin
62. Sorority letter
63. High school outcasts
64. Egg on
65. Huge amount
66. Tolerate
67. Prepare potatoes

DOWN

1. Disasters at the box office
2. Sacred Indian bird
3. Last letter, to Plato
4. Vampire deterrent
5. Yankees' hope
6. Burden
7. Wide of the mark
8. WWII fliers
9. Mideast rulers: Var.
10. Add water
11. Bored a shaft
12. Rhody of song
13. Carmine and scarlet
18. Auctions off
22. 180-degree reversal
24. Liquidate
25. Fearful
27. Yadda, yadda, yadda . . .
28. Gymnastic events
29. Old Slavic dictator
30. Cong. mtg.
31. Prohibited: Var.
32. Hymn finale
33. Knucklehead
37. Farm implement pioneer
39. Groove-billed bird
42. Molasses
44. Splinter groups
47. Western bar
48. Hush!
51. Accustom
52. Gnatlike insect
53. Stand for an oil
54. Eastern adherent
55. Canyon comeback
56. Henry VIII's sixth
57. Highland tongue
60. Psychedelic drug
61. Bucharest coin

❖ **Solution on page 287**

My Italian Restaurant   *Douglas Fink*

ACROSS

1. Cut down
4. Tribal healer
10. Rani garb
14. Parisian pal
15. Make void
16. It's usually a claw or ball
17. Italian cheese
19. Muse's specialty
20. Cuts often grilled
21. Tongue getter?
22. You put the ox before it
23. Smattering
24. Palindromic hit by a palindromic band
25. Thick hairs
26. Holiday preceders
27. It uses 17A and 51A
29. What acid turns litmus
30. Jack Horner's find
31. Approached
32. Hobo's hop
33. Off yonder
34. Positive tick
37. Bill filler
38. Something to shoot for
41. It often uses 17A
43. Boat threatener
44. Tea dippers
45. Catch ya later
46. Heaves
47. Follow furtively
48. "___ the ramparts . . . "
49. If in trouble, you might be under it
50. Spots you might not want to air
51. Italian meat
53. Informal wear
54. Charlize, in *Monster*
55. Feather companion
56. Husking bee supply
57. Least ill
58. Before

DOWN

1. Pet amid wood shavings
2. Playing the ham
3. Showing one's age
4. Adder, for one
5. Towel word
6. Mature
7. X preceder
8. Finally!
9. Adjective at the bar
10. It's long on a keyboard
11. Fish tank bubbler
12. Step advice to the lost
13. Alternately
18. Turns sharply
24. First king of Israel
25. Agent's action verb
27. Arm or stone holder
28. Kind of red or structure
30. Where they always had, in *Casablanca*
32. Unlike a "Baby Got Back" honoree
33. Topnotch
34. Northern
35. Generic soother
36. Skill set teacher
37. CFO concern
38. Artist's aid
39. Among the elite
40. Fix furniture
42. European peninsula
43. Business equivalent of a 4A
46. Word processor key
48. Colorful fish
49. High or low cards
52. I told ya so!

❖ **Solution on page 287**

SOB!!!   *Merle Baker*

ACROSS

1. Superior, perhaps
6. Cognac rating
10. Nephrite
14. Dog
15. With 66A, Neil Diamond song
16. Dumb ___ (birdbrains)
17. Philosophy
20. Salad green
21. Ham option
22. Easy pace
23. Slangy assent
25. Friend of Fidel
28. Costs
34. Break in two
36. McCain, for one
37. Cuzco builder
38. Parceled
40. Flirtatious stare
41. Advice
43. Canyon of the comics
44. It might be cured
47. Buttons on screen
48. Chess pieces: Abbr.
49. Eat like ___
51. Hot drink
55. *Bikini Beach* action
59. Guide in the sky
62. Gyro bread
63. Capacity
64. Piano piece
65. Defraud
66. See 15A
67. Circus performer

DOWN

1. Nave neighbor
2. *The ___ in the Band*
3. Anjou cousin
4. Having eight pins
5. Bette Midler movie
6. It may be African
7. Ump's call
8. David Stockman headed it: Abbr.
9. Pizzeria order
10. Unite
11. One doing the firing
12. Challenge
13. To be: Latin
18. Wear a long face
19. LPGA Hall of Famer Nancy
23. Olden days
24. Geraint's wife
25. Casino purchase
26. SE Asian capital
27. Legendary Spaniard
29. Zesty dip
30. Kind of camp
31. Tee off
32. Have a cow
33. Weak or knock follower
35. Barn topper
38. Skillful
39. Peepers, poetically
42. Godzilla target
43. Coined word
45. Hauled
46. Brilliant fish
50. She played Ninotchka
51. Baker's meas.
52. Hearing related
53. Facts and figures
54. Apothecary's weight
55. Place for hams?
56. Buzzing
57. Give up
58. Part of EMT: Abbr.
60. Greenspan's org.
61. Jungle squeezer

❖ **Solution on page 287**

Jewish Conversion *Douglas Fink*

ACROSS

1. Picked up on
7. Fable fellow
11. Tire letters
14. Omnivore's melange with rice
15. From the beginning
16. Make a selection
17. Teen singer after turning Jewish?
19. *Malcolm X* director
20. Night light
21. Chinese "path"
22. Address for a lady
23. Comedian/game show host after turning Jewish?
28. Bird unbeloved in a Tom Lehrer song
31. Analagous
32. Quite tart
33. One assigned
38. Coal unit
39. Like a séance
40. On a loose leash
41. Like Abscammers
44. Lambchop's Lewis
46. Reduce a sentence?
47. Afternoon social need
48. Puzzle master after turning Jewish?
53. In a casual way
54. Zamboni target
55. "Arise" or "befall"
59. *Titanic* actor, casually
60. Action star after turning Jewish?
64. Isle
65. Moolah
66. One of the Borgias
67. Cliched
68. Eye or camera part
69. Vehemence

DOWN

1. Bridge part
2. Overhang
3. First name in Rex Stout detection
4. A Biblical David, for one
5. House addition
6. Bond portrayer
7. Mayhem
8. Singer DiFranco
9. Toon dog who sounds like Peter Lorre
10. She in a lea
11. Diametrically opposed
12. Say something
13. List filler
18. French quencher
22. American educator Horace ___
24. Apropos name for a thief
25. Fan of this puzzle theme?
26. *Grapes of Wrath* extra
27. Russian fighter
28. Head or liver
29. Clickable thingie
30. Lady's man
33. You need two eyes to judge it
34. Afore
35. Overdramatic pine
36. Shipping container weight
37. Highway sign
39. It's a long story
42. Trust
43. Spots
44. Establish
45. Least clear
47. Deep furrow
48. "Over and out" preceder
49. Perfect
50. *Taxi* actor
51. Henry VIII had six
52. Sleeve filler?
56. Petri dish filler
57. The old grey one ain't what she used to be
58. Ran
60. Stick in the snow
61. La Brea attraction
62. Yalie
63. Two lanterns indicated it

❖ **Solution on page 287**

Catch Some Zs   *Douglas Fink*

ACROSS

1. Old instrument with an individual name
6. Sermon deliverance spot
11. Exercise gait
14. Siberian forest
15. Shower sponge
16. "Caught in the act!"
17. Pawns, for example
18. The Feast of Lots
19. Speed
20. Italian actress with extra cheese?
22. Actress Caldwell
23. Eye woe
24. Sidewalk woe
25. Current event?
27. Grind
29. Senator Specter
32. Beach cover-up
36. Initial X in a game?
38. Flying leader
39. Bitter
41. They're not easy to deal with
43. Tailor's concern
44. Vent
46. Veinlike
47. Choppers
49. Norton's workplace
51. It's a lovely place
53. Not opposed
54. Top quality
58. Termination
60. Bearded comedian
63. She's new
64. We, perhaps
65. Best
66. CPA suggestion
67. It may have attachments
68. Mountain nymph
69. Garment
70. Like a toy piano in sound
71. Cruciverbalist Reagle

DOWN

1. The local has many
2. Inferred
3. Glamorous
4. Staring
5. Arp art
6. Kind of wool
7. Least quiet
8. Corrida cry
9. Blazing
10. *Hot Shots!* lead
11. Host who began with Branford Marsalis
12. Antioch's state
13. Hang open
21. Bright annual
26. Empty
27. Yenta's gift
28. Kool-Aid alternative
30. Lots of work
31. Cyrano standout
32. Hombre's house
33. Leary dropped it
34. Sack with a hat?
35. Cornered, in a way
37. 48D
40. USSR successor
42. Each
45. Song part
48. 37D
50. Like a mammoth
52. Judd of music
54. Clear-sky hue
55. Playful mammal
56. Having a center
57. Lyric poem
58. What I do as I write this
59. Fiery fiddler
61. TV's Stiles
62. Show whose ZIP was 02134, not 90210

❖ **Solution on page 287**

Cereal Connection   *Douglas Fink*

ACROSS

1. Go against
7. It helps you water your bed
11. Mensa measures
14. Astral body
15. Ferry passenger
16. Sideline signal
17. Respond to the drill sergeant
20. Coarse
21. Cuts in two
22. Gloss
24. Doctor's specialty?
26. Nautical adverb
27. Corral critter
28. Turkish tribe
29. Blog editors
30. Patronize the patisserie
31. Stable parent
32. London libation
33. A form of antiquing
39. Half of all things
40. Eleanor Roosevelt's first name
41. Happy baby sound
42. Union onuses
45. Social org. on campus
46. ___ *It Like Beckham*
47. Hoo-ha
48. Active one
49. *Concentration* puzzle
50. Sour
52. Rub the wrong way
54. Hit song by Men Without Hats
58. Car collection
59. Fruit known by its appearance
60. Went together
61. Small dashes
62. Ballerina's strong points
63. Like car radio buttons

DOWN

1. Where those in charge are
2. Groaner
3. It goes with a baby
4. Fish-eating hawk
5. Last word in a Dana Carvey question
6. Love expert
7. Rack hanger
8. Best on eBay
9. Host who'd compete for $5,000
10. More than you want to wait
11. Eaves dropper?
12. Poe's raven, for one
13. Detects
18. Put at ease
19. Four o'clock service
22. Blueprint detail
23. Frost
25. Get ready
28. One known for firing
29. Longest armbone
31. Downhill runners
32. Isn't bad
34. The Terminator, for one
35. Renegade leader
36. They go with the floe
37. Bourgeoisie
38. *The ___ Must Be Crazy*
42. Attach
43. Change container
44. Artisans
45. Sleep spot on a ship
46. Hitherto
48. Don ___ (Zorro)
49. More scraped up
51. Boxing match
53. Rope fiber
55. *Angela's Ashes* sequel
56. *Crouching Tiger, Hidden Dragon* director
57. Topic of *Silent Spring*

❖ **Solution on page 287**

Metal Heavy *Lane Gutz*

ACROSS

1. Eastern nurse
5. After penultimate
9. Tipped the bottle
14. Hayloft block
15. Lilaceae family member
16. X marks the spot, often
17. Traveling by ocean liner
18. Ring a bell
19. Nary a soul
20. Metallic area?
23. Formerly known as
24. Will word
25. ___ tone
27. Marino or Gable
28. Music makers
31. URL extension
34. Mexican shawl
36. Word before 51
37. Junction rectifier
39. Sammy Davis Jr. had one
40. Misuse of matches
41. Clay pot
42. Gathered
44. European co.
45. Colorful bird
47. Kool-___
49. Ugh predecessor, often
50. Indication of ironing
54. Retrospectively
56. Metallic bathroom?
58. Pillages
60. Write data
61. Kind of advice
62. Anthem, church style
63. Protection: Var.
64. Civil rights activist Baker
65. Trees you might find bats in
66. Type of sediment
67. Garden vegetable

DOWN

1. You can count on these
2. Layer of stone
3. A, to a Hebrew
4. Piled
5. Ship's head
6. Overhead
7. Individual passages
8. Electronic message conveyers
9. Spoof
10. ___ rata: in proportion
11. Metallic animal?
12. Isolated
13. Ginkgo, for one
21. Magnets can do this
22. Capital of Togo
26. Cleaning lady in Dover
28. Speaks (archaic variant)
29. This glows when excited
30. Yin's partner
31. Sign that a change is needed
32. Agitate
33. Metallic canine?
35. Pops another Viagra
38. Mrs. of spice blends
40. Brest farewell
42. City north of Essen
43. Not kidding
46. Reasons to drink
48. Distressed one?
50. Kind of suit
51. Legal symbol
52. Tiger's treat
53. Move quietly
54. ___ mater
55. Sentimental drivels
57. O. Henry's wise men
59. Green spike

❖ Solution on page 288

Tot Spot   *Douglas Fink*

ACROSS

1. A babe in the woods
6. 63D attractor
11. Put the blades to the blades
14. Lead role for Clooney
15. Captain Kirk, by claim
16. Cache before hatching
17. NPR newsperson
19. Superman foe
20. Needs at JFK
21. Out of date
22. It's in the background
24. Timer sound
26. Not many
28. Ness, for one
29. Flu malady
31. Take a load off
34. Spielberg's first full flick
36. Get by
38. Actor who often plays a villain
39. ___-tze
40. Better halves
46. The 4 out of 5 who recommend are part of this
47. As well
48. Drink for Alice
49. "This way"
51. Sport not for lightweights
53. Atomizer sprays
57. Lecherly look
59. Infamy time
61. It'll never fly
62. Old lantern
65. Place to talk about Jr.'s classes
67. Yesteryear
68. Giant giant
69. Hit song by Three Dog Night
72. Originally named
73. Gathering spots
74. Flower holder
75. What you do before you "Doh!"
76. Car wash result
77. Notice blatantly

DOWN

1. "La Isla ___" (Madonna tune)
2. Biting
3. Good guy
4. Lamb's saying
5. Combined
6. Keeper, not a weeper
7. It's low down
8. Flabbergasts
9. Artist Chagall
10. *Mary Tyler Moore Show* actress
11. Smallest inherent part
12. Encounter loose lips
13. Kind of buildup
18. Little helper
23. Show assent
25. Peachy follower
27. Greetings!
30. Winter runner
32. ___ anemone
33. Bivouac boudoir
35. The Spanish
37. Lizards
40. Biological holder
41. Devotee
42. One who likes to play
43. Rain check kin
44. Family sign
45. Anti-Establishment musical
50. Lively wiggler
52. Dave Thomas
54. Himalayan guide
55. One who does windows
56. Cowboy need
58. Asian veeps
60. Did lunch
62. Evaporated
63. See 6A
64. It'll shed some light
66. Engraving tools
70. Comedienne Fields
71. Cheerio base

❖ **Solution on page 288**

Passing Fads   *Douglas Fink*

ACROSS

1. Big Bad Wolf verb
5. Club entrance permission definer
9. That nice Haskell boy
14. Nash's adjective
15. Soother
16. Merchandise
17. Unscientific survey
19. His stories told a moral
20. Calcutta carriages
21. Plays the huckster
23. Blackbird home, in a nursery tale
24. Freud focus
25. One way up
29. Church veeps
32. Emeritus, briefly
33. Empty selling
34. Ebbs, like luck
35. Herbert's book series
36. Tale in verse
37. Nat or Natalie of song
38. Progressive eBay maneuver
39. Gift givers
40. Subsists
41. 36A, often
42. Microsoft mega-millionaire
43. Roz on *Frasier*
44. Yan's pan
45. Official seal
46. Horse's gait
47. Fool
48. Caesar salad need?
49. Deadly
51. Deserves
55. Like Keebler magic
58. Clothing tag instruction
60. Source
61. 64A instrument
62. Grammarian's thing
63. Do without
64. Sax player's buy
65. Obi-wan's portrayer

DOWN

1. Regis, for one
2. A law ___ itself
3. Lobby plant
4. '20s fad
5. Fails to renew
6. Worldwide workers gp.
7. Perform a '70s fad
8. Made for TV?
9. Blimey!
10. Performs a '90s fad
11. The TRS-80 used it
12. Chapel promise
13. *X-File* skill
18. Times before seeing the doctor
22. Infamous
26. Road less traveled
27. High point
28. Fail to yield
29. RSVP option
30. *21 Jump Street* spinoff
31. Lively Spanish dance
35. Pink slip receiver
38. Adjust Snidely Whiplash's mustache
42. Trial tapper
45. Like some hair
50. Savvy about
52. Kelly Clark or Ruben Studdard
53. Correct
54. Harmony
55. Gee preceder
56. John, to Ringo
57. PETA no-no
59. Calvin & Hobbes bully

❖ **Solution on page 288**

Chapter 14

I Vow to Theme,
My Country

More Off with Their Heads!   Douglas Fink

ACROSS

1. Lawyer's concern
5. Uncaring
10. Rash
14. Lustrous velvet
15. Like a cow
16. Board, as a plane or train
17. Killeth
18. Short jobs
19. Pineapple
20. Rocket ruiner
22. LEM org.
24. Worse than an imp
25. Overhaul
26. Like Stretch Armstrong
28. Girls' sleepover activity
32. Wall hanging
33. Toon store collection
34. Traps
36. "Consider Yourself" musical
40. Mr. Applegate, in *Damn Yankees*
42. Quite smart
44. Bright star of Virgo
45. It cheers you up
47. Scorched
49. James Bond's school
50. Bergen's mouthpiece
52. *The Apprentice* contestant
54. Cabbie's question
57. Killer whale
58. Big name in blocks
59. Water source
61. Changed places
65. Not well-defined
67. Motto
69. Emulate Hans Brinker
70. Big happening
71. Stet, essentially
72. Clint's *High Plains Drifter* costar
73. ___ Gabler
74. Makes champion racehorses, perhaps
75. Superior bargain

DOWN

1. Soho strollers
2. Get the gold
3. Infernal writer?
4. Derided
5. Showing up and downs
6. Like some ruminants
7. ___ go bragh
8. Coal provider?
9. Priest, probably
10. More than ajar
11. African doc
12. Like poor Johnny One-note
13. Lawmakers
21. Thinking man's artist?
23. Venetian street
27. L.I. city
28. Bass basket
29. Crunchy candy
30. Drop in
31. Came to a common place
32. They ponder
35. St. Petersburg's river
37. Title role not to cry for?
38. Surveillance mission
39. Angel's gift
41. Actress Graff
43. Sends to a proofer too early
46. Isle near Sicily
48. Decree
51. Fishing vessel
53. It might be square or curved
54. Do grainery work
55. Pleaded
56. Landlubber's love
60. Garlic serving
61. Hugo or Tony
62. Windy City airport
63. Hartford-based insurer
64. As good as it gets
66. Michael Douglas's wife's middle name
68. Double-curved molding

❖ **Solution on page 288**

The Four Seasonings Douglas Fink

ACROSS

1. Souvlaki meat
5. Belief in a higher power
10. Signs a contract, slangily
14. Like Snidely Whiplash
15. Where chess originated
16. Cool!
17. She was a bad egg
19. Low-lying area
20. Al Roker's line
21. Logical rule
23. Abscam action
26. A bit under the weather
27. Coyote co.
30. Pearls of wisdom
35. Hirsute one's need
36. Almost runs
37. Bobbles the ball
38. Cratchit's son
39. Utmost
40. Soaked
41. Peeves
43. Fixes for good
45. Carny's attraction
46. Is ultra-pricey
48. Chaser of the Duke Brothers
49. Result of a strike?
50. Pauline's dilemma
52. The bad guy in the original *Dirty Harry*
56. Quantity
60. Tiny quantity
61. Play the sycophant
64. Class to learn all the angles
65. UFO odor?
66. Editor's "cut it out!"
67. Disburden
68. Ping thing
69. Polio conqueror

DOWN

1. 501 name
2. Prayers
3. Joan of art
4. Plead sobbingly
5. Anne Frank, for one
6. Donny Osmond has three
7. Rhoda's mom
8. Delta deposit
9. Gold-medal decathlete of '52
10. Entail
11. Close by
12. Do-re-mi
13. Stern counterpart
18. Christine, for one
22. Antiquity
24. Egress announcer
25. It's all in vain
27. Escapade
28. City in a Woody Allen title
29. Shields and Yarnell
31. Fruit colorer
32. A Mr. Noodle portrayer on *Sesame Street*
33. Doctrine
34. Colorado park
42. One use for an attic
43. Mottled cats
44. Dogie, often
45. Puts more ammo in
47. Nurse a drink
51. Mr. Phelps's org.
52. Location
53. Dagwood's boss's wife
54. Regretful Miss of song
55. Aniseed liqueur
57. Eye layer
58. Superbowl winningest coach
59. Journey
62. Actor Silver or Glass
63. Messenger ___

❖ **Solution on page 288**

Stormy Weather   *Merle Baker*

ACROSS

1. Opening sides
6. Independent country from 1932 until 2003
10. Saharan
14. Left at sea?
15. DVD player remote button
16. Eastern royal
17. Toy soldier
18. *Scarface* actor Paul
19. Chocolate shape
20. Himalayan big cat
23. *Lilies of the Field* character
24. Pole, for one
25. Musical style of Lennon's first band
27. Extreme turmoil
31. Highfalutin'
32. Fed. loan agency
33. Switch from plastic to paper?
35. Stud setting
36. Where to get off
38. Putdowns
40. Not bold
43. Part of UCLA
45. Muse with a lyre
47. Jack of *Barney Miller*
48. Shmoo creator
51. Chosen
53. Part of a road show crew
55. North Carolina senator
56. Tap choice
57. Athlete's endurance-developing exercise
62. Shine partner
64. A sci.
65. Folder's words
66. Six-sided state
67. Aunt with a *Cope Book*
68. Cartoonist Trudeau
69. Spirit roamed here
70. Flower holder
71. Plumber's tool

DOWN

1. Certain sports cars, for short
2. " . . . hear ___ drop"
3. Magic charm
4. Shop leisurely
5. Outstanding
6. Stuck fast
7. Do another hitch
8. Paquin and Pavlova
9. Peculiarities
10. Indiana Jones quest
11. Amazon region
12. Slap
13. Original voice of Mickey Mouse
21. Place for icicles
22. Have a meal
26. Shaving stuff
27. Function
28. Office phone syst.
29. Coliseum shout
30. 1944 Preminger film
34. Rod Laver won 11 of these titles
37. *Wind in the Willows* character
39. Sitting spot
41. Want ad abbr.
42. Decked
44. Gush forth
46. Gulf of Mexico sights
48. Warning, old-style
49. Sue Lyon role
50. Values highly
52. Sports artist LeRoy
54. Drink at the bar
58. Stadium cover
59. Nick's partner
60. Izmir resident
61. Eyelid swelling
63. Sounds of surprise

❖ **Solution on page 288**

It's Not Easy   *Merle Baker*

ACROSS

1. Sigh, say
7. Not as much
11. Place for roses
14. Some are grand
15. Pre-college grades
16. "You ___ what you eat"
17. It might be driven
19. *Platoon* setting
20. Hosp. employees
21. German article
22. Caesar's accusation
23. Staff member
25. The sauce
27. News letters
28. Promising words
29. Joanne of *Red River*
30. Runs into
32. '50s auto feature
34. Sounded satisfied
38. Like an unmade bed
40. 1972 U.S. Open champ
42. Krupp works home
43. Conquest of Caesar's
45. Highland tongue
46. Dermal opening
48. Nipper's co.
49. JFK or LBJ
50. Alternative schooling
54. Rockers from Australia
55. Call at sea
56. Munich Mrs.
57. *Oz* airer
58. *Traffic* org.
59. Experiencing difficulty
63. Bread spread
64. Parisian pal
65. Dresses smartly
66. Freudian subjects
67. Thesaurus wds.
68. Genetics pioneer

DOWN

1. NT book
2. First Chinese dynasty
3. Boom opposite
4. Tennis player Agassi
5. Tennis shots
6. NASA counterpart
7. Shackle of a sort
8. Serengeti grazer
9. Sipowicz carries one
10. Misdeed
11. African language group
12. Sister of Clio
13. Object
18. Gaol site
22. Treat the same
23. Care for
24. Milky gems
25. LP player
26. Gershwin et al.
31. Fleet
33. Arrived on the q.t.
35. Uncompromising
36. Reo competitor
37. Considers
39. Toll rd.
41. "Woe is me!"
44. Teen hangouts
47. Word in an FDR speech
50. Pilgrim to Mecca
51. In the future
52. Gallivants
53. Hatch of Utah
54. *Peer Gynt* playwright
57. " . . . nor long remember what we say ___"
59. Eats
60. 45 or 78
61. Ship heading
62. High-speed modem connection

❖ **Solution on page 288**

It's Just a Formality — Douglas Fink

ACROSS

1. Junk e-mail
5. One way to lie
10. Soccer game segment
14. They're near pants pockets
15. Satisfy, as a loan
16. ___ fixe
17. It's under Wayne Manor (male)
20. ___ op
21. Qatari chief
22. Like bad wine or coffee
23. Witticism
24. Light tan
26. Follow a Halloween tradition (male)
33. Is real
34. Tease
35. GP gp.
36. Singer Houston
37. PC rival
38. Main theme
40. Much of it might be about nothing
41. Commandment word
42. Kind of dance or game
43. Miserly one (female)
47. Apple slag
48. It's a terrible burden
49. Like Teflon
52. Channel
53. Life work?
56. Medical report (male)
60. Just doin' nothin'
61. Empress kin
62. Points of interest
63. Rolling stone's lack
64. Pond hoppers
65. Return call

DOWN

1. Nuclear family members
2. Recess activity
3. Something to put on
4. Tumbler's surface
5. Nudges
6. Goal of an aspirin
7. It's next to 0
8. Vet's tour locale
9. Blinker
10. It gets in the way
11. Purim's month
12. Stubbs of the Four Tops
13. Chow on the farm
18. Nourishing
19. Contort
23. Mrs. Tate, to El Puerco
24. Sevareid of the news
25. "Minnie the Moocher" singer
26. Episode start
27. Rust or laughing gas
28. Plain rover
29. Use a soapbox
30. Gate securer
31. *South Pacific* hero
32. *60 Minutes* newsman
37. Think that life is the pits
38. On the face, it gets a big hand
39. Middle world henchmen
41. Negative conjunction
42. They're easy
44. Bib. book
45. Mischievous deity
46. Gave more body to
49. Crawl, perhaps
50. *Love Boat* deck
51. They're unpleasant
52. Spanish lady
53. Assemblage
54. Yen
55. The Rock and Roll Hall of Fame's state
57. Good name for a painter
58. Chinese chair
59. Rathskellar order

❖ Solution on page 288

Shall We Dance? *Douglas Fink*

ACROSS

1. Outlet goer
5. Drink locales
9. Butler portrayer
14. New currency
15. Pelvic bones
16. Curved arches
17. Country-western dance?
19. Sitar pieces
20. Like blue shoes?
21. Freedom
23. They make trains
25. New Indian city?
26. Newspaper editorial hub
30. Greenhouse purchase
33. English horns
34. "Azucar!" singer
36. Important period
37. Shriekers in *The Princess Bride*
38. Overexcited
39. It takes you up when you want to go down
40. N. or S. state
41. Fable ending
42. Haggled quantity
43. Investor's holdings
45. Patisserie purchase
47. Diversion in a car
49. Superhero item, often
50. What you put in
53. Bow
57. Old Roman port on the Tiber
58. Conservative dance?
60. Parade display
61. Part of HOMES
62. ___ contendere
63. Metric weight unit
64. They're struck in the theater
65. Got by, barely

DOWN

1. Chapel chairs
2. Poi party
3. Press
4. They precede departures
5. Badminton need
6. Pub quaff
7. Cambodian currency
8. Dieter's dinner
9. Samsonite actor of old
10. First name in mystery fiction
11. Salad bar dance?
12. Sinker
13. To live, to Livy
18. Revengeful ones, in a movie series
22. Lukewarm
24. Stallone film for which he wasn't nominated for one
26. Dorm residents, often
27. Voodoo
28. Florida dance?
29. Middle Eastern delicacy
31. Stretch
32. Ranee's wear
35. Shade of purple
38. Violinist's need
39. Park perimeter, perhaps
41. Ref
42. Stage of change
44. Math arc
46. Rips
48. Monstrous baddies
50. Cabin quarters, perhaps
51. 1952 Olympic site
52. Certain
54. One way to run
55. Fit
56. State of mind
59. Take a load off

❖Solution on page 288

City-States   *Douglas Fink*

ACROSS

1. They play low
9. Tells a thing or two
15. More than a loving spoonful
16. Type of airline rating
17. Dependable city-state
19. Cool
20. Soup herb
21. Brings to a new level
26. Crossing guards' attire
27. Brings together
28. Beginner band rehearsal
29. A megatrend, according to Faith Popcorn
30. Pub order
33. It sounds like another pub order
36. Northernmost city-state
39. Camel's walking spot?
40. True-blue
41. Feet that flow
42. Got together
43. Less meaty
44. High praise, indeed
47. Patriotic protectorates
50. Fish or fowl
51. Elaine's last name on *Seinfeld*
52. Friendly, social city-state
59. You might choose this
60. Leo V, for one
61. Aye votes
62. They list the ranks

DOWN

1. Turkish title
2. Before now
3. Practically nothing
4. It's not my fault!
5. ___ Red apples
6. Medicinal herbs
7. Implied
8. T-bar release point
9. PlayStation people
10. Hill dweller
11. Headline word for Holmes
12. Calculations with H and O
13. See 10D
14. Tries to get the golden snitch
18. Raises
21. Play to the audience
22. Indian infantryman
23. Flat food
24. Farming prefix
25. Propaganda item
26. Vicious verbosity
28. Pair
30. Like a wallflower
31. Drink in Wonderland
32. Friend of Pooh
33. Those in charge
34. Plant
35. Hideouts
37. Daycare attendee
38. Superboy's gal
42. Prayer figure?
43. Primitive sweepers
44. Relish
45. It has only two ways out
46. Really wants
47. Layer
48. Ready to serve
49. D.C. transit
51. Prohibitions
53. Misbefallin' event
54. Tennis call
55. Darth Vader, once
56. The light side
57. Hansel and Gretel foe
58. They're back after elections

❖ **Solution on page 289**

Goodbye to Mr. Chips   *Douglas Fink*

ACROSS

1. Like artillery trajectories
6. Multitude
10. Sandwich shop
14. Song or poker game
15. It's earned
16. OPEC VIP, perhaps
17. Bad red tape advice
20. Be mindful of
21. Jimmy the Greek's specialty
22. They're nothing much
23. Adlai's rival
24. Farm sci.
25. Using a lintbrush
34. Shakes in the grass?
35. Madeline's street
36. Piggy
37. Ready to serve
38. Turn over
40. It debuted 12/24/1871 in Cairo
41. Bert Bobbsey's twin
42. Barfly
43. The train that stops a lot
44. Showy maneuvers
49. "___ the fields we go . . . "
50. Start of a Grafton book that started a series
51. Bow on screen
54. Without a stitch
56. Qualified
60. Make a pig of oneself?
63. Type of sax
64. First name in building
65. Undesirable weirdo
66. Destroy
67. Wild West cry
68. Oft-collected shell

DOWN

1. Foot part
2. Scoundrel
3. Buttonlike?
4. *National Velvet* author Bagnold
5. Bald eagle threatener, once
6. Muppet chef's homeland
7. Crow's nest call
8. Quiche need
9. Like a ten-lash noodle
10. Fix a dog, but not that way
11. Give off
12. Bart's sister
13. Is vexsome to
18. Puckish one
19. Part of a weather forecast
23. Pledge-takers-to-be
24. Performed like Venus
25. Half of a famous comedy duo
26. Like werewolf influences
27. Italy's last queen
28. They're known for their towers
29. Actress Scacchi
30. People note its spots
31. Carthage neighbor
32. Now
33. Passions
38. Acronym in a Beatle song title
39. A place to stew
40. They mail lots of CDs
43. DJ's vinyl collection
45. Role on *The Honeymooners*
46. Like Tommy
47. Like some escapes
48. George Burns role in France
51. Blacken
52. Humdinger
53. One opposed
54. Kin on the bayou
55. Razor brand
56. Linc's coif
57. Went like the wind
58. 2D's look
59. Observe
61. Ref. for the RAF
62. Org. that gives Stern warnings

❖ **Solution on page 289**

Say Cheese! *Douglas Fink*

ACROSS

1. Fill-in help
6. Farmer Hoggett's dance
9. According to
14. Fool
15. Loan letters
16. Old-fashioned
17. Nickel-and-___
18. Cheesy film villain?
20. Famous judge on TV
21. "You ___ There"
23. Basis
24. Centrist's place
26. Stay too long in the sun
28. What it all adds up to
29. Cheesy race?
31. CEO deg.
33. Calgary's province
35. Rapid grower
36. Main courses
39. What's under the hood
41. *Mr. Moto's Gamble* actress
42. More unfeeling
44. *ER* site
45. Cheesy "Fish Heads" lyric?
49. First step to an ICU
51. It yields what you're looking for
52. First name in detectives
53. Llama kin
55. Half of Bennifer
56. Opera center
57. Cheesy way to lose power?
60. It doesn't hold water
62. Wilma's neighbor
63. Word on a U.S. coin
64. Kind of strength or tube
65. Slalom paths
66. ___ polloi
67. One side in a game at camp

DOWN

1. News tidbit
2. Douglas Fink, for this book
3. Brunch beverage
4. Annabel Lee's fan?
5. Take both sides
6. It's green and often carved
7. Pub choice
8. Dog's warning
9. Stitch in one's side, for instance
10. Places to take a load off
11. One who takes for granted
12. Like Grant (who isn't buried)
13. Hopeful one?
19. Shoot for success
22. Teachers in Tel Aviv
25. Japanese restaurant order
26. Douglas ___
27. Eye part
30. One at ease
32. Promo pieces
34. Muppet on the drums
35. Distorts
36. Sushi order
37. Encased engines
38. Makers of tantaras and wawas
40. Reason for analysis
43. Tribute
46. Resident with rials
47. Like some gymnastic bars
48. Lovely Rita's beat
50. Prep in a pan
51. Clumsy one
53. Singer Lane
54. They're barely above water
55. Sci-fi warriors for good
58. Yuck!
59. *Barney Miller* actor
61. Pigtail ruiner

❖ **Solution on page 289**

Open   Merle Baker

ACROSS

1. Canning needs
5. Southwest sights
10. "For the life ___ . . . "
14. Fail to mention
15. "That's gross!"
16. *The Rocky Horror Picture Show* hero
17. Bob Hoskins role of 1991
18. Replay option
19. Crooned
20. The wet on the village smith's brow
23. Code-breaking org.
24. Fraternity letter
25. Seaman's rough weather gear
27. Towel holder
30. Water color
33. MLK was its president
34. Alvin's cohorts
37. Daytime dramas
40. Oscar-winning Sorvino
41. Anthony and Barbara
43. ___ no good
44. Wordsworth works
46. Uniform color
48. They're busy in Apr.
50. Summit
51. Pompous person
52. Kind of garden
55. Cpl., for one
57. Belt maker's tool
58. George, to Gracie
64. Like some chances
66. Punctuation mark
67. Greenhorn
68. Casino game
69. Actress Tatum ___
70. Sister of Ares
71. Worry
72. Thanks, to Pierre
73. Knock down

DOWN

1. Hall of Fame catcher Gibson
2. Shells and such
3. Nothing in Nantes
4. Pricey
5. Aura
6. Congers
7. Flat-bottomed boat
8. High points
9. Sandbars
10. Out of date: Abbr.
11. Three-time Academy Award–winning director
12. Parson's place
13. Candice's dad
21. Bogus
22. Nervous twitches
26. Rough weather harbinger, maybe
27. Dudley Do-Right's grp.
28. Columbus's home
29. One runs from Queen Victoria to Edward VIII
31. Nullify
32. Cub Scout leader
35. Argentine expanse
36. Impertinent person
38. Bake sale orgs.
39. Sad sounds
42. *Trilby* Evil master of persuasion
45. Opposite of avec
47. Part of NYSE
49. *My Little Margie*, e.g.
52. Soaks up sun
53. Barn baby
54. *Snow White* meanie
56. *Animal House* fratman
59. Pt. of ACLU
60. Apple product
61. Gore Vidal's ___ *Breckinridge*
62. Calif. neighbor
63. Wine attribute
65. Tend to the lawn

❖ **Solution on page 289**

Dull Clues and Entries   *Douglas Fink*

❖ Solution on page 289

ACROSS

1. Roughs it
6. Diving duck
10. See 17A
14. Constellation or star displayer
15. Old harp
16. Red rock
17. See 10A
19. Affirm
20. Lolly's item
21. Mushy food
22. Ernest's unseen friend
23. Indirect movie ad, for one
25. Art room supplies
26. *Pygmalion* playwright
30. Mr. Roarke's assistant
32. Marked by prudence
35. Glut
39. Symbolic nestling?
40. Takes to task
41. Li'l rockers
43. London or Big Apple neighborhood
44. Twain burial site
46. Abby opener?
47. Football's British kin
50. Hopeless case
53. Duel tool
54. See 29D
55. Bait's goal
60. See 10D
61. See 38D
63. Isle ring
64. *The African Queen* scripter
65. Linda Lavin title role
66. Proofreader's "er, never mind"
67. We are united
68. Like a colander

DOWN

1. Concerto conclusion
2. Hot and dry
3. ICBM threat
4. Prod
5. Bullish sound?
6. Clever
7. Mr. Magoo's malady
8. Ones who wander
9. Shed tears
10. See 60A
11. Contemplated place
12. Three-time Wimbledon champ
13. Gets on one's merit
18. Mulder's outfit
24. And so on
25. Impel
26. Design code
27. Frost
28. Seaweed
29. See 54A
31. Cry of reproof
33. Brit's boob tube
34. Thing
36. Anything ___?
37. Light bulb indication
38. See 61A
42. Day-of PR concern
43. Larder item
45. Rooster or alarm clock
47. Parts of a long movie
48. Front-runner foul-up
49. Lamp liver
51. Movie Tarzan of old
52. In the boonies
54. Chew
56. Be #1
57. Garters' centers?
58. Bobbing-for-apples need
59. Writer Zane ___
62. Driving need

More Leapers   *Douglas Fink*

ACROSS

1. "I ___ a clue"
6. O, woe is me!
10. Goad to go
14. Like some personalities
15. It's one on the Mohs scale
16. Raced
17. Fashion designer born 2/29/1948
19. Choir hider
20. Singe
21. Bony
23. Hunter who went stag
27. Ensure there are no loose ends
28. > or C:\, often
29. Museum reconstruction
32. They're not an easy read
33. Carmen mechanic
34. Olympic chant
35. Black stone
36. Worrier's woe, supposedly
37. Poor ore
38. ATM maker
39. It has a small charge
40. Doing well on a test
41. Perhaps we ___ . . .
43. Water channel
44. Dog show concern
45. Had fun
46. Yak
48. Eh
49. Sills solo
50. Singer/talk show host born 2/29/1916
56. Teller's partner
57. Ring or ringing related
58. Pound replacers
59. Leisure
60. Teen who likes it dark, perhaps
61. They're essential

DOWN

1. Beginner's request
2. Darth Vader, as a kid
3. Indian lentil dish
4. Nada
5. Arm extensor muscle
6. Hindu soul
7. Lion's den
8. SST control
9. Ketch kin
10. Report to bring others up to speed
11. Religious ruler at the Renaissance's end born 2/29/1468
12. Sky bear
13. Fishing pole part
18. Strong bar drink
22. Dress mess
23. Dress mess protection
24. Jewish wedding sound
25. Motivator born 2/29/1960
26. NASDAQ rival
27. An old 9D may have one
29. Plant with two seed leaves
30. Income from wealth
31. One way to be run
33. Like elephant observers?
36. Sweet Polly Purebred's pal
37. Li'l tail
39. Out of harm's way
40. Baseballer born 2/29/1924
42. Sophisticated
43. It's binding
45. Make an egg
46. Tease
47. L × W
48. Petty pique
51. Judge in a famous case
52. Painter's concern
53. Mined-over matter
54. Mr. Twilight Zone, to friends
55. Sideways, mirror-image tilde

❖ **Solution on page 289**

Even More Off with Their Heads! Douglas Fink

ACROSS

1. Annoyance
6. Fred's sister
10. Connected locks, perhaps
14. Good manners word
15. Clean up, Hamelin-style
16. Addis ___
17. Type of apple
18. Imitative
19. *Exorcist* daughter
20. Kid
21. They get things
23. Gift
26. Miles of film
27. Designer Cassini
30. More nervous
33. From the top
35. Baby buggies
38. Provider of 23As
39. Newspaper section
40. Stinger
42. Gaps
43. Entryway
44. Least dull
46. Loath
48. Featherlike
49. Joins at the altar
50. Uneducated guess
52. Crude instrument
56. On the sparse side
59. Tippy-top
60. Competitive activity
63. Opera that's not buffa
64. Taste
66. Suggest
67. Mash
68. Typewriter part
69. Pleasing smell
70. Grammarian's concern
71. Lox topping

DOWN

1. Tin-lead alloy
2. Relax!
3. Astrologist's aids
4. ___ majeste
5. Genetically engineered
6. Capable
7. Dry
8. Birthday suit revealer
9. String of support
10. Cradle users
11. Big hiccup
12. "___ O'Riley"
13. "Everything's going according to ___"
21. British measure
22. ___ Spee
24. They scrape the surface
25. Mournful sound
27. De-blubber
28. Daring exploits
29. Shocked
31. The euro replaced it
32. Wane
34. Like some Popsicles
35. Tried to succeed
36. Was a mule?
37. Spy aliases
41. Scope
42. Sicily neighbor
45. His watch had video
47. Type of tester
48. Gulag zone
51. Movie theater distraction
53. Depp, in a 2003 hit film
54. One who is not a divider
55. Chinese Empire offices
56. Volkswagen model
57. "What did you ___?"
58. Wesley Snipes title role
60. Copycat
61. Oz visitor
62. Pack tightly
64. Presidential pooch
65. Applaud

❖ Solution on page 289

Heighs — *Douglas Fink*

ACROSS

1. Movie camera effect
5. Did best boy work
10. Clean off
14. Big-horned goat
15. City on the Mohawk
16. The Buckeye State
17. *Airplane!* star
19. Touch down
20. Pander
21. Like a not-so-great record
23. Less outspoken
26. Intended
27. Very happy
28. They make you very happy
31. Its slag is called pomace
32. Witness
33. Velvet finish
34. Tombstone-shaped logic gates
35. Cursed
36. Farewell interrupter
37. Question to Kermit
38. Things to select from
39. Thin pancake
40. Cop's beat
42. Less vibrant
43. Pooh's pot filler
44. Torso wraps
45. Afraid
47. Get a grip
48. Polar products?
49. *Shaft* and *South Park* star
54. "En garde!" item
55. Berate
56. Highway hauler
57. Casual call
58. Used an aerial
59. Cold-shoulder

DOWN

1. Tree by the ski slope
2. Olivia d'___ (*Wonder Years*/*Something Is Out There* actress)
3. She's new to the scene
4. Carries out
5. Like a bumpy road
6. Upper atmosphere
7. "You're telling a fib!"
8. Far from friendly
9. Like some caps
10. Later!
11. Apathetic cries of submission
12. "___ We Got Fun?"
13. Rye meeter?
18. Even less cooked
22. Duo
23. Bug out, *M*A*S*H*-style
24. Donahue of *Father Knows Best*
25. She ran the Blue Moon Detective Agency
26. Evenly distributes
28. Morning torus
29. Home on the range
30. Looks from Malfoy
32. Sluggo's pal
35. One way to have eggs
36. Cross the line
38. It might make a sub go blub
39. Infatuation
41. Torso wrap
42. Embellished
44. Baseball action, off the field
45. Dance instruction
46. "Bad Boys" is its theme song
47. Stockholder's hope
50. Moo ___ pork
51. Desire
52. Rod Hull's bird
53. Sis or bro

❖ **Solution on page 289**

Tooling Around *Douglas Fink*

ACROSS

1. Carrier in a canal
6. Ness hideout?
10. Astral honey chaser
14. Radiant
15. Litigant
17. Funny-looking fish
19. JFK calc.
20. Missile sites
21. Calculate, by science and/or magic
25. Goop
26. F/X for *The Day the Earth Stood Still*
29. You'll get a charge out of it
30. Political, debatable punch
32. One of Peter, Paul, and Mary
34. The Yellow Brick Road, for one
36. Idle actor
38. Primp, like hair
39. Low-level giver of orders
42. Treat insultingly
43. Humped henchman
44. Stead
46. Continents, for example
48. Edible tubers
50. It's subjective
51. Spots
52. Small bite
54. Exhilarating
56. Without a clue
58. Absolutely nothing
59. Find it in one's heart
66. Single focus
67. She won America's first *American Idol*
68. Lay seating
69. Scatter
70. Take potshots

DOWN

1. Scrooge summation
2. Objector's org.
3. "Losing My Religion" band
4. Played D&D
5. Like ipecac
6. ___-di-dah
7. It gets enrichment
8. Last name in diet gurus
9. Town near Amherst, MA
10. Cries of disapproval
11. Genetic letters
12. Rel. talk
13. Indiana Jones found it
16. Keep away
18. *Friends* role
21. Backup singer for Gladys Knight
22. Street surface
23. Snares
24. Anklebones
26. Resident of an outer planet
27. Cultivates
28. Be outstanding
31. Don ___ (Zorro)
33. Are you for ___?
35. HS class
37. Flowers
40. Crude structures
41. Type of knot
42. "Take on Me" group
45. Rugged vehicle
47. Fallen out of practice
49. Little Pig building material
53. Pauline's problem
55. Show originally titled *These Friends of Mine*
56. Votes like its last three letters
57. Like a gone GI
59. Drench
60. Honest one
61. ENE antipode
62. Collection
63. First name in cotton gins
64. Mountain that sounds like a call to be rescued
65. Baker's loaf

❖ **Solution on page 289**

Catch Some More Zs   *Douglas Fink*

ACROSS

1. Answer to "Where?"
6. Choir spot
10. Bloke
14. Roarer, in a song
15. Scat singer
16. What a 23D does
17. Active Middle Easterner?
19. French friend
20. Look at
21. Noted jurist's middle name
23. Sparks in the theater
26. Flightless birds
29. Italian cars, briefly
30. Like Humpty Dumpty
32. Idle talk
35. Minotaur milieus
36. Goodnight girl
37. Pesky one
40. Wood cutter
41. Rot
42. Faberge Egg owner, perhaps
43. "Runaway" singer's first name
44. Pie nut
45. Incan residence
46. Truth
48. Think tank output
49. Fragrant resin
51. Ring around the cellar
53. Take to court
54. Auel extras
57. Wrath
59. Muscat's nation
60. He's part mandarin and part peach?
66. Assist
67. Hard water?
68. Pith helmets
69. Gaelic
70. Iditarod need
71. Cheer up

DOWN

1. American acquisition
2. Goblin leader?
3. Rod Hull's bird
4. Tear down
5. They help you to break down
6. O in Oahu
7. Ancient
8. Imperfection
9. Story
10. Bough break befaller
11. Results of do-it-yourself electronics?
12. Walled city near Madrid
13. Banana slag
18. Role for Keanu
22. Basilica section
23. See 16A
24. Dodge
25. What Novack tries to do to his cohost?
27. Each
28. Simon Cowell's forte
31. Stick in the ground
33. Bivouac, perhaps
34. Whatever
38. Hong Kong neighbor
39. Text
41. Reader's spot
42. What you chew if you moo
44. Prissy
45. End of Viagra's or Clomid's chemical name
47. French apology
49. Where élèves go
50. Cruddier, like an excuse
52. Goal
55. Cliff endings
56. Empty
58. Hydroxyl compound
61. Lawyer Baird
62. London series ender
63. Tax pro
64. Blackjack request
65. "It's no ___!"

❖ Solution on page 290

Chapter 15

Of Theme I Sing

Scrub Mission *Douglas Fink*

ACROSSS

1. Israeli city
6. Hairline?
10. Use UPS
14. Bribed
15. Nanking nanny
16. Game of chance
17. Ignore
19. "Photography Sketch" actor
20. IT specialty
21. Mixture
23. Good Feelings time
24. Advance screenings
25. Coffee shop orders
29. Gone bad
30. Town tax rate
31. My gal?
32. Exercise actions
35. ___ Red apples
36. Dropped relations
38. PBS donor
39. Metric units
41. Machine part
42. WWII turning point
43. ___ T
44. Tables of contents
46. Square-dance group member
49. Responses against
50. ___ meteor shower
51. Angry one's route
55. Spice holder, perhaps
56. Second-rate
58. No longer green
59. Notice
60. Tuscany town
61. Red reporters of old
62. Beams
63. Halloween option

DOWN

1. Lack of the 2003 recovery
2. Spacious
3. Winter woes
4. Goes from bad to worse
5. Stick
6. Avoid needing to retake
7. Little Jack Horner's final words
8. Sky surveyors
9. A crossword in this book probably has one
10. Place for poles
11. Investment options
12. Relative by marriage
13. They might have many feet
18. Collects
22. Stay away from
24. Skunk
25. Put out
26. Flank
27. Coop interviews
28. Animal pouch
32. Highly innovative
33. ___ moss
34. He or she follower
36. Gem buyer's concern
37. *Night Court* role
40. Teases, in a way
42. Hopeless state
44. Rock fan?
45. Where deer are denizens
46. '60s style
47. Ceramics need that sounds like a country
48. May cause defamation of character
51. ___ and wherefores
52. Palindromist extraordinaire
53. Sushi fish
54. What noir detectives pack
57. *A Tailor of Panama* profession

❖ Solution on page 290

Musical Finales   *Douglas Fink*

ACROSS

1. Jawboned Biblical animal
4. Alfalfa's girlfriend
9. Actress Garbo
14. Utmost
15. Peer
16. Like werewolf influences
17. Educ. savings
18. Bar treat, usually served hot
20. Harbor helpers
22. Ben Stein's *Ferris Bueller* question
23. Galore
24. Throw in
25. RAF subcontractor, generically
26. First name in skating
27. Title Monty Python role
29. Jefferson's home
33. Bun's place
37. Like a live show
38. *Less Than Perfect* star
39. Subway entrance
40. Feller with Teller
41. Andy Griffith's pal
43. Nannies
45. Genetic letters
46. Does, for instance
49. Carnival site
50. Like taste or sugar
54. Heavenly
56. Red shirts, on *Star Trek*
57. Den greeting
59. X for Xenophon
60. Museum sculpture piece
61. Swiss city on the Rhine
62. Motherly one
63. They might get rustled
64. Pieces in the paper
65. Bit of work

DOWN

1. O'Day of jazz
2. Give an edge
3. It's a wrap
4. Quite the gentleman
5. In middle sea?
6. Like a bumpy road
7. Map or back crossers
8. Drink that sounds unwell
9. Ed Wood title role
10. Vallee of song
11. Try to be all that you can be
12. Treat mercilessly
13. Like 56A, often
19. News source during an outage
21. Horse race activity
24. "Over the Rainbow" composer
27. Confuses
28. Tantrum cry
29. Household cleaner
30. What a hole might be in
31. Rod Serling's daughter
32. A daughter of Zeus
34. Number in a Uris title
35. Will Ferrell hit film
36. Born
39. OPEC alternatives
41. Throws in the towel
42. Built
44. Toastmasters member
46. They stand tall on a ship
47. Tie type
48. Put in the pantry
50. Help the environment
51. Special area
52. Upper atmosphere
53. Losing strength, like a battery
55. Trick
56. Zsa Zsa headline verb
58. ARC categorizing system

❖ Solution on page 290

It's All in Vane   Merle Baker

ACROSS

1. Liquor up
6. *Hungarian Rhapsodies* composer
11. Money movement method: Abbr.
14. Off base
15. Name on an old plane
16. Pub pint
17. McIntosh relative
19. With 20A, *Dino* star
20. See 19A
21. Stigma location
23. They may be offered
26. Bruce and Edward
27. Puts forth
28. Spingarn Medal honoree Evers
29. Tempts Providence
30. Fujimori's land
31. Blackfly cousin
34. Height: Abbr.
35. Not blunt
36. Hearst's kidnappers, briefly
37. Indigence
39. Substantial, informally
40. "Norwegian Wood" instrument
42. Used-car transaction
44. Baseless rumor
45. Come together
47. Bunk
48. Whence comes a scent?
49. Wise guys
50. Estuary
51. New Zealand's Mt. Cook, for one
56. TV weekend comedy
57. Swiss mathematician
58. Not so nasty
59. Abbr. preceding a number
60. Birdbrain
61. Four Holy Roman emperors

DOWN

1. Prohibition
2. Music genre
3. Paul or Mick
4. Warsaw Pact country currency
5. Summer wear
6. Angler's gear
7. "Ignorance ___ excuse"
8. KLM alternative
9. Like most flies
10. Causing strain
11. International benevolent society
12. Aptitude
13. Poker players' giveaways
18. They might be tight or loose
22. Go and get
23. Put on again
24. Outcast
25. Pilgrimage site
26. Hanna-Barbera toon
28. General at Gettysburg
30. Oeno- ending
32. Happy as ___
33. Overdue
35. Noteworthy
38. Hindu goddess
40. WWII major landing site
41. Huffy
43. Detects
44. Rib structure
45. Hapless
46. Speak one's mind
47. Olympic skier Phil ___
49. Development stage
52. *True Confessions* director Grosbard
53. Do something
54. Novelist Tolstoy
55. 7 accompaniers

❖ **Solution on page 290**

See 24D *Michael Wiesenberg*

ACROSS

1. Location of 8 of the world's 14 highest mountains
6. Beg
11. Household deity of ancient Rome
14. Yemenite neighbor
15. Actress/singer in *From Russia with Love*
16. U2 hit of 1991
17. Actor/singer Springfield got on horse?
19. Offspring
20. Deer
21. Easy mark
23. "Barefoot" wines
26. Mythical birds
28. Cast holder
29. ___ Z
30. Adam ___ of pop
32. Get a hand for this
33. Blue
34. Taxmen
38. Surroundings
40. Dog's offering
43. Being litigated
45. Paris's ___ de France
46. Silver brother
48. "Uh-uh"
49. Stanford rival
50. Ire
52. Emulate an alleycat
55. Backpacker's shelter
56. Notebook
58. "Peachy"
60. Baseball stat
61. Issuing pink slips to the cephalopods?
66. House wing
67. Like Harvard or Yale
68. Mommy's sister
69. Rocker Shannon ("Runaway")
70. 1958 Cozy Cole hit
71. Get more out of

DOWN

1. And not
2. Sex Pistols' label
3. Acronymic fund-raiser in the news
4. Egyptian crosses
5. It's a bean
6. Mickey's dog
7. What amateur photographers sometimes forget to remove
8. Treebeard in *LOTR*
9. Yeses
10. Pedestal parts
11. Missing in the cinnamon and cumin aisle of the supermarket?
12. Consecrate
13. Go back on
18. Hockey great
22. Sun phenomenon
23. Serene
24. Thine: Fr.
25. What you need to pay to get your shoes back?
27. Screwup
31. Horse's gait
34. ___ Xing
35. Wreck
36. Try
37. Before
39. "___ inside"
41. Watts of Eastern philosophy
42. It might be raised
44. Fakers
46. Detestation
47. Incompetent
51. Overhaul
53. 1964 Beach Boys hit
54. Fall behind
55. Canadian cap
57. Replay rival
59. Michael or Peter
62. Stone carving
63. Burma's first prime minister
64. "___ Monty Python's Flying . . . "
65. Color

❖ Solution on page 290

All Directions Covered   Adrian Powell

ACROSS

1. Oscar Madison's cronies
6. Some distance away
10. Fish preserver
14. Moths-to-be
15. Exam question choice
16. Young Frankenstein's helper
17. Pass legislation
18. Eve's follower
19. Carpenter's groove
20. Small apartment block
22. Prattled
24. Banana treat
26. Do the blanket stitch
27. Not wanted
31. Jewish leader
35. Vaudevillian singer ___ Bayes
36. Rabbit fur
37. Hose material
38. Black marsh bird
39. Machu Picchu locale
41. Lee, the cake lady
42. Thespian's whisper
44. Pelvic bones
45. Cheshire cat's feature
46. Lab dish
47. Zaireans, once
49. Temper
51. Athenian marketplace
52. Like a barroom door
56. Slightly charred
60. Green Gables girl
61. Muffin maker
63. Earthy hue
64. Begin to waken
65. Extremely desperate
66. Financing option
67. Lusty attraction: the ___
68. Otherwise
69. Fruity organic compound

DOWN

1. Gush out
2. Roman moon goddess
3. Milky gemstone
4. Cabbie's nightmares
5. Sting operations
6. Cash stop
7. Some laundry equipment
8. Séance sight
9. Takes a room for a while
10. Crossing guard's duty
11. Lab gel
12. Prospector's aim
13. Stepped
21. Fold of skin
23. Sea swallow
25. Sarcastically contradictory
27. Open a beer
28. Hangman's expertise
29. Legal right
30. Hairstylist's duty, sometimes
32. Traffic jam sound
33. Mussorgsky's "___ Godunov"
34. Wacky
40. Indonesian palms
43. Yeats's home
48. Bird from Baltimore
50. Weather geologically
52. Naval punishment, once
53. Aware of
54. Military group
55. Pure malice
57. Indian mountain pass
58. Old Celtic tongue
59. Venison source
62. Anniversary announcement word

❖ **Solution on page 290**

Framed   *Merle Baker*

ACROSS

1. Discharge
5. Portoferraio's island
9. Extra large
14. Obviously absurd
16. Consume
17. It's obvious
19. Inn type
20. Watches
21. 63D in the UK
22. Walter Reuther's org.
24. Castle protector
27. Ring result, perhaps
33. 3.0, e.g.
35. Contemptuous look
36. Pronouncements
37. Skeleton part
39. Work dough
41. Actor Tamiroff
42. Another ___ in one's belt
44. Rainbow ___
46. Computer attachment?
47. Go all out
50. In-tray item
51. Seminoles' sch.
52. "So that's it!"
54. Financial page letters
58. Thompson and Lazarus
62. 1930 Gershwin musical
66. Turner autobiography
67. Kind of nut
68. Out of it
69. Pale as a ghost
70. Vaccine developer

DOWN

1. One of the *Odd Couple*
2. Cocoon enclosure
3. Delightful place
4. Culminate
5. West end?
6. Rich supply
7. Toiling
8. *Off the Court* author
9. Stick out
10. UCLA rival
11. Remunerative ability
12. Certain sculpture
13. Page of essays
15. Conspiracies
18. Amphibious warfare grp.
23. Signal of a sort
25. Relative of -ish
26. China setting
27. Historic ship
28. Fifty minutes past
29. Name on a lot of caps
30. The golden ___ television
31. Soul man Redding
32. Word following brand or maiden
33. Revs
34. Sit (down)
38. Square-mile fraction
40. Behind
43. Hesitate
45. Go ___ (rot)
48. Zilch
49. Cugat specialties
52. Sale condition
53. URL opener
55. City on the Colorado
56. Soothing spots
57. Outline clearly
59. One of the Three Bears
60. Deep blue
61. Mount Rushmore's st.
63. See 21A
64. Bandleader Kyser
65. Loft contents

❖ **Solution on page 290**

On Top of Old Smokey *Douglas Fink*

ACROSS

1. Postal need
6. Talking cue
10. ___ up (admit)
14. Hourly
15. Bicep neighbor
16. Involved in
17. *West Side Story* gal
18. Wagnerian goddess
19. Enthusiasm
20. Ache aid
22. No
23. Officeholder's authority
25. Oscar Madison, for one
29. Preceder of Number One
30. It's positive
34. They do filling in
36. Etched
37. Purchase for the garden
38. Cafeteria purchase
39. They might go downhill fast
40. Oldest daughter on *Reba*
41. Using it can be draining
42. Verb for Austin Powers
43. Romanian coins
44. Caught
47. Tablet shape
50. Dangerous snake
55. Cold War initials of concern
56. Supplies for sushi coating
57. 1 A.M., say
58. Coyote co.
59. Just hanging out
60. About 1 percent of the atmosphere
61. Hatchling's home
62. It precedes "Ya wanna buy a watch, cheap?"
63. Look at again

DOWN

1. Deposed Irani
2. Voice quality
3. Something to sing about
4. Welcome name?
5. *Dead Men Don't Wear* ___
6. Thieves, in kid comedy films
7. They run away to get together
8. Infuriate
9. It often has a name that's a reduplication
10. Citrusy bar order
11. It's pointless
12. Lead actor or actress
13. *The Man from U.N.C.L.E.*
21. Landing posts
24. Tote
25. Injury reminders
26. Polynesian porch
27. Prevention amount
28. Bobby Vinton hit with his initials
31. Fit for swine
32. *Cat Ballou* actor
33. Rims
35. Grammy-winning Carpenter
36. Horsey (according to *OED*)
38. Anxious
40. Uniting spots, often
42. Frizz may fill them
45. GI bill
46. It's nothing to look forward to
47. Gulf off Iran
48. Bad habit
49. They're dealt, but they're not hands
51. Race loser
52. Work units
53. Burn balm
54. Force unit

❖ **Solution on page 290**

More X Appeal   *Douglas Fink*

ACROSS

1. *JAG* network
4. To-do list items
9. Bird word
14. Cut into
15. Censor
16. Small amounts
17. *When We Were Kings* role
18. Galactica muckamuck
19. Ruth's mother-in-law
20. Beaker for ashes?
23. Quiche need
24. Dinah kitchen-mate
28. Suns
33. Cereal grain
34. Win the love of
36. Maria's preceder
37. Why a censor is needed
42. Now I've got it!
43. ___ moment
44. Distant
48. Cold-blooded ones
52. Leftovers container
54. PlayStation people
55. Impressive bruncheon spread
60. Swell
63. Workshop items
64. Admirer
65. It might be scenic
66. Tanner's wares
67. One-spot
68. Chose
69. Eat away at
70. You there!

DOWN

1. Rubbed the wrong way
2. Fish for the rich
3. With a certain lilt
4. It'll give you a lift
5. *M*A*S*H* actor
6. Ingmar Bergman title noun
7. Dole's '96 running mate
8. Fixes
9. Movie theater
10. Scam artist
11. Bearded judge
12. Castle attack device
13. Trident-shaped letter
21. Anglo-Saxon kingdom
22. Be a yegg
25. Last king of Norway
26. First name in *Scream* stars
27. Hurricane oasis
29. *Witchblade* airer
30. It means trouble
31. Umps with stripes
32. Less at risk
35. Actress Russo
37. Pad ___
38. Deservedly get
39. It might be in the air
40. 55A subject
41. Fan o' the green
42. Where to see the wake
45. Recently
46. Like some vases
47. Repair
49. Bath brush
50. Prep a shoe
51. Aussie city
53. Rapid rotator
56. Film style
57. Idiot
58. Mixed, like colors
59. Latin life
60. Buddy
61. Chop
62. Ump's cry

❖ Solution on page 290

Let's Fly   *Merle Baker*

ACROSS

1. First name in gothic horror
5. Dad
9. Some paintings
14. Traditional knowledge
15. Like Humpty-Dumpty
16. Former Boston Symphony leader
17. Julie's *East of Eden* role
18. News follower
19. Omega alternative
20. Ticket counter handout
23. ___ Little
24. Freud subject
25. "___ you serious?"
28. Sec
31. Outrage
33. "Take a Chance on Me" group
37. Inspection target
39. Coils around
41. Two-time Barrymore costar
42. Associate with
43. Bump-up position
46. Spiffy
47. Let out, as a line
48. Serve additional
50. Caustic compound
51. A lamentation
53. Referees, slangily
58. Airport area
61. High-strung
64. Polly, to Tom Sawyer
65. Spherical start
66. Don Quixote had one
67. Fields expletive
68. Endeavor
69. Tuxedo accessory
70. Overstuff
71. Guitarist Duane ___

DOWN

1. Spills the beans
2. Woody's *Sleeper* disguise
3. Chilean-born pianist Claudio
4. Stiller partner
5. The body ___
6. Baker's need
7. Twinge
8. Incline
9. Mediocre
10. Weapons of war
11. 12D, maybe
12. See 11D
13. Sidney Bechet's instrument
21. Hoops legend, familiarly
22. Part of FEMA
25. Three-time Pulitzer Prize–winning playwright
26. *Giant* ranch
27. Lysergic acid source
29. Lessen
30. Certain club member
32. "Come ___"
33. Horrid
34. Like Great Salt Lake
35. Danseuse's support
36. Vaulted area
38. Artifice
40. James and Jon
44. Drano target
45. Crepes ___
49. Bodybuilding target
52. "Gosh!"
54. Unconcerned
55. Gave thumbs up to
56. Had an intention
57. Like many bars
58. Word with man or boy
59. Intangible quality
60. Punkie
61. Centers of ops.
62. Oater reply
63. Stew bit

❖ **Solution on page 291**

Britishisms 1 *Douglas Fink*

ACROSS

1. Hackneyed
6. Small songbird
10. Study the night before
14. It helps make a positive connection
15. Seabiscuit, for one
16. Where the Wabash is
17. What the Brits call a bed-sitter
20. Seven of them are deadly
21. Gurus
22. Rash
23. Cluster
24. Guy's mate
25. They'll knock you out
29. Thanksgiving attendee
33. The ones here
34. Party pooper
36. Bento box soup
37. What the Brits call argy-bargies
40. "Angelo" instrument
41. Atop
42. Rolling Stones hit
43. Life savings
45. Angled joints
46. Actress Plumb
47. Beach item for a kid
49. The Bambino's legacy
52. Baby powder
53. They show up on an x-ray
57. What the Brits call fruit machines
60. Yadda-yadda in the bibliography
61. Neutral tone
62. A rookie of the year, or to pull out a ballplayer
63. Politician whose name means "welfare" in England
64. Movie about giant ants
65. Title cartoon female in the funny pages

DOWN

1. Low fish?
2. One opposed
3. Any thing
4. Uses an abacus
5. Ho O
6. Waterfront locale
7. Help a plant
8. When things happened
9. Negative conjunction
10. A nice thing to say
11. It'll never fly
12. "___ She Sweet?"
13. Bit of dust
18. *Bloom County* penguin
19. Ruler of yore
23. Where a kid might build a house
24. Expert
25. One of the filmmaking Coens
26. Where I'm pointing
27. A ton
28. Where you might get some good antiques cheap
29. Walt Kelly's possum
30. Suggestion
31. Moving
32. Carrots in the winter
34. Wild West sound
35. Scrap
38. Venetian veep
39. Snail ___
44. Penultimate fairy tale word
45. Transparent mineral
47. Father Mulcahy, for one
48. It's a record
49. College attendee
50. Biblical preposition
51. Actual
52. The guy who can fix the computer
53. Light bulb indication
54. Dryer dirt
55. Rash result
56. Pale
58. Came together
59. *The Associate* network

❖ Solution on page 291

Overhead   *Merle Baker*

1. Legal rights org.
5. Charity
9. Bach creation
14. Fedora feature
15. Triumph
16. Mimics
17. Arrived
18. Opposed
19. Setting occupier
20. A precaution
23. Spot of land in the Seine
24. Boat pronoun
25. Frosh's concern
28. Have
31. Successor to Muhammad
34. Marx cohort
36. It might add a touch of elegance
39. Pin ___ on (incriminate)
40. Fields of comedy
41. Start for horse or man
42. Senseless
43. Lawyer Dershowitz
44. Cooler
46. President Clinton, at times
48. Accord
49. Early home computer ___-80
50. Barcelona bear
51. Resinous deposit
53. Motorists' org.
55. It may lend a rustic air
62. Laborious routine
64. Sleek
65. Exclamations of surprise
66. Draw out
67. Free from bias
68. Boast
69. Broken
70. Ran away
71. Vestments

DOWN

1. Basics
2. Prepare for a test
3. VIP wheels
4. Oscar winner for *Sayonara*
5. Professors' milieu
6. Solitary
7. Pound find
8. CIA workers
9. Attach
10. Doing
11. Legend says he turned down the role of Rick Blaine
12. Server with a spigot
13. Language ending
21. Slur over
22. *Mask* star
26. Flat
27. Trembling trees
28. Page size
29. Complete things
30. Place to make a splash
32. Spiny-leafed plant
33. Some skirts
35. Chain ___
37. Barcelona boy
38. Like some fish
42. Ancient civilization
44. Cliff projection
45. Briefly
47. Gave the slip
52. Worthless matter
54. Addis ___
56. Formerly
57. Restore to soundness
58. New York canal
59. British nobleman
60. Fictional captain
61. E-mail: Abbr.
62. Acquire
63. Vitamin bottle letters

❖ **Solution on page 291**

Bridges *Merle Baker*

ACROSS

1. Kind of team
5. They might be fine
9. Drink add-ins
14. Aspirin target
15. Furniture wood
16. They're on the list
17. Hold back
18. Memorial Day event
19. Wonderland treats
20. Deep singers
23. Be in session
24. Unspecified number
25. Rats
29. ___-bitsy
31. Shout when laying down
34. Story featuring Achilles
35. Phobia start
36. Chief Roman goddess
37. One of " . . . "
40. Lyric poems
41. Slippery
42. Gives the once-over
43. Cartoon Chihuahua
44. Exert influence on
45. Night spot
46. Unspecified individual
47. Part of PBS
48. Emulated the *Times*
56. It might be a goodie
57. Novel plantation
58. Put in other words
59. Company with a keystone-shaped label
60. Uttered
61. Depend
62. Pink Floyd song
63. Canadian prov.
64. Cameo stone

DOWN

1. Window section
2. Pro-Prohibition org.
3. Throat clearer
4. Fill in
5. Billy Strayhorn's "Take the ___"
6. Give a snappy comeback
7. Add (onto)
8. Slant
9. Repetitive recital
10. Lodi location
11. Measly
12. CPR givers
13. Slow leak
21. Half a 45
22. Sports
25. Sun shader
26. Keep clear of
27. Increased
28. Drivers' aids
29. Without warmth
30. Aikman of the Cowboys
31. Culpability
32. Kind of beauty
33. Untrue
35. On the briny
36. Nudges
38. Not as familiar
39. Model's strong point
44. Happy partner
45. Excessively
46. Sheeplike
47. Word with man or hat
48. Role for Liz
49. Norse creator
50. College of England
51. Challenge
52. Infamous emperor
53. Churchill's successor
54. Cunning
55. Entrance to the underworld
56. Resistance unit

❖ **Solution on page 291**

I Ask for Nothing   Adrian Powell

ACROSS

1. Revenue producers
6. Butler's need
10. Boutique
14. Sacred song
15. Play part
16. Persian pixie
17. What Miss Piggy's agent did?
20. Kid's game
21. Good-for-nothing slimeball
22. From Cardiff
23. Carnation supporter
24. Enemy
25. Reaction of horror
28. Trim for royalty
31. Con vote
34. Subsequently
36. With no tape delay
39. What a good accountant should have done?
42. Werewolf time?
43. Hive dweller
44. Building addition
45. Italian nobles
48. Means justifiers
49. Besides
51. Pie crust ingredient
53. Once more
56. Senator's opponent?
58. Security guard's demands
61. What you should have done with a talkative kid
64. Pouting expression
65. From the top
66. Dark shadow
67. Shady trees
68. Officer's establishment
69. Gin game

DOWN

1. Name for a dalmatian
2. Bhutan locale
3. Country's k.d. ___
4. Caribou cousin
5. Bait fish
6. ER's concern
7. Arabian Knights birds
8. Medicinal lily
9. Sudden desire
10. Binge
11. Get better
12. Tolkien monsters
13. Safari helmet material
18. Buck's partners
19. Duet complement
23. Wizard's forte
24. Phobia
25. Blunder
26. Entangled
27. Moonshine maker's need
29. Unbroken horse
30. Bucharest currency
31. Tricky Dicky
32. Change for the better
33. Encouraging words
35. Radiation dose
37. Canadian corporate designation
38. Deducted from gross weight
40. Wonderland bird
41. "___ rang?"
46. Bends in a pipe
47. Delhi dress
49. Mah-jongg pieces
50. Low note?
52. Happen again
53. Career peak
54. Brig in Britain
55. Astringent
56. All there
57. Birds, collectively
58. Silo weapon, briefly
59. College residence
60. Fix the cat
62. Hydroelectric need
63. Outback runner

❖ **Solution on page 291**

The Theater   Merle Baker

ACROSS

1. Affects adversely
6. One may be broken in court
11. Forbid
14. Audiophile's purchase
15. "John Brown's Body" penner
16. Western Indian
17. Midwestern Indian
18. Ancient Greek social centers
19. King James alt.
20. Avant-garde venue
22. Atticus Finch creator
23. Criticize strongly
24. A nearby star
25. Difficult thing
26. Lamb Chop's friend
28. PETA targets
30. Across from: Abbr.
33. Clinton Cabinet member
35. Kindle
38. Confronts Imus
41. 'Tis author
43. Laos neighbors
44. Catch by a longline boat, perhaps
46. Two-time U.S. Open champ
47. Desires
49. Deplete
52. Pearl Harbor locale
54. Flight
56. It's inexplicable
60. Gone by
61. Resort offering
63. Robert Morse title role
64. One training
65. Nintendo competitor
66. "___ a Rebel"
67. Poker player's declaration
68. Kind of position
69. Holy ___
70. None too bright
71. Henry's son

DOWN

1. Island group near Fiji
2. The Misfits actor
3. Sternward
4. Cuban dance tunes
5. Sully
6. Palindromic pop group
7. Ushers
8. Cleaved
9. Interest
10. Start of a children's song
11. Comics' training ground
12. Clueless
13. "When pigs fly!"
21. Giraffe's cousin
25. Pizzazz
27. Clinton Cabinet member
29. Scanner reading: Abbr.
30. When DST ends
31. Tuba note?
32. Old Vic, for one
34. Latin 101 word
36. Browser bookmark
37. Little green men, for short
39. In ___ of
40. W-2 info: Abbr.
42. Brighten
45. Beats
48. Lumber carrier
50. "___ at Any Speed"
51. Like the surface of the moon
52. Statements of fealty
53. Jibe
55. Mideast capital
57. Fall guys
58. Jazzy Carmen
59. Bond film A View to ___
61. Egypt's Port ___
62. Agatha contemporary

❖ Solution on page 291

259

More Britishisms *Douglas Fink*

ACROSS

1. Middle aged one?
6. Move like 25D
10. ___ noire . . .
14. 1945 conference site
15. Part of Nixon's downfall
16. Co. VIP
17. What the Brits call a bunch of fives
20. Slippery wiggler
21. Britain's neighbor, formally
22. *Midnight Cowboy* role
23. ". . . ___ of thieves"
24. *Remote Control* host
26. Collided
29. Dead-end neighborhood?
33. Publisher of this book
34. ___ speak
35. It alters you at the altar
36. What the Brits call has a natter
40. Favor lead-in
41. Low on dough
42. Goaded
43. Present-wrapping need
46. Fixate
47. Dietetic
48. Unseemly
49. Fomenting
52. *Godfather* guy
53. Accomplished
56. What the Brits call back of the beyond
60. Dust Bowl wanderer
61. Float
62. Kind of engagement
63. Mattel dolls
64. Salamanders
65. Word in a J. K. Rowling title

DOWN

1. Trike user
2. Go out of favor
3. Twelfth Hebrew month
4. List ender
5. Least clad
6. He played a thief in *Home Alone*
7. Lack of difficulty
8. MPG rater
9. Sword defeater?
10. Look out!
11. Labyrinth terminus
12. Gumshoes
13. It makes a comeback
18. Told a whopper
19. Scott in 1857 news
23. Shot and such
24. *The ___ Limits*
25. Monster in a 1958 horror film
26. Grates
27. Thrown together for a cause
28. Kiwi hunter
29. Some salmon
30. Blockade
31. Cutters
32. Cutters of another sort, perhaps
34. Where the buys are
37. Munster pet
38. Masseur specialties
39. Gaelic
44. Playground items
45. Little ledge
46. Greek liqueur
48. Little ones in a litter
49. One way to run
50. Try a ten-speed
51. Valhalla veep
52. Go ___ (disappear)
53. "Whip It" group
54. Persia, today
55. Cut it out
57. Baa ma
58. Clod
59. Rabbit concealer

❖ **Solution on page 291**

Even More Britishisms   *Douglas Fink*

ACROSS

1. Hopper
5. Veggie dish
10. A certain sultan's domain
14. For those trying to lose
15. Gulf Arab
16. Lomond or Ness
17. State firmly
18. Places for worms
19. Iroquois Indian
20. What the Brits call Alsatians
23. Archie's command
24. Go through a manuscript
25. Pro ___
27. Achy areas
28. Video host of yore
31. London district
33. It's unrefined
36. What the Brits call a busker
40. Dallas sch.
41. *The Way We ___*
42. Tick off
43. Coolant
46. Care unit?
48. Deduces
50. Disquiet
54. What the Brits call whitener
58. Curlicue-shaped molding
59. Put on the table
60. French films
61. Inquisitive
62. Don't wait for the draft
63. Alternative word
64. Being, to Brutus
65. Evade
66. They stain

DOWN

1. National symbols
2. Rosie's bit
3. SNL comedienne
4. Antiseptic
5. Shakespearean poetry
6. "Rag Mop" brothers
7. Tie down
8. Feed the kitty
9. Theorem crusher
10. Ace place?
11. Fretful
12. Etching materials
13. The ones here
21. Getting ___ start
22. That girl
26. Rockies resort
27. Kate, notably
28. Viper's sound
29. Robo-banker
30. Curmudgeon's characteristic
32. Aloft, poetically
34. Ser. speaker
35. Prior to
37. Like a coin
38. State one's view
39. Backtracked
44. Photo flaw
45. Baseball stat
47. Race
48. Hole follower
49. They've been called off
51. Americanized one
52. Meaning
53. Forest filler
55. Gambling town
56. Place to rake
57. It gets trapped in a trap

❖ **Solution on page 291**

CONTRIBUTORS

DAVE FISHER

Besides creating various puzzles and word games such as cryptic crosswords, acrostic puzzles, and pyramid puzzles, Dave Fisher also maintains one of the most comprehensive Web sites devoted to puzzles and puzzle aficionados. You can visit him online at *puzzles.about.com*.

GRACE BECKER

She graduated from the Wichita State University with a Bachelor of Business Administration degree. She has four children, eight grandchildren, and ten great-grandchildren. She has been addicted to crossword puzzles since her teen years. For the last ten or so years, she has been constructing puzzles.

VIV O. COLLINS

The daughter of Grace Becker, she is a freelance writer whose puzzles have appeared in many publications and on various Web sites.

LANE GUTZ

Lane Gutz is a computer technician from Cedar Rapids, Iowa. He enjoys working with computers, making crossword puzzles, and collecting exotic pets. He extends his thanks to Anna Gutz, Larry Gutz, and Gary Sargent for testing his puzzles prior to submission.

ALAN OLSCHWANG

Alan Olschwang is sixty-two and lives in Huntington Beach, California. He was in the Chicago area until he was forty-two and then spent seven years in Westchester before moving to California. He's been married for thirty-seven years, has three kids, and two grandchildren, with a third on the way. He still works as a lawyer (General Counsel of a company for more than twenty years), having done that since 1966.

LESLIE NICOLL

After years of solving puzzles, Leslie Nicoll decided to learn the game of constructing—which to her surprise and delight, she finds very satisfying. Leslie owns her own business, Maine Desk, LLC, which provides professional editorial assistance to aspiring authors, primarily in nursing and healthcare. She lives in Westbrook,

Maine, with her husband, son, and daughter, and their retired racing greyhound.

SYLVIA THOMPSON

Sylvia Thompson is a senior citizen and also a housewife. She has always enjoyed working with words. She likes to solve crossword puzzles and also likes to create them.

MATTHEW SKOCZEN

Matthew Skoczen was born and raised in Philadelphia, but now lives in Reading, Pennsylvania. He is a teacher and loves to travel when given the chance. He enjoys Broadway, films, and reading. He is also interested in winning an Academy Award someday for Best Screenplay . . . as soon as he writes the film!

ADRIAN POWELL

Adrian Powell has been publishing crosswords and other word puzzles since 1990. He currently produces puzzles on a daily basis for the media in Canada and has appeared in several other publications throughout North America. He now lives in Winnipeg, Manitoba, Canada.

MICHAEL WIESENBERG

Michael Wiesenberg is the author of *The Official Dictionary of Poker*, and three other books, available at finer Web sites and bookstores everywhere. He writes a biweekly column for *The Card Player* magazine. His crossword puzzles appear on several Web sites, including PokerPages.com, and in *LA Direct* and *Advance for Nurses*. He is a technical writer by trade.

ROY LEBAN

Roy Leban has been a software designer, developer, and inventor for more than twenty-five years. In his spare time, he is a photographic artist, ambigramist, gourmet cook, writer, and puzzle constructor. His puzzles have appeared in the *New York Times*, the *Los Angeles Times*, *GAMES Magazine*, and elsewhere.

Appendix B

Resources

If you want to solve or create crossword puzzles, there are some resources you should know about.

The grand collection of everything crossword (that's "everything" with a lowercase "e"—not an Adams Media title) is Ray Hamel's *http://www.primate.wisc.edu/people/hamel/cp.html*. This should help you find anything out there related to crosswords.

If you're just looking to solve crosswords, I'd like to recommend the Newspaper Puzzles section of Dave Fisher's *http://puzzles.about.com/cs/crosswords/*; I think I started out here before miningco ended up under About.com (if you go up a level, you can also find cryptics, diagramless, and other variants).

If you're ready to compete, or just want to meet some of the top solvers and constructors in the country, there's the national tournament held in Stamford, Connecticut, run by Will Shortz; he edits the *New York Times* crosswords and runs "The Puzzler Presents" on NPR. The tournament's Web site is: *www.crosswordtournament.com*.

Like playing with words in general? Perhaps you should check out the National Puzzlers' League (NPL) at *www.puzzlers.org*. I'm not just a client, I'm the . . . wait a minute, I'm just a member.

Wondering what software there is out there for solving or constructing? Crossword Compiler seems to have become the standard, although you may also want to consider Across Lite (a solver), Crossdown, Across, and Crossword Maestro.

Perhaps you're looking for a forum; a place to learn the recommended rules of construction, ask questions, or even solicit special projects. A place to comment on new lingo and people that may be ready to start showing up in puzzles. A place to ask about how dubious a certain grid entry is. The place to go is *http://www.cruciverb.com*, which also has a Basic Rules page and a Sage Advice page, which might easily answer your construction questions.

Maybe you're working on a puzzle (solving or creating) and realize that you need to look something up, like "I know there was a character named ___ in a movie, TV show, or play I saw." Well, for movie and TV, *www. imdb.com* is a must, and *www.itdb.com* is helpful for the theater. You probably want a good dictionary and thesaurus on hand, maybe an atlas, book of quotations, and reader's guide, too.

There used to be a group on the Net called rec.puzzles.crosswords. While old, its information is still useful: *hppt://thinks.com/faq/crosswords*.

There are a lot of good word list files out there for making crossword puzzles with; just make sure that you edit in the good, and edit out the bad from them. The NPL's *www. puzzlers.org/secure/wordlists/dictinfo.php* is a good place to start, and includes Grady Ward's Moby dictionary, the largest dictionary out there, methinks. Or, for some categorized lists, you might want to try *www.phreak.org/html/word lists.shtml* (or *www.cotse.com/tools/wordlists.htm* if you'd rather not unzip the files).

And, of course, my personal plug for my own Web sites at *www.geocities.com/xwdguy* and *www.themecrossword.com*.

Appendix B

Puzzle Answers

page 2 • **The Optimist**

```
G E N G H I S
O D O R A N T
D E T E N T E
S N E A K E R N
        T E R N
T A V E R N S
A L E X
T O R P E D O
A N N E X E D
R E A C T E D
        T O R E
I M P A L E R
N E A T
S A T I A T E
I N T O N E R
S I E N N A S
T E N S E S T
```

page 3 • **Ringmaster**

```
C A R A C A S
A B A L O N E
L E V E L E D
F L E X I N G
        A N T E
O P E N
C A R D I A C
T W E E D L E
        R E A R
S U G G E S T
A P E R
R O M A N C E
I N S H O R E
        A W O L
W A R M
A L A B A M A
L O R E L E I
S H E L T E R
H A R L O T S
```

page 4 • **Dollar Exchange**

```
S C A B   G A P E R   P S A S
T U N A   O H A R E   F O N T
A M E N   C A I R N   C U J O
G I N G E R B R E A D   R O M
E N D O R A   D U D E D U P
    R A Z O R   L E N O
S E W   T Y B A L T   Y U L E
A L A M O   O W E   L A G E R
D I V A   D E L A N O   H O G
    Y U R I   S H A W N
F I G L E A F   S E E S A W
A G R   F R O M S C R A T C H
U L A N   I R A T E   T A T A
L O V E   S C I O N   E R A T
T O Y S   T E M P T   N E S S
```

page 5 • Dukes

```
BURST ACES  THEE
ANEAR ROTC  HOME
STAGECOACH  EVIL
SOL  MAST  MOWERS
     NOTE  FORA
MACERS  RIOBRAVO
AVOWS  BENZ  WREN
PROF  ARTIE  AIRS
LIER  CARS  AGAVE
ELDORADO  CLOSET
     NODS  ROAN
GOATEE  SHIM  ERA
UGLI  MAKEROFMEN
TREE  IDEA  DAUNT
SEER  COWS  EASTS
```

page 6 • Ring Toss

```
SWAT  AGED  LOESS
HIVE  LOLA  APNEA
ATIT  AWES  TERNS
HARDINGHISCASH
SETAE  YEN   GOA
PARDNER  STALER
ASI   VIA   OUI
EXCHANGINGVWS
RES   ODE   AAH
STYMIE  ADASTRA
ATA   ONO   STEAL
FUNDINGFATHERS
RAGON  RULE  LRON
ORLON  ASEA  LATE
STEMS  MESS  ATAD
```

page 7 • Goners

```
DEBT  WORST  PRIM
UVEA  ERATO  REDO
MEAL  LINER  ITEM
BRUCELEEMAJORS
       STELE  ERA
ESP  HAS  ART  NBC
SHOWER  ADO  ASEA
TOMARNOLDPALMER
OOPS  EWE  ENTICE
PTA  ODE  ALI  THY
       DUO  TEALS
RONHOWARDSTERN
THUS  NOMAD  ROUE
HERA  CRETE  ANEW
EASY  ENDER  PSST
```

page 8 • Planetarium

```
RASH  THUG  COVET
EXPO  PERE  ANISE
PLUTOCRAT  TESTA
SENNA  ILSA  SEER
       ERST  EAST
CADS  EARTHMOVER
DRESSAGE  OPINE
REB  OREGANO  STE
ONAIR  AGITATES
MARSEILLES  DARE
       ARNO  RICO
LADD  NOTA  URBAN
OLIOS  SATURNINE
SPARK  EMUS  ETTA
ESSAY  REMS  DEER
```

page 9 • Whirled Leaders

```
DECAL  SAPS  WEPT
EARTO  OTRA  ALLA
PUTINPUTININPUT
    EGO  UNDREAMT
ALA  OOP  TIO  SEL
BICS  FLA  ENCODE
MOTIF  ADAGIO
NIXONNIXONNIX
  PROTEM  GENRE
LEMMAS  TAR  STAR
ORO  YER  NAP  OYS
CARNEGIE  YEA
ASSADASASSADSAD
TEEM  YETI  CAINE
ERLE  SNAP  ERROR
```

page 10 • Vehicular

```
SUMO  ADAPT  LORE
PREP  ROGUE  AHEM
AIDE  CREPE  MINI
INTHESAMEBOAT
PRO  HEM   EDAM
EUCLIDIANPLANE
SIREN  LOIS
ONES  GEODE  IDOL
    GIGO  GOOSE
TRAINOFTHOUGHT
HERB  YOU   GAS
AUTOBIOGRAPHY
BRIM  CLEAR  OBOE
BORA  BLEND  BAAS
AWES  MASTS  OGRE
```

page 11 • Men on Film

```
SWAM  MBAS   ALSO
AIRY  ALGOL  REIN
MLLE  KOALA  POSE
PIERCEBROSNAN
LENSES  SSA   AHI
ERE  DINT  ICEMAN
   PETERSELLERS
PALE   HIE   ISTO
ALECGUINNESS
NEESON  IDLE  IGO
TAJ  BSA  YASSER
CLINTEASTWOOD
OBOE  AERIE  OLDE
RUBE  PAINE  ODER
EBBS  METS   NESS
```

page 12 • Handy

```
OWES  CITY  AMISH
DELI  AREA  DITTO
ORAL  PALMDESERT
RENEWS  LAW  EMIL
   NOUN  HEARSAY
KNUCKLEBALL
EASE  EWE  LESSEN
EVERS  SIB  EPODE
LESSON  NET  LAGS
   FINGERLAKES
PALETTE   FEAT
IDOL  TAD  ASTERN
NAILBITERS  EPEE
TIRES  ECHO  RIDS
ARENA  NOON  SCOT
```

page 13 • Playing the Game

```
DAZED  TLC  SMOTE
OLIVE  AIR  HERON
CANON  NEO  ANTED
KICKINGUPAFUSS
       EMU   SIT
PAWS  MER  MIRAGE
ALA  RECAP  NUDES
PASSINGJUDGMENT
UNPEG  SARAS  LIE
ASSAIL  HER  FEES
       DES   TRA
RUNNINGTHERISK
LEVEE  EYE  SCOPE
IDEAS  ERR  ERWIN
BOATS  RON  WYATT
```

page 14 • **Spice Shop**

```
I R A   D E A L S T O   A M P
G E T   Y E S I C A N   I R E
N U T M E G S T A T E   R M N
O N R E D     E M T S   M A D
B I A S   P U R P L E S A G E
L O C A T E S   S E C T I O N
E N T   H E E L     A L O T
      C U R R Y C O M B
T S A R     E R G O   A M B
E M P O R I A   A R B I T E R
P E P P E R G A M E   T O D O
I L O   A V E R     I O N I A
D T S   G I N G E R B R E A D
L E E   A N T O N Y M   R T E
Y D S   N E S T L E S   S E N
```

page 15 • **Take Charge**

```
T Y P O   T A P I R   S E R F
R E A P   A B I D E   A R I A
A T I T   M O T E S   J I N X
M I L I T A R Y A T T A C K
      M O L T   A O K
S A T I R E   B O R N   A N D
C R E S S   H E R E   S L U R
R E S T O R E B A T T E R Y
A N T S   E R R S   W O R S E
P A Y   S C A D   W I N T E R
      S P Y   E A S E
  U S E A C R E D I T C A R D
G N A T   L E X U S   O L E O
E D I T   E N A C T   L O A N
T O D O   D O M E S   D E L E
```

page 16 • **Top Notch**

```
T E A L   S K A T   S W A B S
E D G E   T A P E   P I T O N
A N O A   A L A N   I N T R O
M A G N I F I C E N T   R I O
      T A F F E T A   G A S P
S C I O N S       M I S C
E L M S     M O D E R A T O R
L I P   S U B R O S A   I D A
F O R T U N A T E   A V O N
      E R I C     D E S E R T
B U S Y   A S S U R E S
E S S   S P E C T A C U L A R
R H I N O   T R I P   A I D E
R E V E L   T O L E   G R I D
A R E T E   O D E S   E A T S
```

page 17 • **Up and Atom**

```
H A S P S   A M B O   P O R E
A L L O T   B U R N   E M I T
J O U L E C A S E S   R A S H
J E R S E Y   H A H   R H E A
      L A R E D O   Y A R N
A B U T   N O S T R U M
S O P H I S T   H E R E T I C
A S T E R       A S I D E
P H O B I A S   D O L O R E S
      O S M O S E D   N E S S
M A S H   E M I L I O
E M I R   L E G   U P C A S T
S P E W   I O N A M E R I C A
A L G A   A N A T   R A D A R
S E E R   S E L L   A G E N T
```

page 20 • **I Hear Voices**

```
A P H I D   U M B E R   C E O
S H I V A   M A O R I   A M N
T O N Y S O P R A N O   N P S
E N D   C A S K   T I T H E
R O U G H S   C O O L C A T
    A L T O C U M U L U S
B E L I E   P A R I S   T I P
A X O N   A I M A T   G I Z A
D I S   J A N E T   D E T E R
  T E N O R E L E V E N
C R O W N E D   I C E C A P
H A U T E   S O L O   L E A
E M T   S T R I P E D B A S S
F P O   E V E N T   E U R O S
S S N   S A C K S   D R A P E
```

page 21 • **Not Out of the Woods Yet**

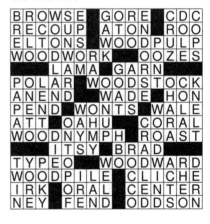

```
B R O W S E   G O R E   C D C
R E C O U P   A T O N   R O O
E L T O N S   W O O D P U L P
W O O D W O R K   O O Z E S
      L A M A   G A R N
P O L A R   W O O D S T O C K
A N E N D   W A D E   H O N
P E N D   W O N T S   W A L E
A T T   O A H U   C O R A L
W O O D N Y M P H   R O A S T
      I T S Y   B R A D
T Y P E O   W O O D W A R D
W O O D P I L E   C L I C H E
I R K   O R A L   C E N T E R
N E Y   F E N D   O D D S O N
```

page 22 • **Late Affirmations**

```
A L M A   D E N T   S C A L A
N E E D   A D A R   P A L E R
D A N D U R Y E A   A S I D O
E S L   N E S   S O D A C A N
S H O O I N   T H I E V E
    N C O   H T S   A F E W
M A S C O T   U V E A   A T E
A S N E R       R O Y A L
S T A   N A P A   E M M E T T
S I K H   B O B   N O N
    E A S E L S   T R I C I A
S T E R I L E   O R E   A H A
L O Y A L   C A M E R A M E N
I D E S T   A R E A   L E A D
M O S S Y   T E N T   G O R P
```

page 23 • **As Seen on TV**

```
R I B   S C U M   S C H E M E
E R A   H I F I   K E E N A N
M A G N A V O X   E R R A N D
    L O R I S   H I T A C H I
W E A S E L   H E N   T U N
O L D Y   I G O R   A L O N G
P L Y   C A R O M   K A R T S
    P A N A S O N I C
A S T E R   B I S O N   H A S
W H E R E   B E A R   D O L L
E E R   E A R   M E A S L Y
S A M S U N G   M A L T A
O R I E N T   S Y L V A N I A
M E N A C E   O N C E   N O R
E D I T O R   W A Y S   A N T
```

page 24 • **Bridge Tutorial**

```
L A C K S   S P A S   E T C H
I N A N E   L I V E   C O R E
O T T E R   A S E A   H U E S
N I S E I   P A S S P O R T S
      A H S   T I E   S E E
D O U B L E H E A D E R
E L L A   S O D   E R E C T S
E L A N D   T I P   S N O O T
R A N C O R   T R E   E L I A
      O P E N H A N D E D L Y
U S E   E G O   I D A
S L A M D U N K S   P L A T E
H O S E   L A N E   P A D R E
E P E E   A G A R   E M A I L
R E S T   R E P S   R A M P S
```

page 25 • **I Like Candy**

page 26 • **Cheese All That**

page 27 • **'50s Pop Music**

page 28 • **Nonsense**

page 29 • **A Little Rearranging**

page 30 • **Aviary Authors**

page 31 • **You Can Say That Again**

page 32 • **No Three-ums 1**

page 33 • **Just In Time**

page 34 • **Metallic**

```
PAPA PEAKS COST
AMIS ONSET ORCA
TINSOLDIER NEAP
ENTER SANA COBS
ROSTRA EURO
    SILVERSCREEN
DAM SLIP SADDLE
ABET ASA SILL
DENIMS ORTS TAL
ALUMINUMFOIL
    ECUS ONEUPS
AMMO BUDS CALLA
LIEU BRONZESTAR
GNAT EERIE ERNO
ADDS DRAPE SASS
```

page 35 • **No Three-ums 2**

```
FILE SCAR GRAPH
IRON TODO LORRE
FEUD ALDA OCEAN
ENSEMBLES OKAYS
SEEDY INTIME
    SWEDEN TWAS
PINATA ARMAMENT
ABOLISH SAVANNA
DETACHED TINDER
STIR ELOPED
    MARINE LATIN
SPLIT PARTYLINE
LOOSE OHIO OGLE
AORTA RULE HEED
BLEST TESS ARTY
```

page 38 • **Too Clumsy**

```
HEIR ASTI SPASM
ALDA LEON COSTA
HoopsKIRT ROTOR
SILICA TOMAHAWK
    DALE TAP
PAM NINCOMPoops
ALEC SOU ALLURE
PETRI SRI EATON
APRONS ICE VEST
SHOCKTRoops REA
    LEA NILE
SARDINIA SALADS
TRAIN SCoopsHOT
AGING ENID IONE
BODES DELE EYES
```

page 39 • **Homophony**

```
SUDS STEAD AJAR
OTOE ORDER COMA
LADE BADGE THUD
THOMASPAINE NSA
INSECT SCRAPER
    DROSS HORA
CAW ERUPT STYLE
OAHU YEARS SNIT
QUAFF TWEED EPA
    TOLD NEXUS
OFASORT TEAMUP
ZIP PARTIALPANE
ZEAL PERON PUPA
ILIE EVENT EVIL
EDNA DIKES DENS
```

page 40 • **Who in the Dickens?**

```
RINSE ASEA ADEN
ANTED ROVE VIBE
MASAI TIER ODOR
    BETSYTROTWOOD
    AOK BOESKY
TOMGRADGRIND
ORALS WRECK BAH
GALE HEALS BRNO
ANT JOLIE TARTY
    LITTLEDORRIT
SCRAMS EOS
CLARAPEGGOTTY
RANI ELLA SOOTH
ANKA LSAT IONIA
PSST LAME ELDER
```

page 41• **In Position**

```
STRAD BONDS RVS
PAOLI INOIL IEL
ACMES TETRA GNU
TOPPRIORITY HUE
    HUP TREATED
PAL POOR ORZO
INEPT LUNA OFFS
SOFA TIRED TWIN
ANTI HOAR SHARI
    ONTO LOVE YET
TANTARA IRE
ORB BOTTOMPRICE
KIA LURER ENTER
YES AGILE NISEI
OLE SHALL TEASE
```

page 42 • **Ask Away**

```
SLOB SCALA DEBT
LOGE PETIT ECRU
ACRE LOATH THEN
WHEREISTHESHOW
    SST ONOR
SIL EPPS ALONSO
ACED EATA ANAIS
WHOISALEXTREBEK
TONNE MELO DONA
ORSONS PERM BAR
    SATO TAM
WHATISJEOPARDY
LIEU CHERI THEE
APER KEELS CELL
WEDS SAREE HALL
```

page 43 • **Fill the Bill**

```
STRAW MAE SCOPE
LAURA ODD CRIED
ATBAT TAG HULLS
PAYMENTREQUEST
    RIO ULT
THATLL WHIZ EVE
AUDIO JAIL STOW
PROPOSEDSTATUTE
ERRS TRES RYDER
RYE IRKS FIXERS
    GNU ADZ
THEATERPROGRAM
CROON TOE NAOMI
HORDE CUR AGAIN
INNER HEY NAMED
```

page 44 • **Br-r-r!**

```
CAVES WABE AVID
AGILE ARAL MENU
LATIN WELLFIXED
FROZENASSET ERE
    ACE ARRESTS
MTA AWNS YOM
IOWA LOMA OOZES
FROSTYRECEPTION
FILTH MARX ETNA
    ORD REUP ISP
VITRIOL DIG
ONO COLDHEARTED
TABLEWARE ZAIRE
EPEE OMAR ZINGY
STYE PAYS ALTOS
```

page 45 • Cooked Books

```
S C R A M   H A L F   E D G E
T E A R Y   U V E A   R E E L
A L I A S   M O S S   I T E M
F I N N E G A N S C A K E
F A Y   L A N   E I N   R H O
    O F R I C E A N D M E N
L E S T   Y S L   A R I A S
O A T H   S M E L T   A N T E
O G R E S   A A R   N E S T
F E A R O F F R Y I N G
A R T   O R E   E P A   I D A
    F E T A M O R P H O S E S
W H O A   M A L I   A L L I S
E A R S   E L A N   N I E C E
E D D Y   D E F G   T O T E S
```

page 46 • Prepare to Act

```
L E A R   C O L I N   S T E M
A X L E   A M O C O   T I L E
S T A G E R I G H T   A T O M
E R R   L E T O   E M I L I O
R A M B L E   S E V E R E
    R A R E   V E T   R A G
J E D I   S E R E N E   O S U
P A R T S   R E N   R U L E S
E V A   H O I S T S   S E C T
G E M   A V E   S A V E
    A L P E R T   S E R I E S
R A C I E R   E S S A   G L O
U C L A   S C H O O L P L A Y
S L U R   E I E I O   I O T A
T U B S   E T E R N   T O E S
```

page 47 • What's Missing?

```
S A S S   P R I O R   H O L M
T R O T   R H O D A   A M I R
A C L U   O U T O N   S A P S
G O O D S A M A R I T A N S
    I A M B   S A G
H A N O I   A M P   B O S S A
A R O U N D   I B M   C N N
F I R S T A I D S T A T I O N
T O M   G A S   A U R O R A
S T A B S   M T S   R A N T S
    L O S   A D A M
Z O O L O G I C A L P A R K
T O N O   L A I R D   I V A N
A L U M   I L I A D   N O G O
M A S S   D A I L Y   G N A T
```

page 48 • Family Films

```
A G H A   P A R D S   D O V E
G E A R   E Q U I P   A V I V
H I R E   A U N T I E M A M E
A S P   F L A T T E N S
S H E A R   S O L D E R E D
T A R B A B Y   S L I M E
    C U R A C A O   N U B
  D A D D Y L O N G L E G S
F A R   N E T T L E D
O Z A R K   S E A G U L L
R E B U I L D S   S Y R I A
    S T E E P E S T   A N D
B R O T H E R R A T   E N I D
A I D E   R E E V E   M I N I
A G E D   S K E E T   S A G E
```

page 49 • Double Duty

```
S P I C   A N T I   J E W E L
P O O R   S U E S   A V I L A
A L T O   S C A M   L I N E N
S E A S H E L L S H O C K E D
    S O R E   O P T
A P R   U T I L I T Y   M S G
S H E A R   L I E   C O H O
C O F F I N N A I L B I T E R
O N A T   A I M   R A T E S
T E X   M U L A T T O   O N E
    O A R   R O W S
I R O N C U R T A I N C A L L
N O O S E   A R I L   O R E O
S U P E R   M I N E   P E N D
T E S T S   P O S T   E A S E
```

page 50 • From Broadway

```
G R A M   E A N E S   S K A T
R A R E   S H U L A   T I L E
A D D S   C A T S C R A D L E
F I E S T A   S A H E L
T O N   A P B   E D I S T O
    G R E A S E M O N K E Y
T O T S   E N C A S E   O R E
S W E A T   K A T   S T A R R
A L E   A T O N E R   I L E S
R E N T C O N T R O L S
S T Y R O N   S A O   A M P
    A M I D E   D U L L E R
C H I C A G O C U B   A L S O
A U N T   H O R S E   N E O N
D E N S   T R U E D   D Y N E
```

page 51 • Getting Around

```
D I L L   C U P P Y   U N T O
I D E A   E N E R O   P E R U
A L A S   C L A I M   T W I T
L E F T F I E L D   S H E A R
    S A L A   E S T E L L E
F A N   S I D E S H O W
A N E W   A E C   E L A P S E
C O S E C   D O C   E L E C T
E N S I L E   L A G   L O A N
    G A D G E T R Y   N B A
E N T H U S E   S E E M
L O A D S   M A K E R I G H T
L O B O   L I M I T   S L A B
E N O W   A N I L E   T U N A
T E R N   W I E L D   Y E A R
```

page 52 • Going Down

```
S T E P   B O A R D   A U K S
H O P E   E N T E R   S T A T
A M I N   A C E V E N T U R A
H E C T A R E S   A R R A Y
    A R C   S A V A N T S
K I N G M A C K E R E L
I S A O   T R A V E L   C B S
S L I N G   U R E   S T R I P
S E L   R E C E N T   R A T E
    Q U E E N S I Z E B E D
R E F U E L S   D E N
A R I A L   T W I D D L E S
J A C K S O N I A N   I O T A
A S H E   O R A N G   E R N S
H E E D   P A S T S   R Y A S
```

page 53 • Heeeeeere's Johnny

```
N A T O   F R O G   H A L T S
A R E A   I S L E   A P O R T
B E N T   E V E N   S P R E E
O N T H E S P O T   S L E E P
B A S S E T   S O L E
    L A G S   B E S T O W
C H E S S   A L S O   E A S E
H A R T   C R E T E   E L L A
I L I A   A B E L   O D E O N
C O N G A S   T O W N
    E C H O   A T T A C H
C R E D O   K N O X V I L L E
R A Z O R   R O P E   P O O L
A K R O N   A V E R   S H A M
B E A R S   S A N S   Y A K S
```

page 56 • All the Same

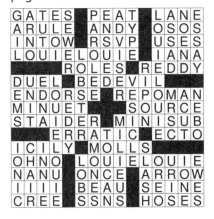

```
GATES PEAT LANE
ARULE ANDY OSOS
INTOW RSVP USES
LOUIELOUIE IANA
    ROLES REDDY
DUEL BEDEVIL
ENDORSE REPOMAN
MINUET  SOURCE
STAIDER MINISUB
  ERRATIC ECTO
ICILY MOLLS
OHNO LOUIELOUIE
NANU ONCE ARROW
IIII BEAU SEINE
CREE SSNS HOSES
```

page 57 • One Good Turn Deserves Another

```
CHARD TAIL LASS
AIMEE ACNE EXPO
STOPMOVING OLAF
ECRU LED GENERA
SHELTER GIGI
    SWINGINGDOOR
COMEIN ENG MAI
ROAST FLO SCARF
ANS POI SPARSE
BACKWARDSTEP
    EAST TRESSES
AMENDS TAI TORI
MOAN KEEPAROUND
APSE ETAL ANNIE
HEEL YALE MEDES
```

page 58 • Cookie Attachments

```
BALI LAPP CHIMP
CLAN ACRE AUDIO
DOUGHSHEETPRESS
ENROUTE VIOLATE
FEATS PENT
   STARE TEASET
SAO LIANA RASH
CUTTERJARRECIPE
ARIA ANGEL DYE
RASPED CODER
    NOSE VIDEO
SEASALT SEEPING
CRUMBTINMONSTER
ANNUL LOON ACME
BETTE ERGS WHYS
```

page 59 • A Dose of 5 cc's

```
RACY DVDS ANTIS
OSHA EINE VEINS
SKEW CLASSICCAR
TOENAIL SCAT
RUS SDAK ENACTS
ATEASE ERN RHEA
  CIA FRUIT USN
COLLISIONCOURSE
ADO LINUS MAC
MITT MEA CARHOP
SCHISM CHIT CPA
   NOEL ANOTHER
CATSCRADLE AONE
AWEEK PALM PIER
DEALS SHEA ERRS
```

page 60 • M&M's

```
ICKY BAJA PRUNE
ALUM ARAB ROSIE
MALCOLMMCDOWELL
BYPASS SECEDES
   CATO CEL
MARIAMONTESSORI
AROAR NEHIS PET
DOWN ASSET ERAS
AME WRIER AMATI
MARSHALLMCLUHAN
   CAB FORA
SCROLLS AMOEBA
MAUREENMCGOVERN
OLDER AGOG AGED
GLESS PREY LSTS
```

page 61 • Three F's for Effort

```
JIFFS ROLLE REP
AGLEE ABOIL AVA
SNORT JEFFFAHEY
PORNOS STEIN
ERA FOGEY NYMPH
RESTFUL ALA
  AFLAME CDROM
PLATO ZIP LUSTS
EELER EXOTIC
RAE DAFTEST
  ROMEO EFFIGY
OFFFLAVOR ARGUE
BAA INEPT COMER
IQS TERSE EGADS
```

page 62 • Urban Jungle

```
SSTS VESTAL ATF
ELON EDERLE SEL
CEDARRAPIDS PRO
TEAROOM VETOERS
SKYLAB TIN RNAS
   AMENRA BAH
IGOT AAA RILING
KOA ACTUPON LOO
EDKOCH MAS ALTO
  FOE LATENT
ATOZ GES WATSON
KOREANS MARIMBA
ERE WALNUTCREEK
RRS ARIOSE ELSE
SET CLEVER SLED
```

page 63 • Leaders and Counts

```
SLIT BALSA FARM
PITA IDIOM IDEA
ALEXANDERI NARC
SAMMS SUED AGUE
   ATE ELLENS
STANISLAUSII
NUN TARP ESTES
ABOVE HIS STILE
PANEL TEEM TOM
  CHRISTIANIII
BOWTIE ATO
ECHO ARCH OMAHA
STAR MUHAMMADIV
TALE ENERO DIDO
SLED REFIT STEW
```

page 64 • Dances We'd Like to See

```
ASAP SPAM START
REBA COTE TAPIR
CAST AMOR EROSE
 BEERBELLYPOLKA
TONNE LOA LET
CATSCAN TRYFOR
URI GAB DOA
DANSEMICAWBER
   PAS DOG YOD
 BARTAB DEAFEAR
ERE GUS TODDY
DANCEOFTHEOURS
SHEOL FEED ROTE
EMAIL ENID APES
LASTS TORY MSRP
```

page 65 • Board Members

```
LOBULAR ENS COP
OCARINA DIE APE
WAYNEKNIGHT  RAE
ESS  LIRE TROLL
    GEESE  FOOL
MAJORS NEO  BETA
ERODE DELI  KEN
CEES LOCAL  WING
CAY  ALAN PANTS
ALBA ITS ARIGHT
   IRON TAROT
HUSKY PLUG  RHO
ASH ELLERYQUEEN
LEO ROE ALUMNAE
ESP SPA LEAPERS
```

page 66 • The Play's the Thing

```
TADA MIDST ALIA
AREA ONICE TONI
RICHARDTHETHIRD
ADO ARESO IONIA
   AMIE LTDS
SHAKESPEARE HOD
OASIS MRED  AWE
LRON OBESE IOLA
ARN BRER  ISLET
RYE LADYMACBETH
   GILA ELAN
STARS MITCH WYE
TITUSANDRONICUS
ELKE HELOT LTRS
PEAL IDEST LUTE
```

page 67 • Blood Type

```
NAIL MELT BEEPS
ACRE AMEN OVULE
THATSJUSTTOOBAD
LESSEES  INLINE
   DRS NET VEER
OUTOFTHEBLUE
AVOW YOUBET ADO
FERNS TRI EGGON
SAN ADDONS RUDY
   STRONGASANOX
CHIC AGS  REV
REDOAK  SNEERAT
ANEWLEASEONLIFE
SCALE LOAF LTRS
HESSE TURF YEOH
```

page 68 • Warning Signs

```
TOLL MUSES POTS
OREO ENOCH AURA
REACHOFCHILDREN
   IOWA OVERSEE
HAM USSR  AVE
EMEER TIC ISLAM
RODE REPAST ALE
ORINCINERATECAN
IAN UPENDS MIST
CLASP DEB BUNKO
   ORB DUCE GAR
WEARIES  ROTE
OBJECTSINMIRROR
ORAL AGREE IOTA
DORY START NEON
```

page 69 • Deserving an A-

```
FUNK ORBIT SEMI
INON BELOW TWIN
EDIE ECOLI PENN
FORENSICEXPERTS
   DEET TUT
EIDER EMI GESTE
SLEEVE COB  PIG
KEEPYOUGUESSING
END NEE GINKGO
RESTS YES DOYEN
   ILL PHEW
MONEYISNOOBJECT
IBID SHIRE ODOR
LONI POSER BIKO
KEEN SWISS STEN
```

page 70 • It's a Laugh

```
DARER SORT RAFT
ELENA TWAS OKRA
THEHEEBIEJEEBIES
AXE ETNA LINES
CIA LAC  ABNER
HARHARHARDASSET
   ODD ROD III
OGRES HUN SPANS
ORE CAB  NOS
HAHAHAWAIIFIVEO
CAPUT RNA  EVA
WISPS GAIT  NET
HOHOHOLDTHELINE
USES NAZI NICER
POSE ODES DEEDS
```

page 71 • Mouth Pieces

```
ACTOR THEM LIFT
BLIGH HOME ISEE
EARLY RBIS PAIN
SWEETTOOTH SAND
   HOW SELECTS
PEATMOSS  SER
OSLO LOOP IVIED
GAIN SUDAN ISLE
OUTGO TATA CUBE
   UKE SCOREPAD
PILESUP  HMO
ANAT CHEWINGGUM
RAVI LOGO ALENE
ILIE INOR LUAUS
SLED DESK DERMA
```

page 74 • Changelings

```
SIAM IRAN ONSET
ANNA CASE REEVE
LATS ETTA BORAX
UNICEDAIRLINES
DECOCT  EAT
   THEDORKETHIC
FLO OARS ERRATA
LUNG YAM  YVES
ALUMNI GAPS EMT
BUSTEDKEATON
   PEA BOOTES
ALLHANDSONDUCK
OXEYE SETA OBOE
RENEW ALIT FEND
CLASS SIRS FROS
```

page 75 • Four-Footed Friends

```
SCAM WARMS MOLE
LOLA EMAIL APES
OVER RASTA RENT
GERMANSHEPHERD
STOOGES  ASA
   SER ALIT ADS
LACE AGATE RYE
SCOTTISHTERRIER
ARR ALIAS EASE
TON ROSS  ROT
   BLT GEORGIA
IRISHWOLFHOUND
IDES MAGEE FIND
SEAL OILER ISEE
MADE STEMS TERR
```

page 76 • Air Force

```
CLAD  POLKA  SLIM
HOBO  AREAL  TORE
ICED  RIANT  ORAL
COLORSOFTHEWIND
      EELS  ONE
LICENSE  BUD  OSS
ERODE  SAG  OPIE
GONEWITHTHEWIND
ONAN  SAY  PENCE
SSN  PAR  PIONEER
     CAB  SEND
CANDLEINTHEWIND
ATOR  LOIRE  OVER
TITO  LOPER  RAMA
STEM  AISLE  KNOB
```

page 77 • Multiple Choice

```
GATE  MARSH  STLO
ARID  ASONE  TRIO
SINGLESBAR  RITZ
PAYEE  ERE  EPEE
     OVER  LOCAL
INQUIRED  NYMETS
ROUT  INFO  ASPIC
OVA  DEALSIN  LEA
NADIR  LAID  SAUL
SERMON  TELETYPE
     UPPED  REAR
MOPE  ERA  SISAL
AREA  DOUBLEDATE
ACDC  LORIS  EVEN
MASH  ELAND  SEED
```

page 78 • Oxtail Soup

```
ASWAN  PATEN  FCC
RHINE  IMAGE  LOS
PANDORASBOX  UNI
  KEENEN  ITEMS
MESA  DOORS  SMEE
FRANCO  NUT  SONS
ASP  RENDS  TEXTS
    DESERTFOX
LEPEW  WASAT  POL
IMAM  REF  IODINE
EBRO  ALTOS  ALSO
  RANDD  VANISH
RAD  ANNIELENNOX
ECO  YEARN  STERE
VEX  SRTAS  TYRES
```

page 79 • When in . . .

```
BEER  ATALL  DEAN
ALSO  MOXIE  ETNA
HIPPODROME  CHIT
TONER  LASTCALL
    DRANO  RAN
SUMO  MOTHRA  FGS
ASOF  PILEUP  REC
TENFOLD  IFSTONE
ORO  TEEOFF  AMEN
NSC  TRAVEL  TETE
   HBO  ERECT
CHRYSLER  AESOP
LION  PALINDROME
ELMO  GRAVE  EDER
FLEW  ASYET  DANK
```

page 80 • Tri-State Region

```
TBSP  VOILA  KWAI
AREA  OLMEC  EARN
ROAR  ISAAC  AXIS
SOLIDCOMFORT
ADE  EEN  RUSTIC
LYRIC  JADE  HDL
   RAVIOLI  HALO
GASOLINEPOWERED
LEAN  COLONEL
ORB  PENS  ELUDE
BOUGHS  AMP  NOR
   LIQUIDASSETS
PUZO  UNGER  ASTA
ASIA  ADOPT  ICET
RAPT  DOTTY  LODZ
```

page 81 • The Old Corral

```
NORA  ABATED  CTR
IWON  TIRANA  ARE
ENYA  HOOTGIBSON
CUR  SOLO  LATTE
EPONYM  PEERESS
   GENEAUTRY
THERE  ELBA  DDAY
NORD  ORNOT  RARE
TESS  NOAA  BOLTS
    BOBSTEELE
OILBASE  TALENT
ASIAN  LOUT  VOW
KENMAYNARD  LANI
ERE  NEEDLE  ENOS
NED  ANODES  ASST
```

page 82 • Spare Change

```
SCAR  PRADA  BLAB
ALMA  RIVAL  ISLE
LAMB  OPENS  ODIE
TWOBITACTORS
  IRE  ERE  AHS
MANTISSA  ANORAK
OVA  STOPONADIME
SINE  UPS  DOLT
SANDDOLLARS  SEC
ARIDER  EYETOOTH
DYE  LII  POX
   PENNYLOAFERS
VETO  OLEOS  OREO
AGOG  CEASE  RIAL
TOTO  OTHER  DEMO
```

page 83 • Frequencies

```
FLIP  ABACK  FLAB
ROSA  ROGUE  LARA
ABEL  CLARE  ERIS
TEEM  HARDLYEVER
   DOES  OCALA
ASIANS  ARGUE
TITLE  WREN  MBA
ONCEINABLUEMOON
NEH  TROY  RATON
   ETHER  MIMOSA
ELENA  MONA
NOWANDTHEN  SMOG
DIEM  EBERT  BIBI
ERLE  SABLE  OLEG
DELL  CREEL  YOYO
```

page 84 • No Three-ums 3

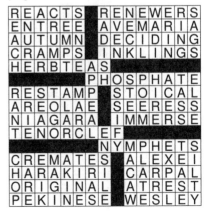

```
REACTS  RENEWERS
ENTREE  AVEMARIA
AUTUMN  DECIDING
CRAMPS  INKLINGS
HERBTEAS
      PHOSPHATE
RESTAMP  STOICAL
AREOLAE  SEERESS
NIAGARA  IMMERSE
TENORCLEF
       NYMPHETS
CREMATES  ALEXEI
HARAKIRI  CARPAL
ORIGINAL  ATREST
PEKINESE  WESLEY
```

page 85 • Just Say It

```
S L A W _ A L T O S _ T A M P
P A P A _ R I A T A _ R H E A
A V E S _ M O U T H P I E C E
S A X H O R N S _ A L P A C A
_ _ _ E R E _ T R A _ D A N
E X P R E S S T R A I N _ _ _
A R E _ S T A R E _ D O W S E
C A R E _ S L I N G _ W H O A
H Y M N S _ U N C L E _ E S S
_ _ _ S T A T E H I G H W A Y
A H A _ E V E _ M O A _ _ _ _
B O R N E O _ L I P S T I C K
U T T E R C H A O S _ I R A N
S L I T _ E M I L E _ N O S E
E Y E S _ T O N E S _ G N A W
```

page 86 • This Bud's for You

```
M O S T _ A D L I B _ A S O F
U N T O _ T I A R A _ L A K E
S O U R G R A P E S _ I L I A
E R N I E E L S _ E A S T E R
_ _ _ A S S _ S L I T S _ _ _
H O B A R T _ A C I D _ H A T
U N I T S _ C R A N E _ A Y E
M I T E _ E A G L E _ O K R A
A C T _ S Y R U P _ T R E E S
N E E _ L E T S _ A V E R S E
_ _ _ R O U T E _ S O S _ _ _
A T H O M E _ S T R E S S E S
C H E Z _ S W E E T T O O T H
D O R E _ T E R R A _ N O N O
C U B S _ S T E E L _ G N A W
```

page 87 • Who Do We Appreciate

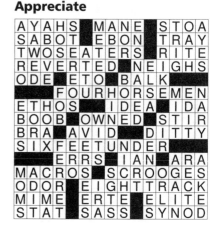

```
A Y A H S _ M A N E _ S T O A
S A B O T _ E B O N _ T R A Y
T W O S E A T E R S _ R I T E
R E V E R T E D _ N E I G H S
O D E _ E T O _ B A L K _ _ _
_ _ _ F O U R H O R S E M E N
E T H O S _ I D E A _ I D A
B O O B _ O W N E D _ S T I R
B R A _ A V I D _ D I T T Y
S I X F E E T U N D E R _ _ _
_ _ _ E R R S _ I A N _ A R A
M A C R O S _ S C R O O G E S
O D O R _ E I G H T T R A C K
M I M E _ E R T E _ E L I T E
S T A T _ S A S S _ S Y N O D
```

page 88 • Joint Venture

```
A R M A D A S _ R E H A N G S
R E A G E N T _ O V E R E A T
A T P E A C E _ T A N T A R A
P A P _ D I A _ _ _ _ T N N
A P E _ S E L _ B A D D E E D
H E R _ E N S _ O R I E N T E
O S S _ A T A N I M P A S S E
_ _ _ _ K A L _ _ _ _ _ _ _
H I S H O L I N E S S _ G I L
I N T O N E S _ R A T _ R C A
T H E B O S S _ P R O _ E E G
L A P _ _ _ _ L A I _ A B A
E S P A N O L _ A C C U S E S
S T E V E N S _ T E A S E R S
S E D A T E D _ E N L A R G E
```

page 89 • T Squares

```
A R M A D A S _ R E H A N G S
R E A G E N T _ O V E R E A T
A T P E A C E _ T A N T A R A
P A P _ D I A _ _ _ _ T N N
A P E _ S E L _ B A D D E E D
H E R _ E N S _ O R I E N T E
O S S _ A T A N I M P A S S E
_ _ _ _ K A L _ _ _ _ _ _ _
H I S H O L I N E S S _ G I L
I N T O N E S _ R A T _ R C A
T H E B O S S _ P R O _ E E G
L A P _ _ _ _ L A I _ A B A
E S P A N O L _ A C C U S E S
S T E V E N S _ T E A S E R S
S E D A T E D _ E N L A R G E
```

page 92 • Actresses

```
A S S A Y _ O R A T E _ J I B
L O I R E _ R O D I N _ U R L
L U C I L L E B A L L _ D I A
_ _ _ L A O S _ _ A B Y S S
T A I L O R S _ A F R I G H T
A R R O W S _ E N I G M A _ _
B R E W S _ S I G N E _ R A M
L A N E _ F A D E D _ F L U E
E Y E _ P A V E R _ L I A R S
_ _ C A L M E R _ M A N N A S
G O A L I E S _ T I R E D L Y
A T S E A _ _ B A N G _ _ _
G O T _ N A T A L I E W O O D
E E L _ C H O R E _ S E W E R
S S E _ Y A W N S _ S E E D Y
```

page 93 • He Fell for It . . .

```
L A I T _ H A N E S _ B E D S
A L D A _ O R F E O _ A Q U A
H O O K C H E C K S _ N U N N
R U L E O U T _ _ O C T A N E
_ _ _ C A M E A T _ H A L E R
R E L A X _ _ I B E A M _ _ _
E D E R _ A P R I L S _ J A M
L I N E O F S C R I M M A G E
Y E T _ H O A R D S _ I D E A
_ _ _ C A R T E _ E X E R T
E L G A R _ S W E R V E _ _ _
T A I P E I _ _ S E E D I N G
H U N T _ S I N K E R B A L L
O R Z O _ B R I E F _ A G E E
S A A R _ N E A R S _ G O R E
```

page 94 • It's a Guy Thing

```
A R MAN D _ T I F F _ C A C A O
D O M E _ I C E R _ A L O I S
A S A MAN _ M E M O _ R A I N MAN
M I D D L E MAN A G E M E N T
S E E S A W _ _ MAN N A _ _ _
_ _ _ P A C MAN _ O K A P I S
A S I A _ R U T A _ E R I C A
C O M MAN D P E R F O R MAN C E S
I H A D A _ D A R N _ I S E E
D O M A I N _ S O C K _ _ _
_ _ _ L O O _ E L G A R T
S P H Y G M O MAN O M E T E R
MAN I T O U _ E D T V _ R A R A
S L A P S _ N I L E _ MAN R A Y
E L S I E _ S E E R _ E I N S
```

page 95 • Take It Off!

```
S T O A T _ E P I C _ J E S T
T U R B O _ R I C O _ O R C A
O D E O N _ A X E L _ B R O S
L O O R I E S _ _ A D B O O K
E R S T _ V E S T _ Y E L P S
_ _ _ E R E _ H O M E R _ _ _
W A L D O _ A U R A _ S P E D
I D A _ B I G D O E R _ E A U
G O W N _ R E D S _ O H A R E
_ _ _ I N A N E _ G N U _ _ _
S I N C E _ T R I M _ M A R S
N G O O D S _ _ S T L I G H T
A L T S _ U R A L _ A D I E U
G O B I _ R O B E _ N O L A N
S O Y A _ F E E T _ D R E S S
```

page 96 • Look Both Ways

```
CASS PLOPS BAIL
LOOT EERIE EDDY
ARNO RATED LOSE
STARTUPSTART
PARKA   ANA UPS
  LSAT   METAL
 PRICELISTPRICE
TRON TENOR ICED
HEADCHEESEHEAD
REDYE SAKI
UNS RCA   GABLE
  FOODFISHFOOD
OGLE VOLTA TWIG
VAIN EPEES EIRE
AGED STEMS REED
```

page 97 • Recipe for Success

```
PARTS LOGE  STAB
AWAIT EDIT  PORE
LAYERTHELASAGNA
EYE  EARS   ARSON
   HAKE  CAST
 SIMMERTHESAUCE
AHSO   RARE   TUX
HAH STMARYS IRA
AMO IOUS    SCAM
BUTTERTHEBREAD
  AGEE DUET
ASPIE  DISC  ERS
CHILLTHECHABLIS
TONE  AUNT  POINT
SEED  NETS  SWAGS
```

page 98 • Law & Order Times 3

```
MARTA TMAN  SOAP
ICERS BALE  HALL
MARISKAHARGITAY
IDUNNO  ENDUP
NINA TERA  SWAMP
GAS  ETA    RUTA
  PRESTO  SETSA
  JERRYORBACH
ALANS  ATTACK
MEMO   HTS   POR
YABBA GEOM  IONE
  STEED  ARNOLD
VINCENTDONOFRIO
IDEO  ITIN  CRANE
MATT  DYES  KATES
```

page 99 • All Ears

```
MOTH MEATS  CHAN
ALSO ASSET  OONA
REAR STARE  ROTC
CORNUCOPIA  NEER
   SOP    MRHYDE
HEPCAT  BAYOU
ALLOF JUG  ISSUE
LEER   ERR   KEGS
LEANS ASA  REALM
  SHUNT  GIRLIE
ROTTEN   CAL
AURA  CORNFLOWER
STAR  ALOOF  VALE
ERIC  PASTE  EGAN
SETH  SNEER  NEMO
```

page 100 • The Other Red Meat

```
REDD CAIN  COLIN
EPEE ORSO  ATONE
SITTINGRIBROAST
  RONDO  DARENOT
SHINTO PET  SELL
SETAE CLAIM  DEE
NEUTRINO  SAP
  SECONDSTEAK
  SON  DOESTIME
IRA METED  TILER
COMB SID  CREOLE
EMBRACE  ALONG
CALIFORNIASTRIP
ANEAR EARN  LANE
PORNO DESK  YMCA
```

page 101 • Patriot Game

```
BOSSA POLL  WAGE
ABACI SKYE  ILLS
ROMULusANDREMUS
KEEL  STYX  ELATE
   PRE    DVD
BATTEDATHOusaND
ADIOS TROMP  ROE
NEAR TBONE  DULL
DAR SHAVE  JUBAL
BLACKEYEDSusaNS
   RIM    OTT
ASSAM MENU  SLID
JOHNPHILIPSOusa
AMOK ERIN  OFFER
REPS MESA  OFTEN
```

page 102 • Whatsitz?

```
ZIPS ATOZ  ZAPPA
ELEC NAMU  ICERS
EIRE IRAN  GENUS
SAINTMORITZ  ADE
   TWA    HAMLET
UZI  ALTEREGO
ROBIN ONES  OPIE
GOINGONTHEFRITZ
ELSE SERE  ASTER
  READYMIX  AMA
RAGTAG   NEA
EMI GERMANSPITZ
CANAL AONE  AGUA
OZZIE ZONE  ROTC
NEARS EGAD  TRUK
```

page 103 • No Three-ums 4

```
PESO SECT  TIARA
ARAB OMAR  ANGER
NILE SIRE  STEAM
ICESKATES  TEDDY
CAMEL  TETHER
   EVENLY  SAGE
CROPPED  EMPEROR
AERATE   NECTAR
RESTORE PASTELS
ALOT  EXHALE
  INDEEP  TACOS
HAPPY MARGARINE
USUAL PRIM  TREE
GETGO TYKE  SCUM
EATEN SEAN  YAPS
```

page 104 • G Men

```
PLOD AGHA  BEGIN
AIDE FOOL  EVADE
NEIL FRUG  DALES
GUNTERGRASS  EAT
   ALOE  EKING
ORG KNOT  IDIOTS
PALE TUB  DEGREE
AMEND SOP  SEDAN
LINTEL NED  ROSS
SENECA EDIT  NEE
  GRASP  IVAN
SAO GEORGEGOBEL
TRURO PARR  VOLE
ALLAN PIES  ERLE
BODES ALEE  LEAK
```

page 105 • Advanced Alchemy

```
W H A P   D R E K   F E W E R
W E R E   E I R E   F R A M E
F R E E R A N G E   I N D I A
  D A V I D G O L D F I E L D
    E B B       E T E
A S P   S E A T T L E   P T A
I C E D   A C R E   E A S E L
M A N I N T H E T I N M A S K
A L A M O   E A R N   A L L Y
T E L   A B S T A I N   M A D
      S L O       M O I
P L A T I N U M F I N G E R
R A J A B   P O R C E L A I N
O M A N I   O N E A   O S L O
P E R K S   N A T L   O Y E S
```

page 106 • Gotta Dance!

```
S L O G   Q U I T O   R O S S
W A X Y   U N D I D   I N C A
A V E R   I C O N S   T E A L
G E N E K E L L Y   Z A P P A
      R T E   H E M M E D
S T A S I S   S P I R O
T A R A S   A L L T O R N U P
D I E M   L U A U S   E U R O
S L A M D U N K S   A N T I S
      Y E N T E   F L O S S Y
W A D D L E   K I D
I D E A L   R A Y B O L G E R
E L E V   J A C O B   O R C A
S A R I   A R E T E   T A R P
T I E S   R E S O D   S M U T
```

page 107 • Better Said Than Read

```
H I L O   P L A S M A   L T D
E T T U   A E G E A N   I W O
M O R T A R B O A R D   B I N
    R C A   N S A   F E R N
W H A T D O Y O U C A L L A
T H I N A I R   N D A K
W E N   S N E E   W I G H T
A L G A   G O F E R   R E A R
S P E L L   F R E T   N I E
    T O G S   I C E M I L K
F I S H W I T H N O E Y E S
O S L O   G O I   U N O
U L A   W O O D E N S P O O N
R E V   I L L E S T   I F A T
H T S   T O S S E S   A F S H
```

page 110 • Body Language

```
T O R S O   H A R T   K I E V
A M O U R   A D A R   U V E A
C A S P I A N S E A   W A R D
O N S   S U N   M E A N I E
    P O T O M A C R I V E R
E L N I N O   A W A I T
C O O T S   M E A R S   Q E D
R O S Y   T U S K S   L U A U
U S E   T A S T E   P O I S E
    T A P I R   P R O P E L
P A C I F I C O C E A N
L E A N T O   A R I   C O S
U R N S   C R A T E R L A K E
M I N E   A I D E   I O N I A
P E A L   S P A R   E S T E R
```

page 111 • Not Brand X

```
B R A N D O   T G V   L E A D
L I V E I N   H U E   A Q U A
O D E S S A   E A T   P U R R
B E R T H   A F R O A S I A N
      S E C L U D E D
S S S   S H A G   S O O T H E
T O E S   E N I D   L U R E S
O N T H E W A T E R F R O N T
L A T E X   S I R E   S U R E
E R O D E S   V I B E   T I S
      R E L E V A N T
S U N S T R O K E   C O U P E
O P A L   I I I   M I T R E D
C O M E   A N N   U N E A S E
K N E W   L S D   M A R L O N
```

page 112 • Fruit Stand

```
M O O S   S W A R M S   A M P
A C M E   P A R I A H   R O E
C H E R R Y S T O N E   T U N
S E G U E   E T N A   H E N
R A M A D A   A T T U
    L E M O N S H A R K S
W O R D   S O L O   E L I O T
A G E E   K U D O S   K A L E
R E M U S   N E S T   S N A P
P E A C H S T R E E T
  R E A P   S T U P O R
O R R   D I V A   T U N E S
L E I   O R A N G E S T I C K
L E E   W E T T E R   T O T E
A D D   S A S S E S   S N O W
```

page 113 • Ya Gotta Have It

```
M E N U   O D O R S   E P I C
P O O R   W Y M A N   A U R A
S E T S O N E S H E A R T O N
  S I R     R E C   S B A
D O O N E S H E A R T G O O D
A S H E   A U T H   U I N T A
C H O   U S M C   P A L
E A T O N E S H E A R T O U T
  G B S   E A S Y   F P O
G N A R L   A R C S   A F A R
L O S E O N E S H E A R T T O
O R C   C A R   C D R
B R E A K S O N E S H E A R T
A I N T   A B I D E   N C A R
L S T S   L E T U P   S K Y E
```

page 114 • Inferiority Complex

```
C O M B   P I P E R   M E N D
A B E L   S T O N E   O R E O
N O R A   H A N D M E D O W N
S E E N   A L E   R E S E T
    K I W I   B A R R E L S
L O W E R E C H E L O N
U N I T E D   E V I L   R E B
T U T S   S L Y   S O U R
E S S   D E A L   S A T I R E
    L O O K O U T B E L O W
S U S A N N E   P U C E
P L A T O   S B A   R I A L
U N D E R W A T E R   A C N E
R A I L   E C L A T   G E T S
T R E Y   S H O T S   E D I T
```

page 115 • Suitability

```
A C T S   C A R A   P H O N E
S O R A   O D O R   R O W E D
S P A D E W O R K   E L E V E
A R I   S P R Y   W I D E N
M A N A T E E   S E A S
    H E A R T W A R M I N G
P L I E R S   H A P   S O U
R O O M S   B U Y   R I L E S
O C T   G A M   S A N E S T
D I A M O N D B A C K S
  A G U E   B R I T T L E
S W I R L   E R I S   R A W
H A N O I   C L U B H O U S E
E L T O N   H O P E   D E E R
A L O N G   A N T S   E R R S
```

page 116 • Seeing the Signs

```
RETRO MAL MAGMA
ETHER ALI ALIEN
CARETAKER ECLAT
UPON DECAL ODDS
REBATED AFT
  COLONIZATION
SARTRE OLES NNE
LOESS ALE TRICE
INA IONA HEATER
PERIODONTIST
  ANE ARTIEST
PALM SALSA ONTO
ADOBE COMMANDER
CECIL EVA DAUNT
KNOCK DEN OLEOS
```

page 117 • Spinoff

```
ASTRO CRIB TMAN
DORIS AIDA RIME
MAUDE GOODTIMES
SPED TNT MARIST
  LOWE HOME
GOMERPYLEUSMC
APART OAT EARP
BEN SLEUTHS BOO
ELEM AMI ORION
  TRAPPERJOHNMD
  LLBS EENY
SPOUSE LIB TRAP
THECOLBYS RHODA
OINK TELE YMCAS
PLOY SEER ASKME
```

page 118 • All the World's a Stage

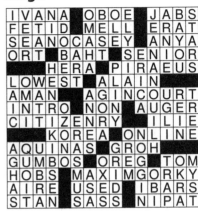

```
IVANA OBOE JABS
FETID MELL ERAT
SEANOCASEY ANYA
ORT BAHT SENIOR
  HERA PIRAEUS
LOWEST ALAIN
AMAN AGINCOURT
INTRO NON AUGER
CITIZENRY ILIE
  KOREA ONLINE
AQUINAS GROH
GUMBOS OREG TOM
HOBS MAXIMGORKY
AIRE USED IBARS
STAN SASS NIPAT
```

page 119 • Weather or Not

```
SALE MAGMA TAPS
LIAR IDLED OLLA
ANNA THUNDERBAY
MUD TEES LOUTS
  SANER WOE MOO
CYCLONEFENCE
PEALS LACTATES
ALPS AMORE SALT
SPEEDIER BELLA
  TORNADOALLEY
APE TET RATSO
PINTA ALOT ROD
SQUALLLINE EDGE
EURO ELLER GERM
SEES DYADS OREO
```

page 120 • Composers

```
LACK SCAR PACER
OBOE WAGE ELOPE
SERGEIPROKOFIEV
EDD UVEA OPINES
  AGED SOLE
RAPPEL SAKE GNP
ASIAN CHAI ARIL
VINCENZOBELLINI
EDGE OARS IBSEN
DES TIRE POETRY
  REDS SANE
ALSACE SALE BOP
VAUGHANWILLIAMS
EVIAN BALE MBAS
RATSO CYST PENT
```

page 121 • Composer Poser

```
MOCHA MATCH ADS
ALAIN INURE TOT
SLANG SORER ONO
HANDELBARS SNUG
  ULEE ESTHETE
EMS ANGST HUSSY
BOAT TOA EON
BACHTOTHEFUTURE
  YES IMF SLAT
DRAMA ABBOT TWA
RACECAR ERIE
OTTS LISZTPRICE
PEI PLOTZ ORDER
IDI EASEL FOLDS
TRI GNOME FLEET
```

page 122 • At the Finish

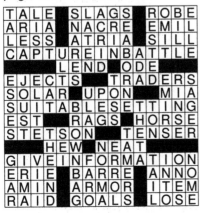

```
TALE SLAGS ROBE
ARIA NACRE EMIL
LESS ATRIA SILL
CAPTUREINBATTLE
  LEND ODE
EJECTS TRADERS
SOLAR UPON MIA
SUITABLESETTING
EST RAGS HORSE
STETSON TENSER
  HEW NEAT
GIVEINFORMATION
ERIE BARRE ANNO
AMIN ARMOR ITEM
RAID GOALS LOSE
```

page 123 • Cash in

```
FLIT DACHA DISC
AIDE ENRON OSHA
BREADBOARD ULAN
LASSES FAIRGAME
ESTER ITS AHMED
  NAVE INF
PING RED STOOGE
SOIREES ALSORAN
SNEERS CLE TESS
  EAT OPTS
GOONS TEO ANGST
ONTHEAIR TROUPE
TITO JACKHAMMER
ACER AREWE ABCS
TERN MASSE DOSE
```

page 124 • Simon Says

```
IBARS TAGS NEWS
RELIC SUET ETAL
ALLAH AREA RAGU
STILLCRAZYAFTER
  SEA ESP
ASH PRIOR PAPAW
SHOO ELF OAFISH
SOUNDSOFSILENCE
AGREES AOL WEIR
MISSM ULTRA DIE
  OWN ISO
SCARBOROUGHFAIR
LACE LENS RONDO
ISLE DACE ANTES
PAUL SLED MESAS
```

page 126 • Stringing Up Lights

```
TESLA SWUM HAJJ
AZTEC WAGE OMOO
BRAKENIGHTKLEIG
SAY HOG   HIRES
    VII TUBAS
FIREGROWSUNMOON
LOATH NEEDS MAE
INFO SLEDS FETA
NIT RAITT EIGHT
GASFOGNEONFLASH
   LASER EFS
ARGUS    AHA SYS
LIMETRAFFICSPOT
EVEN EARL ELEGY
SENT QUAY RADIX
```

page 127 • Male Call

```
COLIN SHAH SCUM
UVULA CANE IRMA
BUCKBOARDS LABS
ALA SPREE WINES
NESS RAMSHACKLE
   AHAB IOTAS
CASBAH STET OIL
SCHAV BEE ELUDE
AHI ELEA DAYTON
  PANEL TRUE
TOMFOOLERY SASS
AVERT BLOAT CIA
TINE BULLDOZING
ANTS ROIL DODGE
RESH AYES DOSES
```

page 128 • On Your Feet!

```
SPED STINT PETE
WEVE HANOI OPAL
ARIA IRATE LINK
PULLUPONESSOCKS
    TRY  DUE
GAP NARC PEBBLE
ASOF ROOK DORIA
FILLEDONESSHOES
FAKIR MENU RAGE
SNAPAT SONS DEL
    THE  RAE
BEDROOMSLIPPERS
ACRE MIKES OLEO
SHUN ALIVE CLAM
HOME SEMIS HARE
```

page 129 • Follow the Money

```
SLIP CHILI FOAL
AUTO LEDON ARTY
PLUM ORLON ADAR
SUPPLYDEPOT ERE
    EYES CAPRIS
UNBIND SCARAB
SEEIN APOSTOLIC
ENL ERASE ANO
DETRIMENT BINGE
  SAMBAS BUNKED
SEAGAL BARK
INN MARKETPLACE
FUDD ZONED ISLE
TREY OPERA NEAL
SERE NEWSY GAMY
```

page 130 • Three in a Series

```
ROOM LAMA SATAN
ASTI ORES NIECE
JOHNQUINCYADAMS
ALEXEI SOAK MET
HER ISM TREK
   SIDED NOISED
IMAC OLEG IDLER
MILLARDFILLMORE
PRIES SORE AGOG
SATRAP ELFIN
  AGUE STP CPR
IBM URLS OSPREY
GROVERCLEVELAND
GIBES IONE ONCE
YESES DEER PEER
```

page 131 • Seasick

```
ETHOS KIWI METE
BROCK IRAN UPON
BIGHADDOCK LEWD
SOSO ANNO GLENS
    DNA  ATE
MACHE PIANOTUNA
ORHERS NUN OPAL
PIER KAFKA VERT
UALR ERR SPENCE
PLAICEMAT ARDOR
   NOT  ANT
BRAGG OSLO TREK
LANA ONPORPOISE
ACTI ICON AGAPE
HEED LETS POLYP
```

page 132 • Fowl Play

```
AVIS ESPY PHAGE
AINT SHOO HOPES
HAHA TURKEYTROT
SLATE NEEDS ODE
  BILL  EISNER
CHICKENDANCE
EAT STOIC SECTS
EVES SNAIL MOUE
SEDAN ENDOW MBA
  GOOSESTEPPER
CARATS  SELA
ERE ALIBI DINAH
DUCKBOARDS EIRE
ABOIL MALE ROIL
RANDY BEET SNAP
```

page 133 • Get a Move On

```
ICER MOOD DABBA
MAXI IBAR ORION
PROPOSEFORMALLY
ATTEND PUEBLO
LEI TONKIN IGO
ARCS IAN GRANT
  HOAGY SEURAT
TOUCHACHORD
SLEAZE KOALA
CELLO EEL LASS
HAL ANDEAN CPT
STPETE ROSTER
CHANGERESIDENCE
HELIO GLEE ROIS
EDENS YOWL EWES
```

page 134 • Casablanca Dreaming

```
ADIOS ALPS UNIX
BERRA FEET SONE
ARMIN RARE ATTN
BRICKANDMORTAR MOA
   GAO  LOCI
ARP LOFTS SISAL
TOI SLOT SASSY
RICKSCAFEAMERICAIN
LAKME SERA TDD
ESSES KINDA RICKEY
  UNTO  IBA
SAP ALASPOORYORICK
CUTE DUPE AMORE
ATRICKY IRON ROGET
NOSE EATS DRILY
```

page 135 • **Ya Gotta Have Heart**

```
SULFA TWIN MSEC
ALIEN HAVE AERO
LTGEN RYES IAGO
LINDARONSTADT
EMUS EWE LISBON
TOM ABA GEM EDO
STEPPE SLID
JOYCECAROLOATES
ISOM SCREAM
MLK PAS GAT DAS
SOONER SER PEPE
HARRIETNELSON
EGAD ENDO REELS
SEMI STEW MARLO
PEAR TORN ASTOR
```

page 136 • **Biblical Blooms**

```
LADY ABIT CLASP
AREA LAME HIDES
LILYOFTHEVALLEY
ALLAH HONOR ARC
SOLS SICKISH
CAB HAHA DOA
YURT FEDS AROMA
STAROFBETHLEHEM
TONER ALAE NINE
ADS ENID ODS
CARDIAC DRIP
ATO NTEST ELVIS
MICHAELMASDAISY
ULCER LULU COIN
STORY OGLE ELSE
```

page 137 • **Almost Physical**

```
RUFFS MARS PEAS
USURP AMAT AXLE
TUNER NINE SPAR
HANDYANDIES USA
SLY NBA PEAR
HEARTYLAUGHS
ACROSS HAE GAIL
LOANS GAM SETTO
VISE RAN UNREST
ARMYRESERVES
USES EEE PTA
BUS NOSYPARKERS
APSE LUAU ENNUI
BOER VENT RICED
ANNA EDGE STERE
```

page 138 • **It Keeps Happening**

```
IDOL GAFF AFRO
CAPED OBOE ERIK
EDINA WORN ROOD
AGAINANDAGAIN
GUT TEE LATHE
EMERALD ATELIER
ERA ADO EWE
OVERANDOVER
ALL GIN LAS
PEDDLER WANTADS
BASRA OAT VAT
TIMEAFTERTIME
SKYE NITE ERASE
OILS ODER DETER
STET SANS EELS
```

page 139 • **Sin City**

```
SPOT TRACE SHOP
LIMO HERON COMA
ATNO ELIOT OPEN
WAIKIKIDNAPPING
IOC IRE
REPAIR HALO VAT
ENOL AOUT NAIVE
SELMANSLAUGHTER
TRYST HARP EARS
SOP OCAS GAMETE
ANO ERR
NEWDELHIJACKING
AVID LOVED ODOR
DELL APACE HERA
ANTE RENTS LAMB
```

page 140 • **Fishy Finish**

```
CARS TROTS TSAR
ALIT AERIE INFO
WATERWHEEL LAOS
SEETO ELSIE FOE
SOMA UMLAUTS
OHIOTURNPIKE
VERN NSA ESTOP
AMO SIESTAS HIE
LINAC AOL SENT
VANILLASHAKE
ECHELON ESPO
DOE ANSER EWING
ULAN CUBANCIGAR
CARE ORATE NOTE
ESSE MEYER GROG
```

page 142 • **Getting Together**

```
CAMP SEWED DOOR
ALAE ERODE ERGO
BONDMARKET CART
ANTAE ENROLLEE
LEANDER ARA
TAPERECORDER
ITS LATENT EASE
SWABS AND URBAN
MIRA RITUAL SUE
STICKINSECTS
HIT SHINDIG
LICENSED MAINE
IDOL CLIPJOINTS
MEMO HORSE LARS
BEER LIEIN SHOO
```

page 143 • **Places, Please**

```
NEMO AGAIN MOHR
ERAS LANCE CREE
AGRA ARNIE FALL
ROCKISLAND ALLA
ASTA GEARBOX
EAR MANX DEL
FLEW IDES SABER
TUBA REBEC NOVA
SMASH DECO DOER
TAT CONN TRA
IMPETUS NCOS
CARL BORDERLAND
AREA ILIAD ABIE
LIEN NACRE CELL
LEND GREYS KEEL
```

page 144 • **Words of Understanding**

```
LAP SEMIS APIAN
EMO TRISH RUDDY
NPR ARNIE TRIMS
GETAROUNDTOIT
TRESTLE BONAMI
HERO TROI ARAT
UNS ALLY ORE
FOLLOWTHELEADER
IDO LARA SAD
NONO LILT ABUT
IMGAME AAMILNE
GRASPATSTRAWS
STOMP LOTTE MIT
PANEL ONEAL ESE
ALENE PERRY SEE
```

page 145 • Right Wings

```
DITTO SLOP CEDE
UNHIP HIRE IRON
SCENE OOPS NILE
THEGREENHORNET
    EAR  ASIA
GAUD OMEN OBESE
AWN IDOL STALAG
MADAMEBUTTERFLY
USURPS DEAR IMP
THEME BEER UNIT
   ONCE  VAN
LORDOFTHEFLIES
LIRA SOHO TASTE
OVAL TREE ECLAT
TELL SEND REELS
```

page 146 • Higher Education

```
STAB DELVE NABS
ERLE ALIEN ALOU
WOMENSINTUITION
STATE  CORDLESS
   LAWN EEL
  THETHIRDDEGREE
CHA OENO  SPEAR
AERO NAACP SASS
TITAN COAT  SET
ONEFORTHEBOOKS
     FER NARC
STREAMER  SCOUT
CHARTANEWCOURSE
AUDI IDAHO RATE
MDSE NYLON SLAM
```

page 147 • Where in the World?

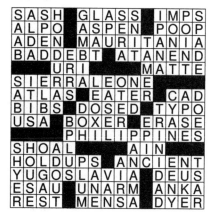

```
SASH GLASS IMPS
ALPO ASPEN POOP
ADEN MAURITANIA
BADDEBT ATANEND
   URI    MATTE
SIERRALEONE
ATLAS EATER CAD
BIBS DOSED TYPO
USA BOXER ERASE
   PHILIPPINES
SHOAL    AIN
HOLDUPS ANCIENT
YUGOSLAVIA DEUS
ESAU UNARM ANKA
REST MENSA DYER
```

page 148 • Ail from Ale

```
LATUS ERMAS PVC
EARNA NEARS EAU
MAILBONDING NCR
  FARLEFT TOTAL
SEEDED LAC BATE
LACES PAILRIDER
AST BAG ITT
TEATROS ROSSSEA
  IDO POS  TSU
BAILSTRAW SPRAT
REND HEN ALEASH
ANGEL TEASETS
NEE SAILSPERSON
DAS TINES PEERS
OST STADT SERTA
```

page 149 • Auto Motive

```
DESI SAMBA ACHE
EXAM TRIOS TOIL
BUMPERCROP HUNK
ADO MISER NERDS
REAGAN   SENT
  LIGHTCAVALRY
ANGEL ERASE III
HORN SLABS KELP
ELI FOLIO SORES
MOTORCONTROL
  TREK  ABACUS
ILIAD DRONE ANT
DIET TRUNKROUTE
EASE WINCE ASIA
ARTS OPTED KEEL
```

page 150 • Bright Ideas

```
DINE BASSO SMOG
IDOL ADIEU PACE
MASERLASER ORTS
  MAMMAS MOTET
UPSET LAVALITE
PETNAME WIG ASS
SLAT ALI SOIL
  TRAFFICSIGNAL
  CLEF EAT CREW
ERR LIE PSALTER
NEONLAMP BOSSY
CASES PLUSES
APSE FLASHLIGHT
SEED DONEE NOIR
EDDY AYERS GAMY
```

page 151 • Off with Their Heads!

```
GLOW LAIRS HURL
LOVE ASCOT ERIA
AGED THANE MISS
RAN TTY ARRACKS
ENSURE   OUT
   RIND RIMIEST
ELENA APED COLE
REM LIMIEST NIN
LAIT TEED RASPS
ENTRIES  YEAR
   ORR   LITHER
RECLEAN RUT AVE
ITAL TOWED EVEN
PARE ELATE NERD
SLED SAGES ANTS
```

page 152 • It's in the Hole

```
MACERS AGOG APSO
IDIOT DRNO SLUR
NIEUW LACEUP PACERS
HALLOWEDPLACE AGO
   FAR ACETONE
MENACED CASINO
COLA ORAL CERTS
HOYT FACETED ADES
INSUM MESA CENT
  ERASER RETRACE
SEEST   DID
CUP TRADINGPLACES
OPAL USER ELISE
BELA TAFT RACECUP
BRACES SPACEY DEPT
```

page 153 • Cow's Word Puzzle

```
REPS DRAW ASSAM
OTIC IOTA MOOSE
INTHEMOOD BARKS
LATEX SPICINESS
   MEET  HAD
SHIEST SPINSTER
TASS CELL COATI
ONA SHMOOZE NHL
ROACH MADE AGEE
MICHIGAN REFOLD
   ONT  BOAR
ANALGESIA SANYO
LEVEL ONTHEMOON
MOORE ACHE EDGE
ANNAS PHEW SEAS
```

page 154 • **From the Director's Chair**

```
S P E C S   A C D C   S R I S
A E S O P   A S E A   T O G A
O N T H E W A T E R F R O N T
  N A N C Y   P R E E M I E
M A T   K L A N   W A I T E
A M E N   E N A C T   K E E N
R E S E E   S P R A T   S R S
    E L I A K A Z A N
M P S   S E R I N   N A M E D
E R O S   S A N K A   G A M E
T O P I C   S Y N C   N P R
C O R T E G E   N A C H O
A F A C E I N T H E C R O W D
L E N O   N I K E   H A L E R
F R O M   O D O R   E M E R Y
```

page 155 • **Moneymaker**

```
M E A N   I B I S   C O S T A
E L B A   N E N E   O C C U R
D O U G H F A C E   B E A T S
E N T A I L   A D S   A L T O
    S N O B   T E N P I N
B R E A D W I N N E R S
O I N K   S C O O P S   A H S
D A V I S   A R N   E G R E T
E L Y   W A R M E D   R I L E
    C A B B A G E P A L M S
J U J U B E   O D I N
U K E S   T I E   U N T O L D
R A S P S   S M A C K E R O O
O S S I A   M I L E   E C O N
R E E D Y   S L I D   S A N S
```

page 156 • **Power Source**

```
G A L A   B A B A S   V A M P
A U E L   A W A I T   A G U E
S T E A M T A B L E   R O S S
P O D I A T R Y   W E I G H T
S S S   J E D   A A R E
    H O R S E T R A D I N G
P A P E R   L A D S   L E O
H E A R   C O E D S   B L A B
E R R   E A R N   F A S T S
W O R L D B E A T E R S
    L E S S   A L A   O R R
T H W A R T   T R A N S K E I
S I A M   A T O M I C M A S S
O K R A   N O L A N   E P E E
S E E S   D O L C E   W I T S
```

page 157 • **Rights of Passage**

```
R O A M   A T T A R   A G E D
O M N I   V E R N E   L O D E
W A Y S T A T I O N   L O I N
E R A T O   P R E S E N T
    E M U S   A W A Y
R O A D B L O C K   S C O T S
E R R   S T L O   C H A L E T
M I L T   R O M E O   T E T E
I B E R I A   E A R N   I R E
T I N A S   S T R E E T C A R
    I L I E   L Y R A
  A L L E N D E   V I A N D
E X A M   P A T H F I N D E R
L E V I   U T T E R   T I R E
F L A X   T E A R Y   S T O W
```

page 160 • **A Spicy Puzzle**

```
A S S T S   A L G O L   D R Y
C H A R O   L O R R E   R A O
T I T A N   L Y I N G   P H D
O P E N S E S A M E   M E S A
U T E S   C E L   C U P
T O N I G H T   K I N G P I N
    T O E   A R L O   E V E
T U T   O L D S A L T   R Y E
B M I   G O O P   M E G
A A M I L N E   E A S I E S T
  C O E   E N D   M M I I
N O U N   D E N V E R M I N T
A P R   N I T R O   E I G E R
P A R   E L R O Y   M C R A E
S L Y   G L E N S   S K E D S
```

page 161 • **A Poker in the Study**

```
M A C H O   A M O S   S H E S
U B O A T   R A N T   L E N O
S A N D B A G G E R   U N D O
E T T A   S O D   E E G
  H I G H S T A K E S G A M E
    O U I   A T T I R E D
A O N   M S D O S   S I S I
C L O S E T O T H E C H E S T
C E I L   L E A V E   S Y S
R I S E S U P   I C H
A C E U P T H E S L E E V E
    T A O   S E E   R I L E
U T A H   P O K E R F A C E D
F O R E   I R E D   B L E N D
O W E D   A I R Y   I D S A Y
```

page 162 • **Frightful**

```
R A M P   S I F T S   D A D A
A R I A   C R O A T   E L E C
P E N N   H O R R O R F I L M
T A X I   I N T A K E   G E E
    C E S S   E L A N D S
B A M B A M   B E R Y L
A B O U T   V O L S   A P E S
S L A T S   O X O   T R I P E
S E N T   S T E N   E M C E E
    O C H E R   C A S T E S
A V E N U E   A L L Y
D I M   E L N I N O   S W A B
D R E A D L O C K S   T A L E
L I N D   A M O L E   E X A M
E D D A   C O N E S   M Y R A
```

page 163 • **Getting Down**

```
E C R U   A T A R I   O F F S
N O U N   B A R O N   I R O N
I N T H E D U M P S   L O C I
D E S I L U   S E T S   M U D
    T I C S   D E C E A S E
F B I   A T T A   P A N G
L I N K   E R G O   R O O S T
O N T H E D A N C E F L O O R
P S H A W   P E E R   A S I A
  E K E D   S A N A   E L M
A D M I R E D   N I T A
R I O   S P I T   E M I L I O
O V U M   O N O N E S L U C K
M E T A   R E G A L   E L O I
A S H E   T R A P S   D U N E
```

page 164 • **Going the Distance**

```
A L B A   A M A N A   G O T H
B E E N   T A R E S   A L S O
Y A R D S T I C K S   R E A R
S P R Y E R   S T U B B O R N
S T Y   E A T   O A R
    I N C H I N G A H E A D
C O N N   T I C   E N M I T Y
A R O S E   S I T   D O N E E
L E V E L S   N O D   N E S S
F O O T S L O G G I N G
    I A N   A G E   L A P
P H O N E M E S   E X P I R E
H O L E   M I L E S T O N E S
I B I S   E D I C T   L E A K
L O O T   R A M O S   O N L Y
```

page 165 • Halloween Happenings

```
WAFT TABS PASHA
EURO INRI ASTON
DRESSEDASAGHOST
SADHU   ITERATE
    MASC ERA
SASH SNAP   MANN
IMPERIALISM ROE
SOAPEDTHEWINDOW
ACT DECORATIONS
LOSS   HURT PREY
   ODE NEST
OCARINA   OSAKA
BOBBEDFORAPPLES
ISLET RUED REEK
STETS OTTO YENS
```

page 166 • Why, Why, Why!

```
HEART VOIR SQMI
ELIHU IPSO AUEL
RADIX ZEAL YALL
AMAZES NYYANKEE
   ODO PLAYER
FAXMODEM OLY
AXLES LAXLY HQS
RIIS JIMMY BERG
ELI SUZIE BOAST
   JAR ENCRYPTS
SHEEDY   ROI
WIZARDRY YASSER
AMIN UHOH DHOLE
BONN TERM ALULA
SMEE YAKS XYLEM
```

page 167 • A Little House Cleaning

```
FLAT STIR TWIT
LIME CONES EASE
ALIT HEAVE AXLE
WASHANDWEAR PEN
SCHEMA ELNINO
   ROPE STEEDS
PAD SPARS EXTOL
ABUT SCOWS TIDE
PESOS HEALS COD
ATTILA   NINA
   BLAMES MIMOSA
GNU VACUUMTUBES
AONE SLAKE LENS
PONY SAVES ESSE
SKYE TEST TEES
```

page 168 • More Changelings

```
MESA DRAPE SHAW
ASIN YESES LONE
SANDINTHECLOWNS
SUE SATYR AGLET
   ELMO SRA
LIMEONMYHANDS
FILMS ATOM RID
LALA MISDO BOZO
ORB CAPO HELEN
SEALSONWHEELS
   PAT HAIR
SOBER MOILS BOA
THEMARSBROTHERS
AIDA AGILE BEAT
BOSN DRESS OSLO
```

page 169 • First Person

```
BATHS LACY ERIK
OCEAN INRE GENE
SHALE ETES OSAY
SELFESTEEM TINE
   ZOO EARNED
BUSHES SUNNI
OGEE OPEN OPERA
ALLAH ETD SPRIG
TILDE KOOP ESSE
   LADEN SORTED
TAHITI ASH
IRON VANITYFAIR
TUBE ENDS EERIE
ABBR ITAL ATEIN
NAYS NIKE HASIT
```

page 170 • Where Does the Time Go?

```
THEIR ALFA SACK
OUTDO LEIS HULA
ONCEUPONA[TIME] IDOL
   AGLETS SPINE
GEISHA CAT TES
RDS [TIME]ISMONEY
AGED TRA TWILLS
SERUM ORB SPOIL
PREFAB KEG SOLO
   FROM[TIME]TO[TIME] FAT
OAF TWO BLEACH
TWIGS REBOOT
HALO ASTITCHIN[TIME]
EKED MEND KEFIR
REDS PLAS SLITS
```

page 171 • The Family

```
DOZEOFF VERANDA
ERITREA IVORIES
FATHERCHRISTMAS
ACHES TOILE
NLER BOOLE SCOW
GER MOTHEREARTH
   PADUA SLATY
PROTEM HASAGO
FROBE CUBED
FAVORITESON EGG
AMEX GUSTY CORE
   PENAL LOCUS
DAUGHTERELEMENT
PLAUDIT REVENGE
SEEMSTO SOIREES
```

page 172 • Fly-byes

```
LOGO CEDAR MALL
IVAN INURE ALOE
PASSENGERPIGEON
   PRE EASIEST
ASNER AVAIL
THECONCORDESST
TAP REEL RAIL
ELAPSES SEVILLE
NOLO FLEE IDA
MIDWAYAIRLINES
   AGENT CREST
MOHEGAN PRO
SPACESTATIONMIR
EACH SAGAN EURO
CLEO ISOUT DDAY
```

page 173 • Signs of a Storm

```
SUBTLE B[RAIN]D[RAIN] [RAIN]ED
UK[RAIN]IAN AHAB GRO
EUCLID BARI AEC
LOTTO YTTRIUM
HER RRS DOGIE
ALAE EATS NETS
SELFREST[RAIN]ED SET
   TARP TREE
[RAIN]ES HEADREST[RAIN]TS
OLIN INRI AFAR
NABOB S[RAIN] OKS
TER[RAIN]MAP WEARE
AIR PASO ENDEAR
DOI ALEC ADESTE
DNA NICK REST[RAIN]S
```

page 174 • Hot Movies

page 176 • In Line

page 177 • It's Patriotic

page 178 • Concealing Little

page 179 • Seeing Double

page 180 • Out of Sorts

page 181 • Just in Case

page 182 • LPs

page 183 • It's Easy!

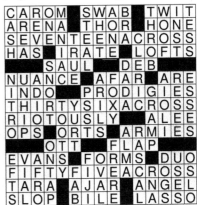

page 184 • It's Not Over

```
S K I M   S L A W S   S L A B
T I D E   P I C O T   H A L O
A T O M   O T H E R   A V E R
B E L O W T H E S U R F A C E
        A T E     G O T
P A R I T Y   E D G Y   J O T
A P A C E   O P A L   S I D E
U N D E R T H E W E A T H E R
S E A S   O M E N   D I A L S
E A R   L A S S   H U R D L E
      Y E S     V O L
B E N E A T H C O N T E M P T
A K I N   E E R I E   M I L E
L E N T   R E E L S   I R A N
I D E A   S L E E T   R E N D
```

page 185 • Three Squares

```
G E T I T   S T I R   C O L A
A L I B I   N U D E   O R E M
L O M A N   A R E A   M I R O
    B R E A K F A S T M E N U
E M U   A L E S   S E A L E R
F A K E R Y   F I N   S R S
T I T O   A P O G E E
    L U N C H C O U N T E R S
    S H A D E R   L Y O N
U N A   I N C   D R Y E Y E
N U T M E G   O K I E   B A Y
L A T E F O R D I N N E R
O N I T   U T I L   T A E B O
A C R E   T E S T   A V A I L
D E E D   S S T S   L E D G E
```

page 186 • Play Option

```
N O P E   S L E E P   W A W A
A L I A   M I L N E   A P E R
P A S S F A I L G R A D I N G
A V A T A R   S I F T   E T E
        L U T E   N O R   C O N
R U N A N E X P E R I M E N T
U M A   N I L   M U M
S P Y O N   T A E   M E D A L
      A E S   I L A   Y I P
K I C K U P O N E S H E E L S
O N O   R I B   V T O L
U F W   A N T E   O R I O L E
F U M B L E A R O U N D F O R
A S E A   T I T A N   E N O S
X E N A   S N E R D   D O M E
```

page 187 • Let's Settle This

```
Y O U N G   B A J A   Z A P S
E L S I E   A L A I   I F S O
A I M E R   K I C K I N G I N
R O C K B R E A K I N G
      R I O   S A D A   A S H
E N F O L D S   L O R E L E I
A I R   E L M   U N P E N
S C I S S O R S C U T T I N G
T E E N A   S A T   N A E
E N N O B L E   D E P R E S S
R E D   R A V E   R A E
      P A P E R C O V E R E D
E A V E S D R O P   E L I Z A
G R E W   O S S A   R I C E D
G E T S   G O E S   S N A K E
```

page 188 • Say It Again, Sam

```
B E D S   P A I D   K Y S E R
O L E O   A B B E   O V E R A
L I S A   S U E R   D O Z E S
E X P R E S S T R A I N
R I O   N E E   I R A N I A N
O R T H O   S P E A K E A S Y
    A L G   E R R S   G I S
T O R Y   A T S E A   T O N E
I D A   C R O C   T E A
V O I C E C O I L   V J D A Y
O R D E R I N   O D E   E L I
      S T A T E C O L L E G E
S A L S A   O R A L   I D O L
T R I N I   W I L E   N E R D
S A T A N   N E E D   T E E S
```

page 189 • The Listener

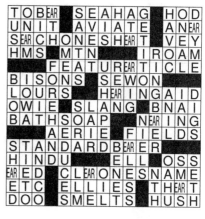

```
T O B E A R   S E A H A G   H O D
U N I T   A V I A T E   A N E A R
S E A R C H O N E S H E A R T   V E Y
H M S   M T N       I R O A M
      F E A T U R E A R T I C L E
B I S O N S   S E W O N
L O U R S   H E A R I N G A I D
O W I E   S L A N G   B N A I
B A T H S O A P   N E A R I N G
      A E R I E   F I E L D S
S T A N D A R D B E A R E R
H I N D U   E L L   O S S
E A R E D   C L E A R O N E S N A M E
E T C   E L L I E S   T H E A R T
D O O   S M E L T S   H U S H
```

page 190 • Running on Empty

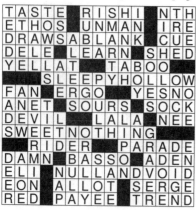

```
T A S T E   R I S H I   N T H
E T H O S   U N M A N   I R E
D R A W S A B L A N K   C U E
D E L E   L E A R N   S H E D
Y E L L A T   T A B O O
      S L E E P Y H O L L O W
F A N   E R G O   Y E S N O
A N E T   S O U R S   S O C K
D E V I L   L A L A   N E E
S W E E T N O T H I N G
    R I D E R   P A R A D E
D A M N   B A S S O   A D E N
E L I   N U L L A N D V O I D
E O N   A L L O T   S E R G E
R E D   P A Y E E   T R E N D
```

page 192 • Small Starts

```
S R O S   R A P   H A H A S
C O M E   I R I S   A R O N I
I B A R   G U L P   J O R G E
F O R E I G N L E G I O N
I T S N O   A A R   S S T
    A N D Y G R I F F I T H
B U D   I R E   B O N E R
O H I O A N S   E V I L O N E
M A S T S   U R I   N O W
B U T C H E R K N I F E
S L A   L O U   A L F I E
    N O R F O L K I S L A N D
O N T H E   N E O N   E T T U
T A L O N   E L L S   N A R C
S A Y S O   E A P   S L O E
```

page 193 • Fuzzy Logic

```
S P A M   F A W N S   C U B A
E L L A   I D E A S   A P E R
C O E D   F E I N T   I S E E
S W E E T T A R T   A N I T A
    S A H L   U R G E D
L A S E R S   S C O T   E V E
I R E N E   C O K E   A D A R
M A C S   R U L E S   L O L A
O B O E   T R O T   B A W L S
S S N   R E V S   C O N N I E
    D O U S E   I O N A
R O B I N   B A B Y G R A N D
O M E N   P A S E O   K N E E
M A S K   C L E A T   I T E M
E N T S   B L A M E   N E R O
```

page 194 • Web of Intrigue

```
STUBS AMA AMBER
TONAL MAR LEAVE
ERICA PRE LOBED
WITHGREATPOWER
    SORCERY
RATA LEASE TESS
AMORAL    PAELLA
COMES    GREAT
EVENSO   BONNIE
REST TORSO SANS
   ATROPOS
 RESPONSIBILITY
HUTCH AID GOOSE
ENNUI TEE NATAL
READD ERR SNARL
```

page 195 • Going Native

```
COMA LOCO PESTE
OVERTIRES ALOUD
MUSKOGEES WOUND
EMS PASSIONPLAY
   SET AGEE
ELMTREES RESETS
CLAY ANDES ERA
LADE CREES ORAL
ANA SALEM DICE
TOMCAT RICKDEES
   ONES HAS
CONSTRUCTOR RYE
ORATE CHEROKEES
SETAE KINDLINGS
HOERS SASS DOGE
```

page 196 • Things Are Looking Up

```
ASSUME BEG DAIS
SCuMMY ERE RITA
TuPPERWAREPARTY
ALP EAu RuM
 PERP VpI pACE
 TROupERS PSHAW
  TOpO EASE ICH
TRAMPLE KITSCHY
BOB YELP LEAK
AULIC DupLEXES
TESH SNO RENT
   HOD COX SLA
HupTWOTHREEFOUR
APIA OSu REBuKE
TSAR MOp SNIpES
```

page 197 • A Two-Step Program

```
SETS WIP AGERS
CLOTHING POPES
ALWAYSKEEPYOUR
GRIN DEY REACT
ALP ORT NRA HEP
BESTFOOTFORWARD
STEAM ALL ILSA
  REKINDLED
SAAR LNG VERGE
ANDYOUROTHERONE
EDO UTE HOR SAL
 SPITZ QOM MESS
OUTOFYOURMOUTH
ACETO CINEASTE
THEAX SPY READ
```

page 198 • Splitsville

```
CAD TAINT KOSAR
ACE ATSEA ENTRE
MCL BORAX NERTS
PERSONALITYTEST
UPATREE HAWAII
STYE LAME OMEN
  LTR CORE ERG
 LEVELHEADED
CTY AMSO POP
AARP ATOR SPCA
SKIRUN ALSORAN
SECONDINCOMMAND
ANIMA NOIRE IDE
VISOR CLARA SLA
ANTSY AOLER EEN
```

page 199 • Sticks and Stones

```
SAUNA ACTS TSAR
UTTER SHEA HERO
STICKSHIFT IRIS
HILT TESLA REDS
ICEAGE ONES
 ROLLINGSTONE
ADD OLIO TETES
LIEF ALTON DINT
MESAS ARIA SEE
STICKINSECTS
  TIME HEEHAW
ALSO AURAE TONE
BEER GRINDSTONE
LAME EASE TEPID
ENID SLEW YESES
```

page 200 • The A List

```
ALOFT MOOT HITE
APNEA ACHE ANON
ANSELADAMS NERD
 CLINE LENSES
AIR ANDREAGASSI
BRED OED RHETT
SMEARS DAME
 ANNAAKHMATOVA
  FLOE ESKIMO
LEAPT NAB SLIP
ALFREDADLER LET
SAFIRE EROSE
SPAN ALVARAALTO
ISIT NOIR MILER
EERS SUZY SLATE
```

page 201 • Initially the Same

```
CLIME DUPE VAST
HAREM INON AHOY
IVANBOESKY NEAR
TANDEM NEA NAVE
  DECAY HADES
BACK NOR ROW
ALOES SLAUGHTER
SURVIVE LEGIBLY
EMPIRICAL STALE
 NEE LAG ERAS
STUBS ADHOC
TINA IRE BOOTEE
ERIC DENNISFUNG
VETO ONTO MANGO
EDEN STEW ONERS
```

page 202 • Creature Features

```
JAMB MASTS FLOP
OREL ALERT RISE
LEIA NITER EASE
TARZANTHEAPEMAN
   EME SPA
NEDROREM SNARES
ALI CELEB WELT
CROCODILEDUNDEE
RONA ADEEM IMA
EYELET SPLENDID
  LOS AKA
THELIONINWINTER
ROUE LINEA TOFU
AURA EDGER ENTS
PROS DEERE SYST
```

page 203 • Enterprising Personalities

```
GLUM ODDS BEMAS
RENO PEEN EXIST
AVID TILE TAMPA
MIXUP GLEE MEIN
  LEONARDSPOCK
ADVERB    NIL
POE KIRKCAMERON
ERIE OED SANE
RANDMCNALLY GUS
 ISA   AUGUST
SCOTTYBOWMAN
KEPI SALE NEWSY
IDIOM BIBB IOTA
MANNA EVER SKEW
PRESS SERA SEWN
```

page 204 • B-Minus

```
BEGS EDAM AFTER
IDEA NISI WORRY
RUSHEDSILKLOUSE
OCTAL CAIN TEES
STEREO   EELS
  ANTIQUEROACH
PAC AINU GRIME
AGHA SNIFF ENOW
REINS PAID TNN
READANDUTTER
  ROAR SLEIGH
ALTO ROOD TERRA
LOWINCOMERACKET
PRIDE PINE HEBE
SENSE STYX ODES
```

page 205 • Animal Behavior

```
ONO DRAW ABBACY
CONDENSE TOUCHE
TRAUMATA MACRON
AMICI USA SKEWS
DARK ITERATE
  ENVELOP DEEP
HEYDAY EST TYPE
ACUTE ODE SHEIK
SHAH ADO PIERCE
HONE SOUREST
 IMPUTER REAP
GESSO ROT FEMME
EXISTS FINANCES
MINUET INCIDENT
STEELY TARN ESS
```

page 206 • Either Way

```
ACRE BASTE MUTT
SHEM IMPEL OKRA
TINA PEELSSLEEP
OMEN ENA EASES
REWARDDRAWER
 TESS BED TAO
GELID BURSTING
ALAN SUITE REAL
PLUGGING NURSE
SAD ALI AGES
 LOOTERRETOOL
STEEL REO EXPO
PORTSSTROP DIAS
UTAH ECOLE IDLE
DOSE AURAS NESS
```

page 207 • Leapers

```
ALE STASH AFTER
CAM ORTHO FRERE
ENE NOLAN LADED
RANDYJACKSON
BIDE ASK CACAOS
  BIN ORT PUN
PASTA GURU ARIA
ANTONIOSABADOJR
TIER NOEL TONAL
TOE BUN PER
INDOOR MOI EAST
 DENNISFARINA
NISEI EDIFY SET
AKRON ADELE LEE
BEING PYRES ERR
```

page 210 • Bad TV

```
PIANO FISH FLAT
AFTERTASTE OATH
IFTVISBADFORYOU
NYU GAITS SLING
  MIRO SHONE
SAXONS CHEER
KNOBS WHYCANYOU
EDU HARMS ALS
WATCHITIN HULLS
  RANTS JAGUAR
 OPART HUSH
GRASP SKIDS RDA
ANYHOSPITALROOM
ZONE RATCHETSUP
ETES ISTH DEARS
```

page 211 • Family Tree

```
SAPID WING PLOP
INANE IDEE RIPE
TONNE SEAN OMEN
ALDERSTATESMAN
REAR PESETAS
 SUER NIL CAW
 BLONDIE CLEAVE
FOILS AND ORPIN
DELETE DOGWOOD
ART RNA RUST
 EARLESS IMPS
HIPPOCRATICOAK
GYRO BOWL BIOTA
EPIC EVIL ISLET
MESH DENY STARE
```

page 212 • Similar Endings

```
OPT DOGMA SMILE
MOO ONAIR COOER
ALP MOULINROUGE
HAITI LESION
ARCANA REPLICAS
 KARL SALERNO
ASSENTED ANN
IWANTYOUTOTSZUJ
LAG PANATELA
ELATERS BURY
DESOLATE STEWED
 MONICA LDOPA
OLYMPICLUGE RON
LOUIE KARAT DDT
DOPER STABS SEE
```

page 213 • X Appeal

```
HERO ALOHA CAIN
OLAV BIDET ONCE
SAFETYNEXT SNOW
ENTRUSTS ORIENT
 ELMS BRONX
CABALS CONDEMNS
AROSE RANEE EAT
SEXY MONEY SAVE
ANY SOUND STRAP
SAGACITY PHIALS
 ERASE SEAL
ANOINT VENDETTA
BURS UNODUETREX
EDGE RULER TAXI
TEES ENTRY OPTS
```